Implementing Design Patterns in C# and .NET 5

*Build Scalable, Fast, and Reliable .NET Applications
Using the Most Common Design Patterns*

Alexandre F. Malavasi Cardoso

www.bpbonline.com

FIRST EDITION 2021
Copyright © BPB Publications, India
ISBN: 978-93-90684-366

LIMITS OF LIABILITY AND DISCLAIMER OF WARRANTY

To View Complete
BPB Publications Catalogue
Scan the QR Code:

Dedicated to

My beloved wife Paula
&
Marli Malavazi and my whole family

About the Author

Alexandre Malavasi has been working in the software development field for the past 15 years. He has participated in many projects as a technical leader and software developer, delivering projects using Microsoft technologies for big companies, including successful projects in South America, Europe and the United States. He is also an accomplished post graduate holding degrees in IT for Business and System Analysis and two master's degrees in Software Engineering with Agile Methods Emphasis and Software Development Process. He is also Microsoft certified in Azure and Web Development technologies. Furthermore, the author takes part as a speaker at IT conferences and writes technical articles on Web Development and related topics. Based on all the contributions to the technical community worldwide, he was nominated as the Most Valuable Professional (MVP) offered by Microsoft.

About the Reviewer

John F. Gnazzo, PE MBA PMP MVP, is a principal software engineering consultant, with Gnazzo Technical Services, Inc. (GTS) located in Minneapolis, Minnesota, USA.

John has over 25 years of application development experience in the development of mission-critical enterprise, mobile device, desktop and Web-based applications, using .NET, C#, C++, JavaScript libraries and frameworks, and SQL Server.

John's role at GTS is to provide an architecture, development, and technical leadership expertise across the full project lifecycle to GTS staff, clientele, and community. John is committed to being a leader in the implementation of enterprise business solutions comprising of contemporary Web, desktop, and mobile technologies.

John has extensive experience in requirement development, application architecture, object-oriented and SOLID design principles, implementation of design patterns, application programming, testing, and DevOps.

John is a registered professional engineer with a Minnesota license, a certified project management professional, a Six Sigma Green Belt, a Microsoft MVP **https://mvp.microsoft.com/en-us/PublicProfile/5001690?fullName=John%20 %20Gnazzo**, and maintains AWS and Microsoft certifications.

John has written many technical blogs, which can be found at **http://www.gnazzo. net/Home/Blogs**, and coding challenges, which can be found at **https://www. teamscs.com/2015/03/c-coding-challenge-1/**.

John has an B.S. Degree in Engineering from the Colorado School of Mines and an MBA specializing in Computer Information Technology from National University.

Acknowledgement

There are a few people I want to thank for the continued and ongoing support they have given me during the writing of this book. First and foremost, I would like to thank my wife for being entirely and continuously supportive since the beginning of this project and my family for encouraging me to write the book —I would not have completed this challenging book without their motivation.

I am grateful to everyone who have worked directly with me during these 15 years, teaching me how to code and always pushing me to a higher level in terms of quality assurance and good software development practices.

My gratitude also goes to the team at BPB for being supportive enough and providing me sufficient time to complete the book through a challenging period between 2020 and 2021 due to the global pandemic crisis that affected everyone, including myself. I am also thankful for allowing me to write my first book, which was undoubtedly a huge personal achievement.

Preface

This book covers many detailed aspects of the Design Patterns and Object-Oriented Programming paradigm concepts using C# and .NET 5, starting from the essential elements of C# and Visual Studio to more advanced software architecture concepts and good practices in coding, including SOLID principles. The key focus is on using design patterns to solve real-scenario challenges, demonstrating how to take advantage of the good practices of the object-oriented paradigm to solve problems with different levels of complexity.

The book describes the theoretical concepts required to understand encapsulation, interfaces, inheritance and other aspects of C# language. It discusses how to solve real problems in software development using design patterns under C# language and .NET platform. It provides a general picture of the advanced resources present in the .NET platform and gives detailed information on the solutions primarily applied in the market regarding multiple strategies for reliable software development processes.

The first six chapters will start from the basic concepts of C# language and .NET platform, including SOLID principles and object-oriented programming paradigm. Then, it will focus on practical examples of the necessary and preliminary notions of good practices in software development to prepare the reader for more advanced implementation presented in the later chapters of design patterns and software architecture.

The eleven chapters of the book gives a good exposure the reader to the most used design patterns in C# language and .NET platform with practical examples and real scenarios with a step by step approach. Last but not the least, it will have some sections regarding recommendations and good practices for .NET applications in cases where the design patterns need to be applied.

The primary goal is to get the reader familiar with the design patterns using C# language in applications based on .NET focused on solving real problems and demonstrating practical examples. You will learn the following in the seventeen chapters of this book:

Chapter 1 explains the fundamental concepts of C# language in detail, including a guide on Visual Studio installation and environment configuration to start the journey into .NET Core. The chapter covers operators, variables, object types, iterations and error handling in the C# language.

Chapter 2 focuses on the essential aspects that a developer needs to get started with the .NET platform, right from the installation steps to understand how it works. It will also give a detailed history of .NET Core versions, multi-platform concepts and aspects of cloud solutions built on .NET.

Chapter 3 describes the basic concepts of object-oriented programming paradigm, including classes, constructors, methods, inheritance, static classes, structs and polymorphism. It will also discuss the good practices regarding the object-oriented programming using C# language along with practical examples.

Chapter 4 focuses on interfaces in C# language including good practices and real-life examples. It will also discuss testability and extensibility in software development, which are quite close to the best practices in terms of interfaces.

Chapter 5 explains the basic concepts of encapsulation and polymorphism in C# language including real-life examples, best practices and correlations between those concepts and the SOLID principles.

Chapter 6 describes the SOLID principles using real-life examples in C# language and hands-on scenarios. It will also discuss the good practices behind each principle of single responsibility, open-close, Liskov substitution and dependency inversion.

Chapter 7 provides a profound explanation of the Abstract Factory design pattern in C# language. It will also discuss the practical examples based on a real-life scenario and explain how to apply this pattern to solve a medium complexity problem.

Chapter 8 explains the Singleton design pattern in detail using practical examples in C# language and .NET. It will also show how to use this pattern in ASP.Net Core applications combined with the dependency injection concept.

Chapter 9 focuses on the Prototype design pattern demonstrating with practical and real-life examples the difference between shallow and deep copy of objects, including implementing a scenario that requires the use of this pattern to keep an extensible and testable software architecture.

Chapter 10 describes in detail the Factory Method design pattern using practical examples in C# language and .NET platform. It will also explain the scenarios where the use of this pattern is recommended including advices and good practices.

Chapter 11 elucidates the Adapter design pattern, one of the most used patterns in software development, mainly in database providers. It will also give real-life examples and practical exercises in a hands-on style.

Chapter 12 explains the composite design pattern. It will also provide practical examples based on real-life scenarios, demonstrate good practices of object-oriented paradigm using C# language and explain how to apply this pattern combined with advanced software architecture concepts.

Chapter 13 discusses the proxy design pattern and how it can be used to solve problems commonly found in many companies and projects based on C# language and .NET Core.

Chapter 14 tells about the command pattern and gives the reader a practical example based on a real-life scenario. It will also provide theoretical details found on this pattern and its importance to .NET Core applications in the market.

Chapter 15 focuses on the strategy design pattern, explaining the scenario in which the use of this pattern is recommended. It will also discuss details of the pattern through a practical example based on real-scenario software requirements.

Chapter 16 explains the observer design pattern in detail, demonstrating how to use it in legacy projects based on C# language and .NET platform. It will also help the reader apply this pattern in many applications through practical examples based on real-life scenarios.

Chapter 17 focuses on good general practices and recommendations for implementing applications using design patterns in projects based on C# language and .NET Core. It will also give an overview of extra design patterns, such as chain of responsibility, façade, builder, bridge, and decorator design patterns.

Downloading the code bundle and coloured images:

Please follow the link to download the
Code Bundle and the *Coloured Images* of the book:

https://rebrand.ly/df6fc1

Errata

We take immense pride in our work at BPB Publications and follow best practices to ensure the accuracy of our content to provide with an indulging reading experience to our subscribers. Our readers are our mirrors, and we use their inputs to reflect and improve upon human errors, if any, that may have occurred during the publishing processes involved. To let us maintain the quality and help us reach out to any readers who might be having difficulties due to any unforeseen errors, please write to us at :

errata@bpbonline.com

Your support, suggestions and feedbacks are highly appreciated by the BPB Publications' Family.

Did you know that BPB offers eBook versions of every book published, with PDF and ePub files available? You can upgrade to the eBook version at www.bpbonline.com and as a print book customer, you are entitled to a discount on the eBook copy. Get in touch with us at :

business@bpbonline.com for more details.

At **www.bpbonline.com**, you can also read a collection of free technical articles, sign up for a range of free newsletters, and receive exclusive discounts and offers on BPB books and eBooks.

BPB is searching for authors like you

If you're interested in becoming an author for BPB, please visit **www.bpbonline.com** and apply today. We have worked with thousands of developers and tech professionals, just like you, to help them share their insight with the global tech community. You can make a general application, apply for a specific hot topic that we are recruiting an author for, or submit your own idea.

The code bundle for the book is also hosted on GitHub at **https://github.com/bpbpublications/Implementing-Design-Patterns-in-C-and-.NET-5**. In case there's an update to the code, it will be updated on the existing GitHub repository.

We also have other code bundles from our rich catalog of books and videos available at **https://github.com/bpbpublications**. Check them out!

PIRACY

If you come across any illegal copies of our works in any form on the internet, we would be grateful if you would provide us with the location address or website name. Please contact us at **business@bpbonline.com** with a link to the material.

If you are interested in becoming an author

If there is a topic that you have expertise in, and you are interested in either writing or contributing to a book, please visit **www.bpbonline.com**.

REVIEWS

Please leave a review. Once you have read and used this book, why not leave a review on the site that you purchased it from? Potential readers can then see and use your unbiased opinion to make purchase decisions, we at BPB can understand what you think about our products, and our authors can see your feedback on their book. Thank you!

For more information about BPB, please visit **www.bpbonline.com**.

Table of Contents

CHAPTER 1
C#
Fundamentals

With this chapter, we are starting our journey into design patterns using C# 9.0 and .NET 5, walking through the basic concepts of programming in C#, giving you familiarity with the language, main operations, and instructions that will help you understand what you need to make progress in the next sections of this book, such as object-oriented programming, design patterns, and .NET platform. You will learn how to create and work with variables, operators, logical and conditional statements. Additionally, you will have the opportunity to have a practical experience in implementing basic programs in C#.

Getting familiar with the basic and fundamental concepts of C# will allow you to understand how to apply the complex design patterns that will meet the most common real scenarios in enterprise projects.

Structure

In this chapter, we will discuss the following topics:

- Visual Studio 2019 and Visual Studio Code installation instructions
- Introduction to Visual Studio 2019
- Introduction to Visual Studio Code
- Basic operations in C#

- Object types in C#
- Loops and iterations in C#
- Error handling in C#

Objectives

After studying this unit, you should be able to:

- Install and setup the Visual Studio IDE and Visual Studio Code
- Create and build applications using Visual Studio
- Understand and use the basic operations using C# language

Tools and environment setup

To get started with software development in .NET 5 and C# 9.0, you must install the latest Visual Studio 2019 version, a complete **Integrated Development Environment (IDE)** for creating, compiling, and building your .NET projects. Visual Studio is available for Windows and macOS, and both of them are available in the Express Edition for studying purposes. The tool can be downloaded from the official Visual Studio website.

Further more, Microsoft has provided Visual Studio Code, an alternative light version of editor for .NET and C# applications, which is available not only for Windows and macOS, but also for various Linux distributions. Considering this editor is an open-source extensible project, the technical community, IT professionals, and companies around the globe have created numerous free extensions for different languages apart from C# itself. Therefore, it is a suitable tool to create cross-platform applications, without any compatibility concern. Visual Studio Code can be downloaded on the official website for free.

Installing Visual Studio 2019

After downloading Visual Studio 2019 from the official website, you must take the following steps for its installation:

1. Double-click on the downloaded executable file. Make sure your user on the operating system has permissions to install the software.

2. Choose the desired workloads to be installed and setup together with Visual Studio. For the examples of this book, the following workloads must be installed:

   o   ASP.NET and web development

o .NET desktop development

o Universal Windows Platform development

o .NET Core cross-platform development

After making this step in the installation, the workload list will be shown as the following screenshot:

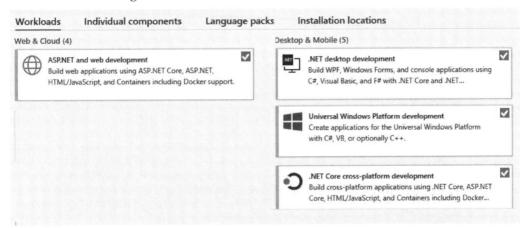

Figure 1.1: Visual Studio 2019 workloads

3. After choosing the necessary workloads, click on the **Install** option.

4. Usually, Visual Studio is configured to use the same language as the operating system language. If you would like to setup a different one, you can do that in the **Language Packs** option, where other ones will be available. For the examples of this book, Visual Studio was configured to English language.

   After finishing the installation, you will be already able to create .NET 5 solutions using all the project type available in Visual Studio.

Once Visual Studio 2019 is installed, you do not need to install the latest stable version of .NET SDK, as it is already a part of the Visual Studio installation. By default, Visual Studio updates and follows the newest features introduced into .NET, such as library updates, minor and major changes, and new project templates. Even though, the library updates do not automatically apply to your existent projects. Each project targets a specific .NET version, and Visual Studio updates and modifies just the IDE, and not the configurations for the existing projects.

Installing Visual Studio Code

Visual Studio Code is a cross-platform alternative to Visual Studio IDE and it is a good option if you want a light weight editor for .NET Core projects. The companies and communities have provided many extensions that allow us to work with many distinct languages and it has become one of the most popular editors to software developers. Also, it is available for any operation system, such as Linux, macOS, and Windows. After downloading the executable from the official Website, you must take the following steps:

1. Double-click in the downloaded executable file. Make sure your user in the operation system has permissions to install the software.

2. Download Visual Studio extension for C# and Azure, as seen in the following screenshot:

Figure 1.2: *Visual Studio Code extensions*

You must have an internet connection to search the extensions on the **Extensions** tab. After typing the extension name, just choose the install option to complete the process.

Introduction to Visual Studio 2019

The Visual Studio 2019 is a powerful IDE, which allows you to create, build, debug and deploy your .NET applications in one place, including access to external resources such as databases and Azure features. In addition, it contains many project templates to get started with software development, including project types based on .NET. To access those templates, just click on the **File** option on the superior menu and choose the options **New Project**, as seen in the following screenshot:

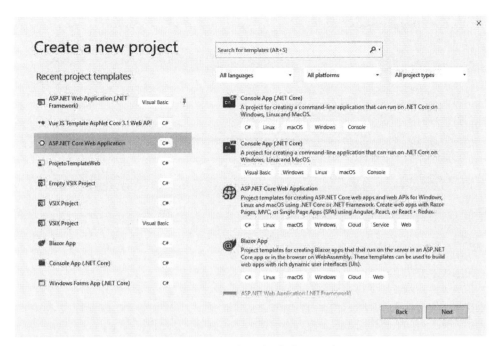

Figure 1.3: *Visual Studio Code extensions*

After installing the Visual Studio 2019, the most popular project templates for .NET Core such as Console App application, Asp.Net Core Web API Application and Blazor App are available to use. Each project template has other sub-types to choose from. Those templates are time saving and help to configure and create new projects using Visual Studio.

> Many free extra templates are shared by open-source communities, companies and individual developers on Visual Studio Marketplace website. Also, Visual Studio extensions for many purposes can be downloaded on the same website to get the best experience in software development and get integrations with third-part tools. They are also available for Visual Studio and Azure Devops.

After creating a simple project from the template list, you are redirected to the integrated environment for developing your code, having in a common place the text editor with code suggestions support and access to files and external resources, as seen in the following screenshot:

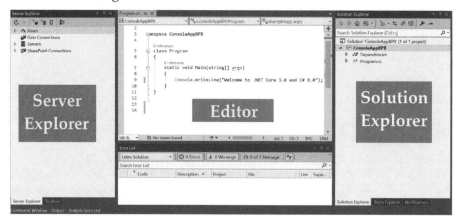

Figure 1.4: *Visual Studio features*

On the **Solution Explorer** side-bar, you can access all the existent folders and files of your solution. Additionally, it is possible to see all the linked projects in case you have multiple ones as a part of the software development. Further more, this view allows to have access to extra options regarding the projects, such as the installation of extra packages and external third-party libraries using the Nuget Package, which can be done by right-clicking the project and choosing the **Manage Package** option, as seen on *figure 1.5*:

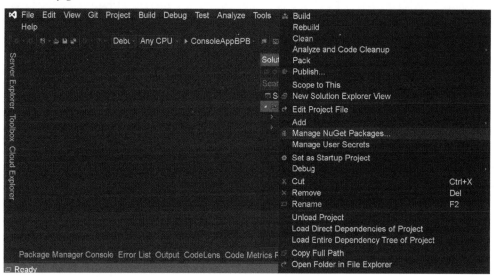

Figure 1.5: *Nuget Packages option*

After that, a new window is available where is possible to search and install Nuget packages, choosing the desired version, as seen on *figure 1.6*:

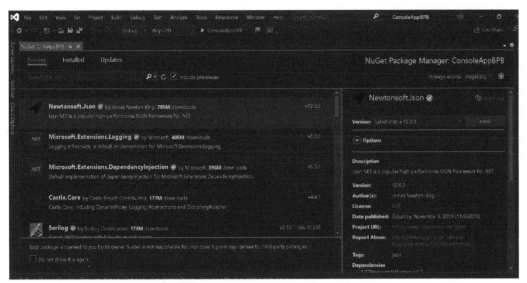

Figure 1.6: *Nuget Packages window*

Another interesting option is to install packages using command-line, which makes the process much easier once there is familiarity with the available commands. Under the Nuget Packages Console that appears on the bottom, it is possible to use the **dotnet install** command followed by name of the package, as seen on *figure 1.7*:

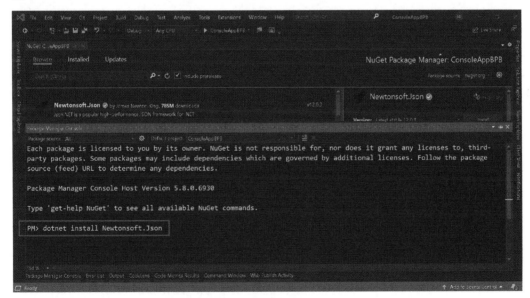

Figure 1.7: *Nuget Package Console*

On the other hand, , the **Editor** side-bar is the place where you develop your code and can get tips on code syntax, indentation, code suggestions, previous codification error messages and navigate into classes, functions and methods, as seen on the *figure 1.4*. The editor is totally customizable, and many settings can be changed such as background color, contrast, and font-size.

Finally, on the **Server Explorer** side-bar is possible to connect to external resources, databases, servers, cloud resources and on-premise features. That way you can keep all the work in a unique and shared place and it has a great value to get high productivity. In the Toolbar there are options to run the application, save pendent changes, modify the debug mode, comment code lines, open new files and undo recent added code in the editor, as seen on *figure 1.8*:

Figure 1.8: *Visual Studio toolbar*

The .NET platform allows to build applications using F#, a language based on the functional paradigm, and in addition allows us to use Vb.NET, a language largely used in .NET projects since the beginning of the platform. On the project creation dialog, the Visual Studio provide us specific templates regarding the same type of projects, but based on other languages, apart from C#, as seen on *figure 1.9*:

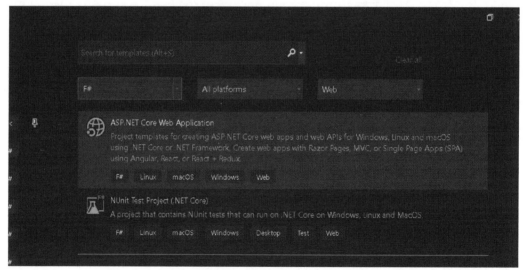

Figure 1.9: *F# application*

On the given example on *figure 1.9*, the Visual Studio creates an Asp.Net Core application based on F# language instead of C#. However, in case there is other projects on the solution target to C# language, it is possible to share references and reuse the code on the F# project considering they are compatible under the .NET platform.

The Visual Studio is a complete IDE for .NET applications. It does require to have extra tools to build and execute programs based on C# or any other language supported by .NET platform. Additionally, it is possible to create and integrate different projects even if they are written using other languages.

Introduction to Visual Studio Code

At the first moment, Visual Studio Code seems to be quite different from Visual Studio 2019, but both of them have the exact same purpose: create, debug, build, and deploy applications made using many languages and resources. At its core, it contains numerous extensions to get our routine as developers much easier. The main difference between Visual Studio 2019 and Visual Studio Code is regarding to cross-platform development; once Visual Studio Code is available not only in Windows and macOS operating systems, but it is ready to use in Linux as well. Another relevant aspect is the performance of this editor in comparison to a full IDE; on the other hand, you have to individually enable extensions and components, according to what you really need to develop your software. As seen on *figure 1.10*, the sections available in Visual Studio Code are similar to those in Visual Studio:

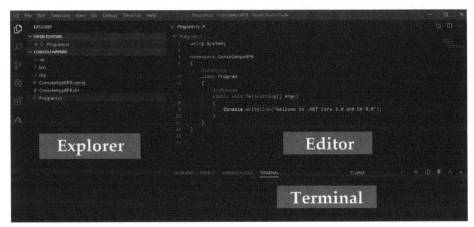

Figure 1.10: *Visual Studio Code*

There are significant differences between Visual Studio Code and Visual Studio IDE. The first one has the purpose of being a light code editor that can be used on Linux, macOS, and Windows, which is an interesting option for low-resources machines. The second one is focused on being a complete integrated environment where it is possible to have almost everything we need for development in a single place, including database access, extra options for deployment, build, and advanced visual options in order to keep all the necessary tools in a single application.

The companies and open-source projects provided many extensions for Visual Studio Code since its creation. That means it is gradually becoming a more complex editor. However, all the extra features that are out of scope of a simple editor need to be enabled and installed as a separate extension. The central idea of Visual Studio Code is to keep it light, simple, productive, and high performing by loading on it only the tools we need.

On the **Explorer** sidebar, you can access all the existent folders and files of your project. Also, it is possible to see all the linked projects, in case you have multiple ones as part of the software development process. As seen in *figure 1.5*, the **Editor** sidebar is the place where you develop your code and can get tips on code syntax, indentation, code suggestions, and previous codification error messages and navigate into classes, functions, and methods. The editor is totally customizable, and many settings can be changed, such as the background color, contrast, and fontsize. Considering you have installed the C# language extension, the editor is ready to highlight the most important parts of your underlying code, showing in distinct colors the classes, methods, primitive types, and static text such as String, Integer, or even the custom classes you will create. For other programming languages, distinct extensions were released as open-source projects, but for all the examples of this book, the C# extension is enough to obtain the wanted results.

Visual Studio Code is a command-line-based editor, which means that once you have familiarity with the commands, you can benefit from quickly running your application, build and create new files without using mouse clicks for that. It is an important functionality to be productive and manage better your development environment. All the commands can be executed on the **Terminal** sidebar, and on the output window are shown the results and the status of the commands. Because of the facility to use the editor combined with command lines by terminal, Visual Studio became the most popular software editor in the world, and it has been well received even by developers who do not use .NET Core and C# for software development. Considering the editor is a cross-platform and open-source project, it has been largely used by Linux users and for software development in various programming languages and platforms.

Furthermore, Visual Studio Code supports deployment and source control, being easily integrated with GitHub, GitLab, and Azure DevOps.

> **Visual Studio was the used IDE to create, run, and build all the code examples of this book, but you can get the same result using Visual Studio in a similar way, using the command lines present in the appendices of this book.**

The traditional and complete Visual Studio 2019 IDE version depends on the existent specification in files whose extension is `.sln` (solution file) and specific extensions for projects such as `.csproj` for C# library projects. Although, Visual Studio Code allows you to run code by only opening simple folders and files, which is useful in case you want just to run other languages apart from Microsoft technologies.

Regarding productivity and menu options, Visual Studio Code is more flexible, as it contains many predefined commands to get files, search across files and contents, debug and deployment options, and to manage and add new extensions, as shown in *figure 1.11*:

Figure 1.11: *Visual Studio Code - User Interface*

Visual Studio Code is the most popular code editor in the market, and the features available are increasing fast because of the active technical community behind the project, providing a lot of extensions and new integrations.

History of the .NET platform

The .NET platform was created long before web applications became popular and even before the first version of the C# language. If we pay attention to the massive adoption of .NET these days, it gives the impression that the scenario was always like this, especially for those who did not experience software development around the beginning of the 1990s. Looking back almost three decades ago, when other programming languages like Java and PHP stood out, the first for generalist cross-platform software development and the second for the web applications, it seemed essential for Microsoft to enter this great market of the development tools. The first version of the .NET platform was then launched as a beta product in 2000. And finally, in February of 2002, the official 1.0 version was released, supporting Windows 98, Windows Millennium, and Windows XP. The most important feature of the first version was the **Common Language Runtime** (**CLR**), which allowed developers to create .NET applications using more than one programming language. The .NET platform was able to execute it using CLR and to convert it into **Common Intermediate Language** (**CIL**), also called **Intermediate Language** (**IL**). Therefore, it was possible to share libraries written in C# and components written in Visual Basic in the same project. Being able to use multiple programming languages in the same program did not necessarily mean being able to create multiplatform software using .NET at this time, whereas it was possible to run and develop the .NET Framework applications only on the Windows OS.

In the second quarter of 2003, the first relevant update to the.NET Frame work version (.NET 1.1) was released, and the support for **Open Database Connectivity (ODBC)** was introduced, following standard requirements for database integrations in .NET applications. Up to this point, the .NET platform did not have wide adoption in the market, and important features should be released to meet the most modern software development demands and trends.

In January of 2006, Microsoft launched version 2.0 of .NET Framework and other important tools and products, such as Visual Studio 2005, a more stable release of the new SQL Server database 2005, and Biz Talk. One of the most important improvements of this version was the support to 64-bit computer architecture and new features on C# language, such as partial class, new authentication options for Asp.Net, and "Data table" objects, which allowed us to make database operations in memory using datasets.

Along side these new features, Visual Studio was becoming mature and complete, being a full IDE, even for programmers who work with languages different from C# and Visual Basic. Also, the Asp.Net Web Forms started having a large adoption among developers who had experience with desktop applications and were migrating to Web development. Visual Studio 2005 already contained features to quickly drag and drop visual Web components and add events to those interactively in the environment. This way of developing applications was very similar to desktop application development, and for that reason, developers who were not familiar with Web development before could start developing their first Web applications without huge effort in learning Web development.

The Asp.Net Web Forms occupied an important space in the .NET Framework before the Asp.Net **Model View Controller (MVC)** was introduced to the platform. The web pages navigation based on forms were common at the beginning of the Web, and it essentially consisted in a user sending request from the Web browser, and the server returns a response, keeping the state of the Web controls for giving to users a continued experience navigating on the web page and interacting with its controllers. In that case, the server was totally responsible for processing the HTML and all the dynamic data. This technology used the View State approach to store the values of all server-side components. Additionally, the Asp .Net Web Forms provided the option to use separated files between the HTML and the logic code for each page. That was considered an innovation, and years after that, the separation of responsibilities in the application would be better provided with ASP.Net MVC.

In November of 2006, .NET Framework 3.0 was released, including relevant features regarding desktop development and web services. At this time, the **JavaScript Object Notation (JSON)** was not used for integrating services based on the Web protocol. The **Extensible Markup Language (XML)** was largely used for standard communication between systems, and the **Windows Communication Foundation (WCF)** became the official web service of the .NET Framework. The WCF became obsolete once .NET replaced it with the Web **Application Programming Interface (API)**, following the most modern patterns being adopted in the market.

One of the benefits of the WCF was its integration with Visual Studio tools, which allowed us to import third-party endpoints via an address and generate classes in C# language corresponding to the objects specified in an external web service, even that it was written in other languages. The functionality was focused on interpreting the XML of the third-partyweb service specification and creating objects and their properties, without being necessary to write any code line. Additionally, the **Service Import** tool automatically generated the methods in C# language to open connection and send requests to the external web service, parsing the response to objects in C#. It was an extremely productive tool, and it was hugely important for the popularity of the .NET Framework in the market. Till these days, there are a great number of companies that were still having web services developed using the WCF as a legacy project. The same situation happens with ASP.Net Web Forms applications, considering a lot of companies adopted it to large projects and did not migrate them yet to a newer version of the .NET Framework project types or .NET Core.

Another important technology that was introduced to .NET Framework 3.0 was the **Windows Presentation Foundation (WPF)** project type, a new way to create desktop applications using the **Extensible Application Markup Language (XAML)** and develop rich user interface applications using 3D computer graphics hardware. It was an alternative to the traditional Windows Form Desktop applications existent in the .NET platform. Despite other project types of .NET Framework 3.0 becoming only legacy projects and not having continued updates till .NET Core, the WPF was still largely used by companies and .NET developers because it continuously received updates and had full support in .NET Core, not only in the .NET Framework.

.NET Framework 3.5 was released in November of 2007, bringing performance improvements for desktop applications. Additionally, the first version of Entity Framework was introduced, giving the possibility of better communicating with databases and being an alternative to **Object-Relational Mapping (ORM)** of other distinct platforms. However, a new release of Entity Framework was launched only in 2008 at the same time as the .NET Framework Service Pack 1, including updates after technical community feedbacks, with this version not being mature enough to be largely adopted in many companies across the globe. The ORM concept and its importance were widely accepted on the market, and huge improvements on Entity Framework became extremely necessary at this point, mainly to give reliability and stability to the product.

After only one year, Microsoft provided version 4.0 of .NET Framework, but it did not represent any break changes and did not have many new features, different from.NET Framework 4.5 that was released in August of 2012, containing many improvements for Web applications, desktop development, and native components for Windows 8 operating system. Among all the new features, the new functionalities for Asp .Net applications stood out, including support to HTML5 for Web Forms and support to Web Socket protocol, which represented a large step to follow the most modern Web standard practices at that point. Also, with this version of the .NET Framework, it was possible to use asynchronous HTTP requests and responses.

Finally, in July of 2015, .NET Framework 4.6 was released, being the last big version of this platform before the first version of .NET Core, despite having small updates after that in the versions 4.7 and 4.8. The 4.6 version introduced support to Azure SQL Server distributed transactions, improvements related to WPF user interface, and support for localization of data annotations attributes in Asp.Net.

The .NET Core versions

Considering at that time in 2015, the market for information technology and software development was changing to become compatible cross-platform concepts, the fact the .NET Framework had support only for Windows operating system represented a significant limitation for its evolution. It was largely accepted by companies, developers, and technical communities that it was mandatory for any software development technology to be capable of being executed in any operating system, multiple devices, and having interoperability with other technologies and platforms.

Meeting these new requirements, Microsoft launched in June of 2006 the first version of .NET Core, a disruptive platform that allows to develop and run .NET applications on Linux and macOS. The .NET libraries for C# and Vb.NET were completely re-written from scratch, including a new version of Asp.Net projects and Entity Framework, both of them renamed to Asp.Net Core and Entity Framework Core, following the new brand of the .NET platform.

Additionally, all the **.NET Core libraries** and their projects became an open-source project, with the code being totally shared on GitHub, making it possible for anyone to contribute to the evolution of the technology reporting issues of this new version. This represents a big milestone for .NET developers, considering only the Asp.Net MVC project was considered opensource at this point, and it significantly contributes to .NET adoption by developers from other technologies.

.NET Core 1.1 was released in November of the same year; it contained many solutions for issues reported by developers and companies and was focused on supporting more variety of Linux distributions. Also, the Entity Framework was improved to support Azure and SQL Server 2016 databases.

In August of 2017, .NET Core 2.0 was launched, containing the possibility to integrate with the legacy .NET Framework libraries using .NET Standard and also improving the cross-platform support with new features. Additionally, this version brought the new Razor Pages Web project, an alternative to the traditional Asp.Net MVC project type for creating Web applications within the .NET Core platform. At this point,

.NET Core became a mature platform being largely adopted by companies and .NET developers. The support to cross-platform development was the key of .NET Core, joined with Visual Studio Code and new command-line options. Definitely and officially, developers were able to create .NET applications that run literally everywhere, participating in the evolution of the next versions of it on the GitHub repository and taking the benefits of performance that were added to .NET Core in comparison to .NET Framework.

The .NET Standard was a common API specification for .NET libraries that would allow us to use them across all .NET projects. It means that different types of projects would be able to share libraries between them with the .NET Standard, including implementations between .NET Framework and .NET Core projects. The .NET Core and .NET Standard are distinct things. The first one is not compatible with original .NET Framework libraries, and the second one was made to be a bridge between all .NET versions. Therefore, considering there is no compatibility between .NET Core and .NET Framework, the best strategy to migrate .NET Framework applications to .NET Core is to create libraries in the .NET Standard. In that way, it is possible to keep your old implementation without break changes and use the same libraries in .NET Core projects in case the migration would gradually occur.

As you can see in *figure 1.12*, the .NET Standard represents the intersection between .NET Framework and .NET Core projects, and it already contains relevant compatibility in version 2.0:

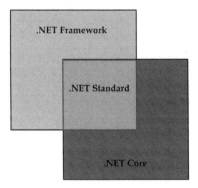

Figure 1.12: .NET Standard

Each new version of the .NET Standard added universal compatibility in .NET projects in general: .NET Core, .NET Framework, Mono, Xamarin, and Unit. Its specification is the base feature for any .NET library considering all the products, including mobile development and games. The .NET Standard 2.0 supports interoperability with .NET Framework 4.6.1 or later versions. Therefore, in projects that are using an older version of the .NET Framework, such as 2.0 or 3.5, they are not able to use .NET Standard libraries. It is recommended to migrate the project to the 4.6.1 version before starting any migration to .NET Core.

Since the first version, the .NET Core had many improvements, and significant new features were released at the same time as the compatibility with cross-platform development was strictly followed. .NET Core 3.0 represented the biggest jump in the creation of modern software, considering in this version were added support to Windows Form application, WPF, **Artificial Intelligence (AI)**, and development for the **Internet of Things (IoT)**. In the next chapters of this book, you will have the opportunity to have a deepdive in all these types of projects and understand the performance improvements that were applied to C# 8.0, which is part of this.NET Core version.

In November of 2020, Microsoft already released .NET 5, which represents the beginning of a new era in software development using the .NET platform once all the effort for cross-platform development reached their maturity and stability. It means that all .NET libraries are fully migrated to cross-platform development at this point, and the intention to have 100% of the .NET project as opensource is close to being met.

.NET 5

Among all the .NET versions, .NET 5 represents an evolution of .NET Core 3.1 and .NET Framework 4.8, being a huge milestone in terms of consolidation of all the effort regarding cross-platform development that started in the .NET platform since .NET Core 1.0. Therefore, it is possible to say that .NET 5 is a complete unification of the .NET ecosystem, combining new features and relevant improvements in terms of performance.

The unified platform has a central key point the cross-platform aspects, which does not only mean compatibility across multiple different operating systems, but in terms of multiple devices and platforms, such as desktop, Web, cloud, gaming, IoT, AI, and others.

Considering the .NET Standard becomes more fully supported at this point, .NET 5 represents a complete API provider that supports implementation for any type of runtime used in the .NET platform. It give us the opportunity to share libraries between .NET 5 applications and legacy projects built on .NET Framework as far as they share a common layer built in the .NET Standard.

The achievement of a multi-platform application using .NET required a complex re-architecture of the entire .NET platform, bringing at the same time significant improvements in terms of performance for existing features presented on C#, even the most commons ones such as type conversions, parallelization, and others. In this chapter, you will have the opportunity to create the most common project types based on .NET 5, and you can combine all these types of projects with all design patterns explained along with this book.

Introduction to C# language

The best way to learn any programming language is to create real applications for practicing and apply in real scenarios the knowledge you have got. Firstof all, there are basic concepts that apply to any programming language, including C# languages, such as variables, statements, loops, blocks, and iterations. In the next sections of this chapter, you will have the opportunity to create multiple C# applications, and in the meantime, all the basic concepts will be explained.

C# is a stringly typed language, which means it requires to have all the variables with specific type when it is created. Therefore, if you create a variable to store only numbers and try to store text content on it, the compile will show an error indicating that the value of the variable does not correspond to the variable type. In computer programming, there are weakly typed languages as well, which are not pre-compiled, but the type is checked dynamically once the application is running. As a stronglytyped language, in C# language, you must specify the type of any variable created in the program, indicating the type of values that will be stored on it.

A variable in programming language could store simple data structures such as numbers and strings but could also contain complex data as files, lists of custom objects, and much more. Their correct use represents an important point in software development considering they are closely related to the way we interact with the memory in any application, and they could represent a good measure on how readable the software is in terms of coding. It is essential to follow good practices and conventions related to variable names, not only for this specific small part of the software, but for other structures used in C#. Always use meaningful names across the system, applying camel case pattern for classes (for example, **MyBpbBook**) and upper case for constants (for example,**MAX_ITEMS_ORDER = 3**). Make your code easy to read by others and even by yourself.

The following screenshot represents a simple creation and value assignment for a C# variable:

```
static void Main(string[] args)
{

    string myMessage = "I'm reading the Design Patterns with .NET book";
    double dotNetVersion = 3.0;

    Console.WriteLine($"My Message {myMessage}");
    Console.WriteLine($".NET Version: {dotNetVersion}");
}
```

Figure 1.13: C# variables

Lines 10 and 11 represent two different variables in C# from distinct types. The first one is a variable of the string type, and it is storing the content "**I'm reading the Design Patterns in .NET Core 3.0 book.**" The value must be around quotes, because that is a pattern for any string in C# language. Referencing to the second variable (line 11), it is storing a decimal value (3.0), and because it is not a string, the value does not need to use quotes. The variable should be named according to its purpose, and it can be used in other parts of the program within the same context, such as the same method scope or other methods in case this variable is created as a global one.

There are many types of variables in C# language, and each one has a specific reason to be used. The following topics contain the most popular types and their detailed explanation with examples:

- **object**: It is the most basic type in C# language because all the other types are derived from it. It is possible to assign values of any type to it. It was made to be completely generic, and it is largely used in dynamic types, manly for assignments when the content has unknown type.

- **int**: This type was created to store integer numbers, positive or negative. As what happens with any variable type, there are limits (maximum and minimum values) that can be stored on it. In that case, the minimum value is -2,147,483,648 and the maximum value is 2,147,483,647. This limitation helps to prevent security issues and to optimize the memory usage. Each time a variable is created in the program, a space is reserved in the memory to store the value. For that reason, it is high recommended to choose the suitable variable type for any variable used in the system. Additionally, it is possible to use integer types with other sizes in C# language. For instance, the short type allows us to store a number between -32,768 and 32,767 (**System.Int16**), the long type allows us to store an integer between 9,223,372,036,854,775,808 and 9,223,372,036,854,775,807 (**System.Int64**), and there are much more options. The correct one to use in a specific routine depends directly on the requirements of the data in terms of precision and size. Usually, the type **int** is more often used, being a 32-bit number (**System.Int32**). However, the right choice regarding the integer type is important and essential in order to avoid runtime issues in production projects.

- **bool**: It has the purpose to store Boolean values (true or false), as it follows in the following screenshot:

Figure 1.14: C# bool variables

Line 9 represents a bool variable storing a "**true**" value, and Line 10 is printing on the console the value of the underlying variable.

- **string**: As in the example of *figure 1.8*, this type was made to store a sequence of Unicode characters and requires use of quotes around the value. It will indicate to the compile that is effectively a string content. Additionally, it is possible to use the String class instead to achieve similar results. Both of them contain similar properties, but considering the **String** type, with capital letter, is a complex type, it will be handled differently on the memory in a less efficient way in certain scenarios that requires a strict use of machine resources and relevant scale workload. Each primitive type on C# language has their correspondent class under the System namespace, for instance **System.String**, **System.Int32** and many others.

- **byte**: It is a type used for storing unsigned integers values that start with "0" (minimum value) and "255" (maximum value). It is commonly used to manipulate file bytes in arrays of that type (**byte**) and in low-level programming.

- **char**: It was created to store a single Unicode character, different from the string type that stores a sequence of those. The utilization of this type is useful for allocating less space in the memory if the content is just a simple Unicode character. If the quantity of characters in a variable is predefined and it would have just one Unicode character, choose this type of variable instead of the **string** type.

- **float**: It is used to store numbers with precision between 6 and 9 digits, and the maximum size is just 4 bytes.

- **double**: It stores numbers with precision between 15 and 17 digits, and the maximum size is 8 bytes.

- **decimal**: It stores numbers with precision between 28 and 29 digits, and the maximum size is 16 bytes.

Each type is suitable for a specific type of data. For instance, the decimal type is largely used to store monetary information. The *figure 1.15* gives an example of the most common uses, as it follows:

```
static void Main(string[] args)
{
    decimal dollarValue = 3.5m; //DOLLAR VALUE
    decimal price = 103.45m; //PRICE EXAMPLE FOR MONETARY VALUE
    float floatValue = 1.07f; //FLOAT VALUE
    float floatSecondValue = 70.9F; //FLOAT VALUE
    double scale = 67.5; //DOUBLE VALUE

    Console.WriteLine($"Dollar value: {dollarValue}");
    Console.WriteLine($"Price: {price}");
    Console.WriteLine($"Float value: {floatValue}");
    Console.WriteLine($"Float second value: {floatSecondValue}");
    Console.WriteLine($"Scale: {scale}");
}
```

Figure 1.15: *Type examples*

All the types represented between the topics 1 and 8 are considered primitive types in C# language, as they represent the simplest structure in this program language to store data. Each type uses specific size in memory after its creation, and the .NET Core platform handles the clean-up of them in a high-performance way once they are considered reference types.

> In C# language, there are differences between variables of value type and reference type. The primitive types (int, string, bool, etc.) are considered value types once their value is stored in its own memory space. On the other hand, the reference type has a reference placed in the memory, and its underlying value is placed in a different memory space. Being familiar with these differences is important when the scenario requires a development of highdemand and better performance.

If the incorrect value type is being assigned to a variable of certain type, the compile will show an error, and the program will not run. It represents a huge advantage to use strongly typed language as C#, because it is possible to figure out programming issues earlier in comparison to the languages that accept only dynamic types, whose values are verified in runtime. The following image contains the samples of the creation and assignment of each variable shown and explained so far, focused only in primitive types and in the most frequently used types in C# programming language, as seen in *figure 1.16*:

```csharp
static void Main(string[] args)
{
    decimal dollarValue = 3.5m; //DOLLAR VALUE
    decimal price = 103.45m; //PRICE EXAMPLE FOR MONETARY VALUE
    float floatValue = 1.07f; //FLOAT VALUE
    float floatSecondValue = 70.9F; //FLOAT VALUE
    double scale = 67.5; //DOUBLE VALUE

    Console.WriteLine($"Dollar value: {dollarValue}");
    Console.WriteLine($"Price: {price}");
    Console.WriteLine($"Float value: {floatValue}");
    Console.WriteLine($"Float second value: {floatSecondValue}");
    Console.WriteLine($"Scale: {scale}");
}
```

Figure 1.16: Primitive types in C#

Meanwhile, the reference type variables are used to store more complex data and are stored differently in the memory from value type variables. A part from the primitive types, it is possible to create variables of your own custom types or even of other available native complex types in C# language such as a list, array, and others. Essentially, the syntax to create reference types is the same, declaring the type before the name of the variable.

> Despite of string and object being primitive types, they are considered reference types in C# language in the same time as class, interface, and delegate types. Therefore, there is no mandatory relation between value types and primitive types.

The following topics contain the most popular native reference types and their detailed explanation with examples:

- **Array**: This type has the purpose to store a collection of objects, being possible to have multiple values in a single variable, optimizing the time in the manipulation of a huge amount of values using distinct multiple variables. To create an array, you must declare the variable type followed by the square brackets, and the values can be assigned separated from each other by a comma. As seen in the following screenshot, to manipulate the values in the array, you must use any available iteration statement in C# language (loops, **foreach** and **for**), which will be explained in detail further in this book.

```
1       using System;
2
3       namespace CSharpFundamentalsSample
4       {
          0 references
5         class Program
6         {
            0 references
7           static void Main(string[] args)
8           {
9               string[] daysOfWeek = {
10                  "Monday",
11                  "Tuesday",
12                  "Wednesday",
13                  "Thursday",
14                  "Friday",
15                  "Saturday",
16                  "Sunday"
17              };
18          }
19        }
20      }
```

Figure 1.17: Array in C#

- **List**: It is a complex object that allows us to manipulate elements as a list and access those values by index. This type contains a bunch of extension features to search elements on the list, sorting, and making various operations. It is one of the most used types in C# because many programs have in common the need to manipulate a list of elements coming from database and other sources. When the list is created, the type of the elements should be defined and the values can be assigned using the method **Add**, which belongs to the **List** class. This type supports a wide variety of operations, and those operations are the main difference between that type and array variables. Both of them can get similar results in the manipulation of a list of elements, but the complex type List contains more advanced options to insert, add, remove, and search items in the list without explicitly referring their indexes. It prevents errors in dynamic operations once arrays always have a specific range of values. The *figure 1.18* has an example of the **List** variable type and the way to assign elements to it:

```
1   using System;
2   using System.Collections.Generic;
3
4   namespace CSharpFundamentalsSample
5   {
6       class Program
7       {
8           static void Main(string[] args)
9           {
10              List<string> daysOfWeek = new List<string>();
11              daysOfWeek.Add("Monday");
12              daysOfWeek.Add("Tuesday");
13              daysOfWeek.Add("Wednesday");
14              daysOfWeek.Add("Thursday");
15              daysOfWeek.Add("Friday");
16              daysOfWeek.Add("Saturday");
17              daysOfWeek.Add("Sunday");
18          }
19      }
20  }
```

Figure 1.18: List in C#

Lists in C# are under the **System.Collections.Generic** name space, and any type can be used combined with the list type as it accepts as argument a **Generic** type. A Generic type can be specified determining a type parameter with in brackets, as seen in *figure 1.19*:

```
1   namespace CSharpFundamentalsSample
2   {
3       public class MyGenericClass<T>
4       {
5           public T MyData { get; set; }
6       }
7   }
```

Figure 1.19: Generic type class

In the instance creation of the **My Generic Class**, a specific type must be passed, and the **My Data** property will assume the same type, as *figure 1.20* shows:

```
5   class Program
6   {
7       static void Main(string[] args)
8       {
9
10          MyGenericClass<string> myGenericClassOne = new MyGenericClass<string>();
11          myGenericClassOne.MyData = "String Value";
12          Console.WriteLine($"This a string: {myGenericClassOne.MyData}");
13
14          MyGenericClass<int> myGenericClassTwo = new MyGenericClass<int>();
15          myGenericClassTwo.MyData = 10;
16          Console.WriteLine($"This an integer: {myGenericClassTwo.MyData}");
17      }
18  }
19
```

Figure 1.20: Generic type example

In the given example, a first object is created passing the **string** type as the argument for the **Generic** type, which means that the underlying **MyData** property for this instance assumes that it has **string** type. The same happens with the second object called **My Generic Class Two**, which receives the integer type as argument, automatically reflects on the related **My Data** property for that object.

- **Class**: In C# language, it is possible to create your own types considering it is an object-oriented language. There are many particular concepts related to class that will be explained detailed in *Chapter 4: Interfaces in C#* of this book, but only to get started with classes, you must know that they are one of the reference types in C# language, and their correct use and construction is the most important part of any software using C# language. Through classes, it is possible to define properties, visibility, constructors, and other inherent concepts to object-oriented programming. For now, it is essential to understand it as one of the available types in C#. The following screenshot contains an example of a class called **Book**, which has six properties: **Id**, **Title**, **Creation**, **Author**, **Summary**, and **IsbnNumber**. You must realize that the types of properties correspond to primitive or complex type, depending on the kind of information that should be stored on them. The **Author** property represents a complex type of **Author** class; therefore, it refers to another entity, as seen in *figure 1.21*:

```csharp
1        using System;
2
3        namespace CSharpFundamentalsSample
4        {
         2 references
5            class Book
6            {
                 0 references
7                public int Id { get; set; }
                 0 references
8                public string Title { get; set; }
                 0 references
9                public DateTime Creation { get; set; }
                 0 references
10               public Author Author { get; set; }
                 0 references
11               public string Summary { get; set; }
                 0 references
12               public int IsbnNumber { get; set; }
13           }
14       }
15
```

Figure 1.21: Class in C#

- **Other types**: There are other reference types in C# such as delegates and interfaces, which will be explained in detail in the next chapters. They involve more advanced concepts, and many examples of them can be found in *Chapters 3: Basic Concepts of Object-Oriented Programming, Chapter 4: Interfaces in C#*, and *Chapter 5: Encapsulation and Polymorphism in C#*.

Understanding the most basic types will allow you to get started with performance enhancements in C# language and will help you to follow the best practices of coding.

Loops, operation, and iterations

There are many ways in C# language to manipulate a list of objects and execute recursive logical programming to meet the specific requirements and significantly reduce the number of necessary code lines for certain implementations that are needed to make operations many times. In the following topics, you will have the opportunity to walk through the most common statements to execute repetitive operations and will understand the difference between them.

while statement

With the **while** statement, is possible to execute operations till the predefined condition is not satisfied (**false**). The program will test the condition in the beginning of the loop, and if the result is true, the loop will still be executing. Its use is pretty similar to other statements in C# language for loop operations, but the syntax used for the condition is clear enough for the developer who is trying to interpret and debugging the code. In the following screenshot, there is an example of a **while** statement, which has a condition to keep running till the condition is not satisfied (number greater than 25), as seen in *figure 1.22*:

```
 1      using System;
 2
 3      namespace CSharpFundamentalsSample
 4      {
            0 references
 5          class Program
 6          {
                0 references
 7              static void Main(string[] args)
 8              {
 9                  int timesExecuted = 0;
10
11                  while (timesExecuted < 25)
12                  {
13                      Console.WriteLine("Time(s) " + timesExecuted);
14                      timesExecuted++;
15                  }
16
17              }
18          }
19      }
```

Figure 1.22: While in C#

The above code has the purpose of printing the message **Time (s)** followed by the time of loop execution, and it should run until the number of times. Therefore, the operation will happen 25 times considering the initial value of the variable **times Executed** is **0** and the variable is increasing one number on each iteration, as it is possible to see in Line 14.

do-while statement

The **do-while** instruction is very similar to the regular **while** statement, except that the logical code within the block will be run before the code that tests if the predefined condition is satisfied. The following screenshot contains the exact same purpose and logic programming of the previous example, but using **do-while** instead, as shown in *figure 1.23*:

```
1       using System;
2
3       namespace CSharpFundamentalsSample
4       {
            0 references
5           class Program
6           {
                0 references
7               static void Main(string[] args)
8               {
9                   int timesExecuted = 0;
10
11                  do
12                  {
13                      Console.WriteLine("Time(s) " + timesExecuted);
14                      timesExecuted++;
15                  }
16                  while (timesExecuted < 25);
17
18                  Console.ReadLine();
19              }
20          }
21      }
```

Figure 1.23: do-while in C#

This type of loop is useful when a certain operation needs to be done before the condition is tested by the routine, and that represents the main difference from the while statement.

In this simple routine, the initial value of **timesExecuted** is **0,** and the body is executed with out testing the condition for the first time. With in the body, the value of **timesExecuted** in one number, which means that routine, will be executed 25 times. In specific scenarios, the condition tested by the **while** could be never satisfied, and it will cause an infinite loop.

for loop

In a programming language, there are many ways to get similar results, and this premise applies to loop operation in C#. Apart from the **while** and **do-while** statements, it is possible to make similar operations using the**for** loop, which allow us to execute repetitive operations when the number of times for the loop is known before it starts to run. To use this type of loop, you must create a **for** statement following these requirements:

- A variable that contains the initial value for the iterations should be created inside the **for** statement.

- The condition to be tested and satisfied should use the variable created for the initial iteration.

- The times of the executions should be incremental and predefined.

To clearly understand this type of loop operation, you must see *figure 1.24*, which contains similar purposes to the previous examples:

```csharp
using System;

namespace CSharpFundamentalsSample
{
    class Program
    {
        static void Main(string[] args)
        {
            for(int timesExecuted = 0; timesExecuted < 25; timesExecuted++)
            {
                Console.WriteLine("Time(s) " + timesExecuted);
            }
        }
    }
}
```

Figure 1.24: For loop in C#

As seen in *figure 1.24*, the variable **timesExecuted** is declared inside the **for** loop instruction, and the incrementation process occurs after the condition that needs to be satisfied. If you compare to the previous explained loops in C#, it seems to be simpler and easier to read than the other ones, but it has the same purpose, which is printing content 25 times in the screen. Therefore, there are many ways to reach the same target in logical operations, and you must choose the suitable one for your own scenario in enterprise solutions.

foreach statement

The **foreach** loop can be used to execute operations in a list of elements and in any type that implements the **IEnumerable<T>** interface in C#. The *figure 1.25* represents how it works executing a block of code for each individual item in a list:

```
Program.cs  ⊕ ×
CS CSharpFundamentalsSample                                    ▾  CSharpFundamentalsSample.
    1    ⊟using System;
    2     using System.Collections.Generic;
    3
    4    ⊟namespace CSharpFundamentalsSample
    5     {
              0 references
    6    ⊟      class Program
    7           {
                  0 references
    8    ⊟          static void Main(string[] args)
    9               {
   10                   List<string> daysOfWeek = new List<string>();
   11                   daysOfWeek.Add("Monday");
   12                   daysOfWeek.Add("Tuesday");
   13                   daysOfWeek.Add("Wednesday");
   14                   daysOfWeek.Add("Thursday");
   15                   daysOfWeek.Add("Friday");
   16                   daysOfWeek.Add("Saturday");
   17                   daysOfWeek.Add("Sunday");
   18
   19    ⊟              foreach(string day in daysOfWeek)
   20                   {
   21                       Console.WriteLine("Day of Week:" + day);
   22                   }
   23               }
   24           }
   25     }
```

Figure 1.25: Foreach in C# *

As seen in the **foreach** statement sample, in line 10 is created a list of string items, and between lines 11 and 19, it is populated with the days of week, from Monday to Sunday. Finally, a **foreach** instruction is executed one time for each individual item on the list. That means the block of the codethat prints the **Day of Week** runs 7 times. In general, loop implementations have the advantage to write less code in case it would contain repetitive logical operations. In this example, instead of specifying the **Console.WriteLine** instruction 7 times (one for each day), it was specified just once.

Operators

Operators are largely used not only in mathematical operations, but also in programming languages to make arithmetic operations, comparison between values, and specify conditions for Boolean values. The C# language contains a huge number of operators, and in the next topics, you will have the opportunity to walk through the main types, their usage, and helpful examples.

Arithmetic operators

This type is used to make the addition, subtraction, division, multiplication, and other popular and conventional arithmetic operations. It is possible to specify these operations using variables or oven directly using values, as seen in *figure 1.26*:

```
using System;

namespace CSharpFundamentalsSample
{
    class Program
    {
        static void Main(string[] args)
        {
            int number1 = 50;
            int number2 = 25;

            int totalSubtraction = number1 - number2; // 25
            int totalAddition = number1 + number2; // 75
            int totalMultiplication = number1 * number2; //1.250
            int totalDivision = number1 / number2; // 2

            Console.WriteLine("Total subtraction: " + totalSubtraction);
            Console.WriteLine("Total addition: " + totalAddition);
            Console.WriteLine("Total multiplication: " + totalMultiplication);
            Console.WriteLine("Total division: " + totalDivision);

            Console.ReadLine();
        }
    }
}
```

Figure 1.26: Arithmetic operators in C#

As seen in the above screenshot, between lines 12 and 15, variables were created to store the total of the arithmetic operations of two numbers: variables **number1** and **number2**. It is important to note that the total variables should be created to support the underlying correct result operation. If at least one of the two numbers had decimal value (for example, **25.4**), the variable total should be from the decimal type or even a float variable depending on the quantity of characters.

Assignment operator

The most common operator is the **equal** operator, which is used to assign value to a variable, as shown in *figure 1.27*:

```
Program.cs    ↔ ×
CSharpFundamentalsSample                                              CSharpFundamentalsSample.Program
    1        using System;
    2
    3      ⊟namespace CSharpFundamentalsSample
    4       {
              0 references
    5      ⊟     class Program
    6             {
                    0 references
    7      ⊟         static void Main(string[] args)
    8                 {
    9                     string myMessage = "My variable is assigned with this value";
   10
   11                     int myNumber = 5;
   12
   13                     int x, y, z;
   14
   15                     x = y = z = 10;
   16
   17                     Console.WriteLine("My Message:" + myMessage);
   18                     Console.WriteLine("My Number:" + myNumber);
   19                     Console.WriteLine("Variable X:" + x);
   20                     Console.WriteLine("Variable Y:" + y);
   21                     Console.WriteLine("Variable Z:" + z);
   22                 }
   23             }
   24       }
```

Figure 1.27: Assignment operator in C#

The assignment operator is frequently used as well for conditional and comparison statements, but using two operators instead, combined, as seen in *figure 1.28*:

```
    7      ⊟     static void Main(string[] args)
    8             {
    9
   10                 DateTime today = DateTime.Now;
   11
   12      ⊟         if(today.Day == 4)
   13                 {
   14                     Console.WriteLine("This is day number for");
   15                 }
   16             }
   17
```

Figure 1.28: Equal operator

In the given example, line 12 uses the operator == in order to verify if the property **Day** is equal to the number **4**. Therefore, the equal operator has a different meaning in this context, not being an assignment operator.

In line 9, a **string** variable called **myMessage** is created, and a value has been assigned to it using the operator =. The same process is happening in line 11, but with an **int** type. There is the possibility to assign a value to multiple variables in sequence using the equal operator, which means that all the variables will have the same value in the final. As seen in line 15, the **int** variables are being assigned to the value **10**. Therefore, the equal operator in C# language is not necessarily used only for arithmetic operations, but to set values as well. The variable always will be placed on the left side and the value on the right side.

Relation operators

One of the most common logical implementations in any programming language is Boolean expressions, considering a system could have a routine that should follow specific logic based on certain conditions. To help with this target, the C# language contains many relational operators that allow us to make comparison between values, from the simplest operation to the most complex ones, according to what is needed. The following table contains all the relational operators that can be used in C# language:

Name	Operator	Example	Expected result
Equal to	==	25 == 25	True
Not equal to	!=	25 != 10	True
Less than	<	25 < 15	False
Greater than	>	25 > 15	True
Less than or equal to	<=	25 <=25	True
Greater than or equal to	>=	25 >=25	True

Table 1.1: Relational operators in C#

Regarding the equal to operator, in C# language, it is important to know that to make a comparison between two values; two equal operators should be used. In that way, the compile will recognize it as a comparison and not as a value assignment. Also, the operator ! can be used to reverse the Boolean value for any statement. The *figure 1.29* contains examples of each relational operator in C#:

```
static void Main(string[] args)
{
    DateTime today = DateTime.Now;

    bool resultOperation = today.Day != 4;

    if (resultOperation == true)
    {
        Console.WriteLine("This day is not four");
    }

}
```

Figure 1.29: Relational operators in C#

As seen in *figure 1.29*, a variable called **resultOperation** is created to store the Boolean result of each relational operation.

Logical operators

Logical operators are used to combine multiple relational operators in compound conditions. They are just Boolean statements that return true or false value. This kind of operator is largely used in loops and decision statements in logical implementations, when one or more conditions in a sentence should be satisfied.

The **AND** and **OR** operators can be combined to make different comparisons, and depending on the order of them, the statement can return different results.

As an example, imagine a program had a specific operation that should be run only if the day of week is Monday or Tuesday. The **OR** operator can be used in that case, as seen in *figure 1.30*:

```
using System;

namespace CSharpFundamentalsSample
{
    0 references
    class Program
    {
        0 references
        static void Main(string[] args)
        {

            var currentDayofWeek = DateTime.Now.DayOfWeek;

            if(currentDayofWeek == DayOfWeek.Monday || currentDayofWeek == DayOfWeek.Tuesday)
            {
                //MY CUSTOM LOGIC IMPLEMENTATION
            }

        }
    }
}
```

Figure 1.30: "OR" operator in C#

As seen in the code line 12, there is an **if** statement containing two comparison expressions separated by the keyword **||**, which is in C# equivalent to the **OR** operator. In that case, the code inside the **if** block will run only when at least one of the two conditions is satisfied: if the day of the week is **Monday** or **Tuesday**.

Otherwise, in the case of multiple conditions being tested and all of them being true, the operator **AND** can be used. The keyword for that operator in C# is **&&,** as *figure 1.31* shows:

```
using System;

namespace CSharpFundamentalsSample
{
    0 references
    class Program
    {
        0 references
        static void Main(string[] args)
        {

            var currentDayofWeek = DateTime.Now.DayOfWeek;
            var currentHour = DateTime.Now.Hour;

            if(currentDayofWeek == DayOfWeek.Saturday && currentHour > 6)
            {
                //MY CUSTOM LOGIC IMPLEMENTATION
            }

        }
    }
}
```

Figure 1.31: "AND" operator in C#

In that example, the condition to execute the block of code inside the **if** statement will be satisfied only if the current day of week is **Saturday** and the current hour is greater than 6.

Unary operators

The C# language has operators that have the purpose of making operations using a single operand. It saves time to write specific routines such as to increment a number, invert the value of a Boolean value, decrement a number, and others.

To add an extra number to a integer variable in C#, the operator **++** can be used, and it is possible to use the two minus operators to subtract one a variable that contains a number value, as seen in *figure 1.32*:

```csharp
using System;

namespace CSharpFundamentalsSample
{
    class Program
    {
        static void Main(string[] args)
        {
            int numberExample = 25;

            numberExample++; // Variable has the value 26

            numberExample--; // Variable has the value 25 again

            numberExample--; // Variable has the value 24
        }
    }
}
```

Figure 1.32: Unary operators in C#

The preceding implementation is the same as if it was adding one value to the variable using arithmetic operator as: **numberExample = numberExample + 1**. Surely, the unary operator syntax is much more optimized in terms of the amount of needed code to get the similar result.

Ternary operators

Another operator that helps to reduce the used line of codes in logical statements is the ternary operator that can replace **if** statements for comparison in the cases where the condition results in the assignment of a variable. As the example in the following screenshot, there is a variable called **message** from the **string** type, and its value is a ternary expression using the operators **?** and **:**. If the comparison condition is satisfied, it is assigning the message **Today is Monday,** and if is not, the assigned value is **Today is not Monday**, as seen in *figure 1.33*:

```
1        using System;
2
3        namespace CSharpFundamentalsSample
4        {
             0 references
5            class Program
6            {
                 0 references
7                static void Main(string[] args)
8                {
9                    var dayOfWeek = DateTime.Now.DayOfWeek;
10
11                   string message = dayOfWeek == DayOfWeek.Monday ? "Today is Monday" : "Today is not Monday";
12
13                   Console.WriteLine(message);
14               }
15           }
16       }
```

Figure 1.33: *Ternary operators in C#*

It is not recommended to use conditions using ternary operators in the cases that the condition is complex and contains compound statements. It would make the code hard to read. Use the **if** statement instead, as the intention of the logic operation will be explicitly exposed in future changes in the underlying part of the code.

Compound assignment operators

As what happens with the ternary and unary operators, the bitwise type helps to reduce the number of coded lines, and it makes certain operations easier to be made. Any arithmetic operator followed by the equal operator = means to the compile in C# language that the arithmetic operation before the equal operator should be applied to its own variable value. The *figure 1.34* contains an example of the compound assignment operator for + (addition) and (multiplication):

```
int firstExample = 25;
firstExample += 10; // 25 + 10

int secondExample = 15;
secondExample *= 5; // 15 * 5
```

Figure 1.34: *Compound assignment operators*

In case the logical implementation contains a complex operation, the use of compound assignment operators can difficult the reading of the algorithm by developers who will maintain the code. Therefore, consider using explicit variables for complex math operations in case it contains many parts and conditions.

if statement

The C# language contains a bunch of operators for making different conditions in Boolean expressions. This is a clear indication of the importance of controlling the behavior of the software by implementing precise statements, even for complex conditions. To properly use the operators, you must know the **if** statement, which allows us to execute a specific part of code if a certain condition is satisfied. Otherwise, it is possible to specify an implementation that will be run in case of the condition not being met. This kind of logical statement is one of the most common operations in any programming language, and C# language has a clear syntax, as seen in *figure 1.35*:

```
15      var dayOfWeek = DateTime.Now.DayOfWeek;
16
17      if(dayOfWeek == DayOfWeek.Saturday)
18      {
19          Console.WriteLine("Today is Saturday");
20      }
21      else
22      {
23          Console.WriteLine("Today is not Saturday");
24      }
25
26      if (DateTime.Now.Day == 1)
27          Console.WriteLine("Today is the first day of the month");
```

Figure 1.35: Compound assignment operators

In this example, a specific block of code will run if the day of week is equal **Saturday,** and a different block will run if the condition has a false result. Using it exactly like that is suitable mainly in the cases when there are clearly two distinct things that should be executed depend on the condition result. It follows the pattern if-then-**else**, and it is one of the most used features in C#.

If a logical requirement contains many sub-conditions inside of an **if** or **else** statements, it is recommended to use other language structures such as **switch**, which will be explained in the next topic. Depending on the complexity, many levels and sub-levels of conditions in a single one routine could turn the code hard to read, and errors might be introduced while changes are made.

switch case

The **switch** case statement is suitable to use if a logical implementation contains multiple options to choose from, there by only one will have its block of code executed, in other words, the option that matches with the predefined value for comparison. The **switch** case is largely used if a value should be tested by many conditions or even if it has more than two or three conditions, as the example in *figure 1.36*:

```
 9          var dayOfWeek = DateTime.Now.DayOfWeek;
10
11          switch(dayOfWeek)
12          {
13              case DayOfWeek.Monday:
14                  Console.WriteLine("Today is Monday");
15                  break;
16              case DayOfWeek.Tuesday:
17                  Console.WriteLine("Today is Tuesday");
18                  break;
19              case DayOfWeek.Wednesday:
20                  Console.WriteLine("Today is Wednesday");
21                  break;
22              case DayOfWeek.Thursday:
23                  Console.WriteLine("Today is Thursday");
24                  break;
25              case DayOfWeek.Friday:
26                  Console.WriteLine("Today is Friday");
27                  break;
28              case DayOfWeek.Saturday:
29                  Console.WriteLine("Today is Saturday");
30                  break;
31              case DayOfWeek.Sunday:
32                  Console.WriteLine("Today is Sunday");
33                  break;
34          }
```

Figure 1.36: Switch statement

In this example, a value (day of week) is tested against 7 options, one for each **case** in the instruction, and if one of the conditions is satisfied, the program will execute the block of code specified between the underlying **case** and the **break**. It is very useful to expose system requirements in the cases that the work flow could contain multiple options and the routine that should be executed for each one is slightly different. Using a **switch** statement for multiple options instead of an **if** statement is a good practice in C# programming language. If in the example presented in *figure 1.37*, the **if** statement was used, the code would look like that, which is not recommended:

```
var dayOfWeek = DateTime.Now.DayOfWeek;

if(dayOfWeek == DayOfWeek.Monday)
{
    Console.WriteLine("Today is Monday");
}
else
{
    if (dayOfWeek == DayOfWeek.Tuesday)
    {
        Console.WriteLine("Today is Tuesday");
    }
    else
    {
        if (dayOfWeek == DayOfWeek.Wednesday)
        {
            Console.WriteLine("Today is Wednesday");
        }
        else
        {
            if (dayOfWeek == DayOfWeek.Thursday)
            {
                Console.WriteLine("Today is Thursday");
            }
            else
            {
                if (dayOfWeek == DayOfWeek.Friday)
                {
                    Console.WriteLine("Today is MondFridayay");
                }
                else
                {
                    if (dayOfWeek == DayOfWeek.Saturday)
                    {
                        Console.WriteLine("Today is Saturday");
                    }
                    else
                    {
                        if (dayOfWeek == DayOfWeek.Sunday)
                        {
                            Console.WriteLine("Today is Sunday");
                        }
                    }
                }
            }
        }
    }
}
```

Figure 1.37: Switch statement

This implementation works the same way as the previous example, but it contains a significantly greater number of lines, and it is much more complex to read. Therefore, it is recommended to use the **switch** statement when a value needs to be tested against multiple values.

Error handling

Every software existent in the market could have implementation errors, unexpected behaviors and execution issues. There are many possible causes for them, such as conversion type error, leak memory issues, data problem, wrong conversion type, etc. Each programming language has a particular way of handling those possible errors, and mapping those could notably contribute to have more stable software.

The C# language contains native implementations to properly catch all the errors that a program may have and shows worthwhile and detailed information on the cause of the exception and if it is related to native .NET Core libraries, it also contains suggestions to fix the errors. It is common to use in any software development third-party libraries and use resources from other systems, such as database, external services, and others. The integration with those third parties usually requires networking connection for communication or even availability of them. Therefore, a system should have a reliable way to prevent the exceptions that could happen during this process, and the program must implement a custom routine in case some issue appears in any part of the software.

Error handling in C# language must use three combined blocks of code: **try**, **catch**, and **finally** keywords, which represent ways of making proper custom actions in case a software failure occurs. The implementation exceptioncan be applied in many levels of our application, and it is important to spend enough time to plan properly on the best strategy for error handling in your software project.

Exception

In software development, exceptions are all the errors that could happen in the application. They make it possible to control our custom implementation of any error that might happen in the execution and give a specific direction to it.

In the following screenshot, there is an example of exception handling implementation. In that case, the method is receiving a person age value and handles the possible exceptions throwing an exception to the system if the **age** is invalid, as seen in *figure 1.38*:

```
18    static bool ValidAge(int age)
19    {
20        if(age < 0)
21        {
22            throw new ArgumentOutOfRangeException("The age must be greater than 0");
23        }
24
25        return true;
26    }
```

Figure 1.38: Throw exception

The .NET Core libraries contain a lot of exception classes that are inherited from the main class **System.Exception**. In this example, an **Argument Out Of Range Exception** was used, passing a custom message error to the system referencing the cause of the issue. In that case, it is not allowed to have a minus number for the **age** value. An exception can be intentionally thrown, or it might come from an unexpected behavior of the software.

The **try** and **catch** blocks should be used by the part of code that is using effectively the method to validate the **age**. The rule to throw the exception was implemented in the child method, and the following contains an example on how to use the **try** and **catch** block to make custom actions in case of an error happens, as *figure 1.39* shows:

```
1    using System;
2
3    namespace CSharpFundamentalsSample
4    {
5        class Program
6        {
7            static void Main(string[] args)
8            {
9                int age = 25;
10
11                try
12                {
13                    ValidAge(age);
14                }
15                catch(ArgumentOutOfRangeException ex)
16                {
17                    Console.Write("You must specify a valid value for the age information. Info:" + ex.Message);
18                }
19                catch(Exception ex)
20                {
21                    Console.WriteLine("Unexpected error: " + ex.Message);
22                }
23
24            }
25
```

Figure 1.39: Throw exception

As seen in the example, the **ValidAge** method was called inside the **try** block code, and if an exception occurs, the system will execute the underlying **catch** block, according to the type of exception. If the error has a known cause, it is showing a specific message related to the invalid value. If the exception does not have a known cause, the system is showing a message in the console with generic information. In real scenarios, in case the method throws a custom exception as if the **age** is a minus number, the program could have a routine to show to the users the error in the form of a validation message.

Exception handling is one of the most important parts of any software project, because usually, it is related directly to user experience. Therefore, all the possible exceptions must be mapped in the development phase, and an action should be taken in all the cases according to the defined system requirements.

When the system is using external resources or even has integrations with third-party systems, usually a routine should be implemented to prevent the dispose issues of the objects in the memory. For instance, if there is an error to record something into an external database, it is recommended to close the connection with this database, with the process being made successfully or not. To handle that properly, you must use the **finally** block, which will be executed in all the cases, even if an exception was thrown, as seen in *figure 1.40*:

```csharp
1   using System;
2
3   namespace CSharpFundamentalsSample
4   {
5       class Program
6       {
7           static void Main(string[] args)
8           {
9               int age = 25;
10
11              try
12              {
13                  ValidAge(age);
14
15                  SavePerson();
16              }
17              catch(ArgumentOutOfRangeException ex)
18              {
19                  Console.Write("You must specify a valid value for the age information. Info:" + ex.Message);
20              }
21              catch(Exception ex)
22              {
23                  Console.WriteLine("Unexpected error: " + ex.Message);
24              }
25              finally
26              {
27                  CloseDbConnection();
28              }
29
30          }
31
```

Figure 1.40: Throw exception

In the previous screenshot, is possible to see that after calling the validation method inside the try block, the system is calling the **SavePerson** method, which in a real scenarios would have a database operation that requires open connection and depends on the network availability. Even if the operation fails, the system will always close the connection with the database, as seen in *figure 1.31* between Lines 25 and 27. The **finally** block code is being executed in all the cases, respecting the order of try and catch previous blocks.

Namespaces

A namespace in C# language is a feature that gives us the possibility to separate and keep a set of classes based on the logical criteria. Every class is under a specific name space; the ones we create our selves or the ones provided by the .NET platform. To define a name space, just specify a path separated by a period, before the name of the class, as seen in *figure 1.41*:

```
5    namespace DesignPatternsBook.Models
6    {
        3 references
7        public class MyClass
8        {
            0 references
9            public List<string> MyList { get; set; }
10       }
11   }
```

Figure 1.41: *Namespace definition*

In the given example, the **MyClass** class is under the namespace **DesignPatternsBook.Models**. Therefore, in this context, it would be logical to consistently keep all the models under the same name space. In case the class needs to be used by another name space, a using directive can be used in order to get visibility of the related class, as shown in *figure 1.42*:

```
1    using System;
2    using DesignPatternsBook.Models;
3
4
5    namespace CSharpFundamentalsSample
6    {
        0 references
7        class Program
8        {
            0 references
9            static void Main(string[] args)
10           {
11
12               MyClass myClass = new MyClass();
13           }
```

Figure 1.42: *Namespace use*

The use of namespace allows to organize complex projects in order to keep the classes under a similar box.

New features on C# 9.0

.NET 5 brought to C# language a bunch of interesting and useful features that have being claimed by technical communities, developers, and companies for a long time. One of them is the use of top-level statements, which simplifies the creation of sample applications by removing all the unnecessary code, as seen in *figure 1.43*:

```
Program.cs
ConsoleApp10
1    using System;
2
3    Console.WriteLine("My simple program");
4    Console.ReadLine();
5
6
```

Figure 1.43: *Top-level statements*

The previous example represents a standard console application, but without the traditional **Program** class called, including the **main** method. The *figure 1.44* shows how it was until .NET Core 3.1:

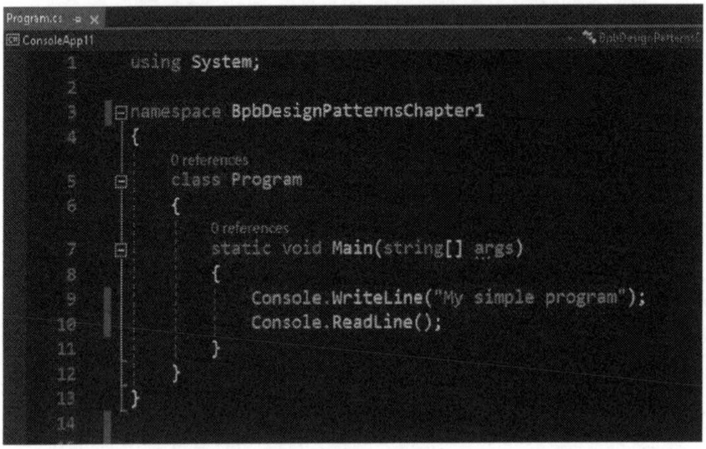

Figure 1.44: Top-level statements

The simple **Program** in the .NET 3.1 version has 13 lines instead of only 4 compared to the .NET 5 version. The same simplification exists in other languages such as Python, and it is now a part of the .NET platform as well since C# 9.0.

Additionally, C# 9.0 provides a better way to create new objects, simplifying the call of constructor methods. The *figure 1.45* shows the difference between C# 9.0 and the previous versions regarding the instantiation of new objects:

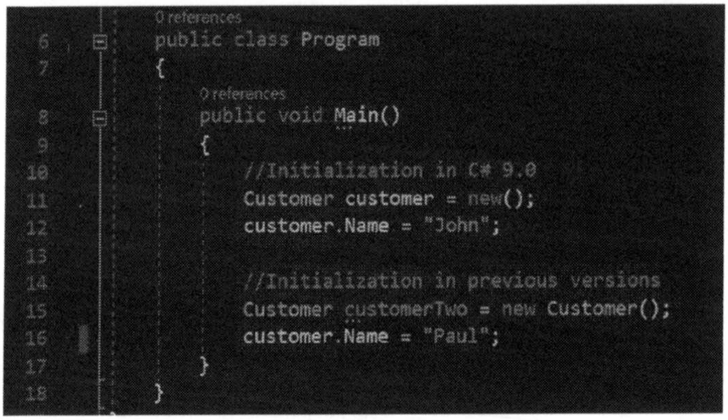

Figure 1.45: Top-level statements

With the version of C# language, it is possible to create new objects using the keyword **new** with out specifying the type of the class. This new way to create objects is a good alternative in the cases where there is a need for creation of complex object types, such as dictionaries and complex lists, being an interesting simplification in terms of syntax.

Another new feature of C# 9.0 is the use of record types, which gives us the possibility to create immutable objects with implicit read-only properties, being a useful alternative to data transfer objects in many scenarios. To create a record type, it is mandatory to use the record keyword, as presented in *figure 1.46*:

```
namespace BookDesignPattenrs
{
    public record Product
    {
        public int Id { get; }
        public string Title { get; }
        public double Price { get;}

        public Product(int id, string title, double price) => (Id, Title, Price) = (id, title, pric
    }
}
```

Figure 1.46: Record type

At the first moment, it seems a normal class structure, but it is slightly different from a usual one. A **read-only** keyword was not specified in any property; however, they are read-only members, as the setter statement was not declared. Additionally, the record type gives us the chance of creating clones or copies of an object using the **with** keyword, as seen in *figure 1.47*:

```
public class Program
{
    public void Main()
    {
        Product productOne = new Product(1, "Product 2", 100);

        Product productTwo = productOne with { Title = "Product 2" };
    }
}
```

Figure 1.47: Use of "with" keyword

The use of the **with** keyword allows us to clone an object modifying the properties that are not read-only. A similar syntax can be found in JavaScript and other languages, and the combination of record types and the **this** keyword represents a timesaver in terms of clone operations and a better use of memory as well.

Beyond the features covered in more detail in this book, this new version of C# introduced the support for code generators, being possible to create analyzers ontop of the standard C# compile implementation. It is a powerful alternative for integrations, reusability, and creation of custom components that require a close interaction with low-deep native implementation in C# language.

Conclusion

The C# language contains the basic instructions that allow us to develop and implement any standard functionality presented in any software. Despite every program having distinct requirements; the majority of the applications must represent a group of simple and basic operations that have support in C# language.

In this chapter, you learned the very important and fundamental concepts of C#, such as variables, logical statement, operators, error handling, and different types of loops and iterations. Now, you are able to learn more advanced concepts of coding with C# and get started to the next related topics.

In the next chapter, you will learn about the .NET Core platform and will have the opportunity to know the most common project types presented on the platform for Web applications, mobile development, desktop implementations, and much more.

Points to remember

- To develop .NET Core applications, you must install the latest version of Visual Studio or Visual Studio Code.

- The C# language contains features to handle exceptions and system errors that may happens in the software execution.

- To get started with C#, you must be familiar with the variable types, loop statement, operators, and error handling.

Multiple-choice questions

1. **Which option contains only the relational operators:**

    a. $==, !=, >, <$

    b. $!=, >, <,$ if

    c. Switch, for, foreach, equal

    d. None of these

2. **Which type of variable is used to store true and false values:**

    a. String

    b. Int

    c. Bool

    d. Decimal

3. **What is the value of the variable "isValid" in the following code:**
   ```
   int age = 25;
   var isValid = age > 18;
   ```
    a. False

    b. True

    c. 25

    d. 18

4. After the following code, what is the final value of the number variable?

    ```
    int number = 78;
    number++;
    ```

    a. 78
    b. 77
    c. 80
    d. 79

5. Imagine you have a routine in your code that should connect to a database. Considering a networking issue could be happen, in which block of code is recommendable to close the connection with the database:

    a. Inside the **try** block
    b. Inside the **catch** block
    c. Inside the **finally** block

Answer

1. a
2. c
3. b
4. d
5. c

Questions

1. What are the available loop statements in C#?

2. What is the best alternative to implement a logical statement that could have more than three conditions?

3. What are the **try catch** blocks used for?

Key terms

*   **Exceptions**: Errors that could happen in software execution.

*   **Operators**: The C# language contains many operators that allow to make arithmetic operations, simplify iterations, and testing conditions.

CHAPTER 2
Introduction to .NET 5

With this chapter, we are starting our journey into the cross-platform and modern .NET 5. The .NET platform has changed to provide powerful libraries that allow us to build applications for any operating system and even multiple different devices, taking the benefits of the best practices of software development. You will learn how to set up the environment for building .NET 5 applications and understand cross-platform concepts, which is one of the main advantages of this platform. Considering the software development market has changed to become focused on open-source projects, it is essential and extremely important to find out how .NET 5 works and how you can build robust cross-platform enterprise applications using this impressive technology.

Structure

In this chapter, we will discuss the following topics:

- Multi-platform concepts
- Main aspects of .NET 5 applications
- Overview of project types on .NET 5

Objectives

After studying this unit, you should be able to:

- Understanding multi-platform concepts
- Discuss the available .NET 5 project types
- Create the most basic projects in .NET 5

2.1 Understanding multi-platform concepts

With the beginning of cloud-based applications in the last decade, the market competition significantly changed from a battle for a software license to cloud system infrastructure services to support the high demand for scalability, modern applications, big data, globalization, and openmarket. Therefore, the interest in profitability is not focused on the operating system anymore, but on reliable infrastructure, as many companies are changing their business model to provide solutions based on the **Software as a Service (SaaS)** concept.

None the less, the big IT companies are still releasing and creating new operating systems, the attention is completely on open-source projects nowadays, and any modern application must be able to run in Linux, macOS, and Windows platforms. Further more, with the rise of the **Internet of Things (IoT)**, the types of devices where applications can be run are much more diverse and have made the software development process more complex. Not long ago, the biggest concern of every Web developer was to get success in running the same application in multiple different browsers properly, and it still represents a huge challenge. But, although the Web applications are accessed from multiple operating systems, usually, the application was hosted on a server, whose specifications were under control, using a single one operating system and platform. This scenario rapidly moved to another more complex one, based in a cross-platform environment with the purpose of having more compatibility, decrease the costs, and deliver applications faster to a more relevant number of users across the globe, using the micro-service architecture.

Therefore, to attend these new requirements, Microsoft provided the .NET 5 platform, a rich and powerful technology that was made to run literally every where and in any operating system, rewriting all the libraries presenting on the .NET Framework and getting better results in terms of performance. At the very beginning of the C# language and .NET Framework, they were completely made to support only the Windows platform, which was a clear limitation for adoption in the market because, in specific scenarios, to build desktop applications, the projects of this type require to be written twice or even more times redundantly and, therefore, increase the costs of any project. In order to attend the creation of multi-platform applications, Microsoft created .NET Core 1.0, and after that upgrades to that, until the current .NET 5, which represents a consolidation of all .NET Core versions: 1.0, 2.0, 2.2, 3.0, and finally, .NET 5.

Building applications using .NET 5 allows you to write a unique application that can be hosted on any platform, in many types of devices, distinct cloud infrastructures, and to consume it in plenty of Web APIs. It represented a revolutionary change for the .NET world and placed this technology in a prominent position in the market. Also, another important movement of .NET was the fact that it became an open-source project. So, individuals, companies, and academic institutions could contribute to the evolution of the platform, and because it became true, the .NET community has been one of the most active communities in the world.

2.2 Overview of the principal project types in .NET 5

To get started with .NET 5, we must be aware of the main type of projects it supports. Along with the examples of this book, you will have the opportunity to create various types of applications for multiple platforms (Web, desktop, and mobile), and this section represents only a brief overview of all the types that can be used for building enterprise applications. By default, the Visual Studio already contains specific project templates to facilitate the creation of .NET 5 projects. Some of them are provided by Microsoft, and other ones by the technical community as open-source projects.

Once you start a new project using Visual Studio, the following options will be available, as seen in the following screenshot:

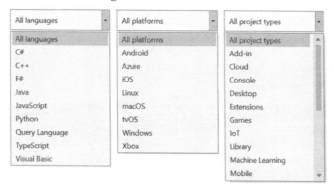

Figure 2.1: Visual Studio project options

As you can see, a wide variety of programming languages, platforms, and project types are available for .NET 5 applications, including mobile app development, desktop applications, Web development, machine learning, and games.

2.2.1 Console application

To get started with the .NET 5 project types, we will create a simple Console App, a standard project for desktop applications that allows us to run applications in the background and to integrate it with simple user interaction. To create the project, after opening the Visual Studio and having access to the project type list (*figure 2.1*), you must choose the C# language and Windows platform. It will filter the results to show only the applicable types. Once .NET 5 represents an evolution of .NETCore 3.1, depending on your Visual Studio version, the name of the project template will contain the keyword **Core**, despite the project can be set to .NET 5 without restriction. Additionally, you can type the word **Console** in the search box. That way, you will get the Console application template types, as you can see in the following screenshot:

Figure 2.2: Console Application

If you are not familiar with C# language, it will be your first opportunity to get started with the language, its structure, keywords, and statements. Once you confirm in the application creation dialog the name of the project and make it to the next steps, the result is a simple Console Application containing only one class called **Program. cs**. To see the content of the class, just open the file by double-clicking on it, and the Visual Studio will show the class in the code editor section, as shown in *figure 2.3*:

```
namespace BookDesignPattenrs
{
    0 references
    public class Program
    {
        0 references
        public static void Main()
        {
            Console.WriteLine("I'm learning .NET 5");
            Console.Read();
        }
    }
}
```

Figure 2.3: Program.cs

Every C# application is organized by namespaces, referred to in *figure 1.10* in the first line. A regular enterprise application might have a lot of libraries, packages, and various used namespaces for different purposes. Their names and paths follow a logical sequence hierarchically, and they might belong natively to C# language, as the namespace **System**, and other ones could belong to a custom or third-party implementation.

> **Following and using good name conventions for namespaces, classes, methods, and variables is one of the most important best practices of coding, and it is valid for any programming language. Always use meaningful names across the system, applying the camel case pattern for classes (for example,MyBpbBook) and upper case for constants (for example, MAX_ITEMS_ORDER = 3). Make your code easy to read by others and even by yourself.**

Line 3 contains the custom namespace reference for our project (**ConsoleAppBook**), and it usually is the name of the project or the company organization name, depending on the architecture of the application and the technical decision made by the team. By default, the Console Application has a main class called **Program** and a static method called **Main**, which will run once the application is started. The content of the **Main** class in the example is a **Console.WriteLine**, a method that will print the content "**I'm learning .NET Core**"on the screen, and the **Console.Read** method will ask the user for a typed entry.

Once it is running by Visual Studio using the option **Start Debugging** in the Debug superior menu option, the application starts, and it shows in the console the printed phrase specified in the method **Main**, as the following screenshot:

Figure 2.4: Console application debug

Another known type of project template in the .NET platform is the Windows Forms project, which allows us to create rich desktop applications using visual components, easily integrated with native desktop components for Windows and other platforms. The first version of .NET Core (1.0 and 2.x) did not support Windows Forms applications, but it was fully introduced since .NET Core 3.0 version, following relevant improvements in .NET 5.Comparing with .NET Core versions, one of the most relevant improvements introduced since .NET 3.0 is related to self-contained executable files, which means the application is built with self-contained mode enable, and the .NET will generate a single file with all the libraries and files that the application is using. The executable will contain all the necessary project dependencies, such as .NET native libraries and third-party implementations. There fore, the machine where the application will be installed does not need to have any extra library or .NET installation. The executable contains everything necessary. It facilitates the deployment, installation, maintenance, and even software updates in any environment, and it works properly not only for the Windows OS but even for Linux and macOS.

2.2.2 Windows Forms

To get started with the creation of Windows Forms applications, you must go to the creation template dialog already shown in this chapter, search for Windows Forms, and the results will show the Windows Forms project type as a suggestion, as seen in the following screenshot:

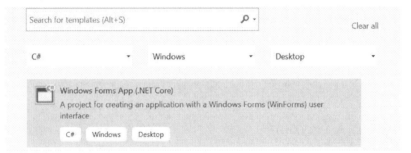

Figure 2.5: Windows Forms

The Visual Studio provides a large list of visual components that can be used in Windows Forms applications. Considering that almost all the enterprise applications share the same or at least similar visual components, the available list is really useful and helpful. Among them, there are specific ones for common form controls such as **TextBox**, **Label**, and **ListView**. It also contains a bunch of options to use native operation systems features likea media player, embedded browser, file and folders manipulations, and much more. To access the full available list, just go to the left sidebar on Visual Studio and open the **Toolbox** tab over there.

You can drag and drop components directly into the form and change their properties visually or access the **Properties** tab, selecting a component and clicking on the **Properties** tab in the right sidebar, as you can see in the following screenshot:

Figure 2.6: Visual Studio sections for Windows Forms

To include a logical statement to your components, you must double-click on the control to access the source code control associated with the component. Each visual control has custom events associated with the component type, and considering you can start your logical coding in a design mode, Windows Forms is one of the easiest ways to learn C# language because you can quickly see the results of your code working. Also, once the project is created in Visual Studio, the program is ready to run with out extra configurations, increasing productivity and deployment rate. As a cross-platform solution, a Windows Forms application built in .NET 5 is ready to be used and installed in any platform, such as Linux, macOS, and Windows operation system.

To get started with the Windows Forms application development, once you have created the application in Visual Studio, drag and drop a **TextBox** and **Button** controls to the form; you can position those as you want. Selecting each control, just go to the **Properties** tab on the right sidebar and change the **Name** property to **txtName** for the **TextBox** and **myButton** for the button control. After doing that and pressing the **Start** button on the superior toolbox, the Windows Forms application will run, and the design is going to look like the following screenshot:

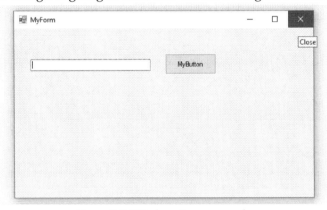

Figure 2.7: Windows Forms example

As a concept and following a programmer perspective, the Windows Forms project type was made to be simple and fast to create. Different from Web development, you can create in visual mode all the screens of your system and code just the logical part of the events, methods, and buttons such as database call operations, communicating with external APIs, or even making business operations to meet the user system requirement.

Once you have a brief contact with two desktop project types in .NET 5 (Console and Windows Forms), there are other project types that you must know regarding Web development. The first is the Asp.Net Core Web API project type, which allows us to create **Application Programming Interface (API)** applications based on REST, meeting all the most modern requirements for Web services, security, and performance.

REST is the contraction of Representational State Transfer, which is a standard architecture to build and define Web services. The biggest advantage of this approach is the interoperability across many languages and platforms. Also, most of all, the modern Web APIs are based on JSON (JavaScript Object Notation), a largely used pattern for data object transfer between systems. All modern languages provide methods to handle JSON objects properly. It became the most popular way to integrate systems.

2.2.3 Asp.Net Core Web application

To create a Web API project in .NET 5, you must search Asp.Net Core on the search box in the Visual Studio project creation dialog, give it a name, and it will be redirected to the list of available Web project types in .NET 5. Choose the API type and finish the final step, as seen in the following screenshot:

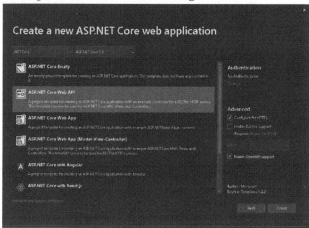

Figure 2.8: Asp.Net Core 5.0 Web API

Once the creation is complete, the Visual Studio generates a Web API with a basic structure based on the Model View Controller architecture, which will be explained further in this book. Each API has multiple methods called end points as well. Each exposed method could contain security settings, allowed HTTP verbs configured and also logical programming to make the necessary operations according to the main target of each endpoint. To create a new end point, you must take these steps:

1. Create a new **Controller** clicking the right mouse button on the **Controller** folder shown in the **Solution Explorer** right side bar. There are a few controller types, but it needs to be of the kind API Controller Empty.

2. Give a name to the controller, for instance, **CustomerController** and save it.

3. Visual Studio will generate a `Controller` class without a method. To insert one, create a public method returning a string type and return an underlying string content for testing.

4. After creating a public method, it is necessary to specify the HTTP verb allowed for this method, for instance, **HttpGet**, which specifies that this method should be called using the **GET** method by the application, which will use this API. Usually, different HTTP verbs are used for distinct purposes: for example, **POST** is used for inserting data, and **GET** for retrieving data by the API.

5. Once all the steps are done, your code will look like the following screenshot:

```
CustomerController.cs  -p  ×
WebAPIBook
1    using System;
2    using System.Collections.Generic;
3    using System.Linq;
4    using System.Threading.Tasks;
5    using Microsoft.AspNetCore.Http;
6    using Microsoft.AspNetCore.Mvc;
7
8    namespace WebAPIBook.Controllers
9    {
10       [Route("api/[controller]/[action]")]
11       [ApiController]
         0 references
12       public class CustomerController : ControllerBase
13       {
14           [HttpGet]
             0 references
15           public string GetName()
16           {
17               return "Customer Name";
18           }
19       }
```

Figure 2.9: Asp.Net Core Web API code

For organizational purposes, usually, all the controllers in a Web API project share the same namespace as **WebAPIBook**, as you can see in Line number 8. Also, each controller must use annotations above the class name to indicate to the .NET Core application **ApiController** that this controller should be accessed as a Web API endpoint. Additionally, you can specify the route or the path that will be used for accessing all the methods in this controller. In this example, the route is the domain followed by the suffix API, controller name, and method name, as you can see in Line 10. After running the project, the path for this example will be **https://localhost/api/customer/getname**. Running the application over this URL, the result is as the following screenshot:

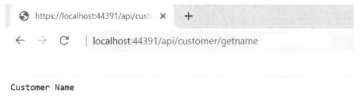

Figure 2.10: Asp.Net Core Web API results

The API method returned the content specified on it, respecting the type of return and the custom logic implemented. In more complex scenarios, which you will implement further following the samples in this book, the API would get a customer name connecting to a database, and it would populate a Customer object to return the data. The controllers usually contain logical programming targeting other layers in the applications.

Another common project type in .NET is the traditional Asp.Net Core **MVC (Model View Controller)** project, one of the most popular templates in Visual Studio, considering that it has been largely used by many companies, even for the migrated projects from the legacy .NET Framework versions.

> The MVC pattern is one of the most famous architectures for Web applications, not only in the .NET platform. This approach follows important best practices of programming, such as separations of responsibilities between application layers, and it is helpful to scale the system in complexity, being possible to keep parallel teams working in the same project without a huge impact or merging issues.

To get started with the Asp.Net Core MVC project, you must create a new project of that kind in Visual Studio. In the project creation dialog, search for `Asp.Net` and choose the option **Asp.Net Core Web Application**, as seen in the following screenshot:

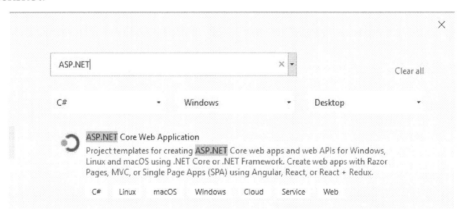

Figure 2.11: Asp.Net Core MVC project

In the next step, after defining the project name, choose the template called Web Application (Model View Controller). Once the project is created, Visual Studio would generate the default folder and file structure for a standard MVC application. There are three main folders in the project: Model, View, and Controller, corresponding to the MVC architecture.

The Model has the responsibility to keep the state of the application according to certain system requirements, and the other layers of the application have the responsibility to populate and manage the model properly. The View has the responsibility to render the user interface, such as HTML, CSS, and JavaScript. By default, in Asp.Net Core MVC projects, the Razor engine is used to mix .NET Core code with HTML. This approach makes it possible to implement and use logical programming in C# inside the Views and interact with HTML elements. Finally, the Controller has the purpose of managing the routes and user actions such as page requests, form submissions, and other types of data requests and user interactions. Once an action is requested by the user, it is managed by a specific controller depending on the path that was specified and associated with it. Each controller could contain and support many actions, each one having its own responsibility and logical programming implementation.

To create your first custom MVC application, just make the following steps:

1. In Visual Studio Solution Explorer, click the right mouse button on the **Models** folder and choose the option to add class giving the name **Book**. It will generate an empty **book** class. You must create the properties of the class, as seen in the next screenshot:

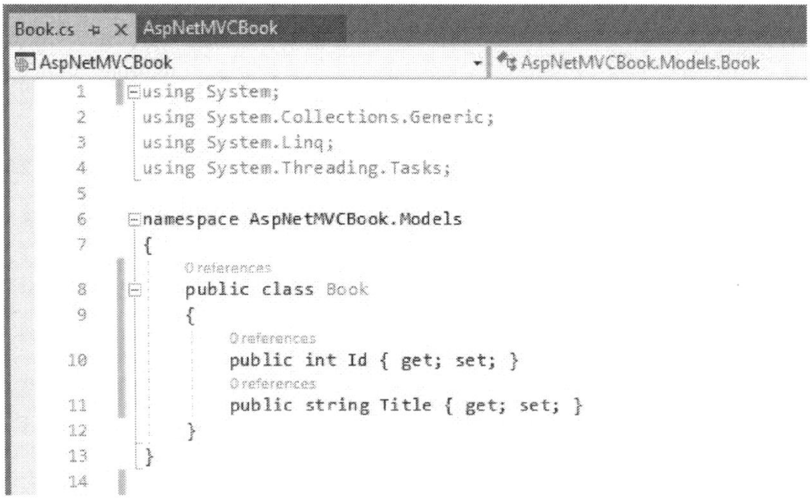

Figure 2.12: Book Model

As you can see in *figure 2.12*, two properties were created for the **Book** class: **Id** and **Title**. They will be used to render the book information on the View after the logical process has been done by the Controller.

2. In Visual Studio Solution Explorer, click the right mouse button on the Controllers folder and choose the option to add an empty MVC Controller, giving the name **BookController**. It will generate an empty controller class. By default, the scaffolding functionality generates an Index method without implementation. As the purpose of this example is to show a book in the View, we must implement it in the Controller, returning to the View an

instance of the **Book** model class. To get this result, the class should have the following implementation, as seen in the following screenshot:

```
BookController.cs + X
AspNetMVCBook                                    AspNetMVCBook.Controllers.BookController        Index()
     1    using AspNetMVCBook.Models;
     2    using Microsoft.AspNetCore.Mvc;
     3
     4    namespace AspNetMVCBook.Controllers
     5    {
              0 references
     6        public class BookController : Controller
     7        {
                  0 references
     8            public IActionResult Index()
     9            {
    10                Book book = new Book()
    11                {
    12                    Id = 1,
    13                    Title = "Building Enterprise Applications with .NET Core"
    14                };
    15
    16                return View(book);
    17            }
    18        }
    19    }
```

Figure 2.13: Book Controller

As you can see in *figure 2.13*, an instance of **Book** class was created inside the Index method with the properties being populated with specific sample values. As the View will use that information, the book object was passed as a parameter in the return View instruction in line 16.

3. The last step is to create the View itself to have a complete MVC sample. Click the right mouse button on the **Views** folder and create a new folder called **Book**. In Asp.Net Core MVC applications, the **Views** folder is strongly associated with the Controllers. All the Views that will be handled by a specific controller should be placed in a folder with the same controller name inside the **Views** folder. Each action that returns a View must be present in the **View** folder associated with the Controller. After creating the **Book** folder, add a new View file clicking the right mouse button on the **Book** folder, and choose the option View giving the name **Index**, whose value is the same as the existent method in the **Book** Controller.

Considering the View contains HTML code, and it can interact with the server-side code using the Razor engine, a View must mix Razor code syntax and the necessary code to make the presentation part of our project. Also, as the sample controller has a method, which returns a populated **book** object to the view, you must refer which type of model is associated with the view in the top of the file, and you can call the model properties using the Razor statement, as you can see in the following screenshot:

```
Index.cshtml  -□ X
    1     @model AspNetMVCBook.Models.Book
    2     @{
    3         ViewData["Title"] = "Index";
    4     }
    5
    6     <h1>My Book</h1>
    7     <br />
    8     <b>Book Id: </b> @Model.Id
    9     <br />
   10     <b>Book Title:</b> @Model.Title
   11
   12
   13
```

Figure 2.14: Book View

Between lines 6 and 10, there is the necessary code to show the book information properties with the values populated by the Controller. The View only receives the data from the Controller, and it is not recommended having that much logic implementation on it, as the main responsibility of the View is to render data and presenting it to the user. Finally, after running the project in Visual Studio and typing the path of our controller (book following by the index), it is possible to see the following results, as seen in the following screenshot:

Figure 2.15: Asp.Net MVC result

Another pretty popular project type for .NET Core applications is the Razor project that allows us to benefit from the Razor engine, but with the full MVC architecture not being mandatory. This type of project is suitable for small and simple projects or for the ones that just need to have a presentation layer consuming external APIs, considering the huge complexity of logical programming is delegated to a third project.

To create a **Razor Pages** project, go to Visual Studio project creation dialog and choose the option Asp.Net Core Web Application, and after that, the **Web Application** type. A simple Web project will be created containing a folder called **Pages**, where your views will be placed. As shown in the following screenshot, the structure is simpler than an MVC project, and it does not follow any architecture pattern:

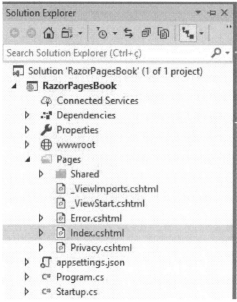

Figure 2.16: *Razor pages*

If you want to use models and controllers associated with the views, you must refer their code inside the Razor Page. Considering each page contains its logic implementation, each page can be considered as an independent component. It is a good option for simple data input and for non-complex logic operations. Also, this project type increases the time spent in building applications because it does not require configuring routes and strongly naming folders and files in the correct places.

Each view has associated its own server-side code file with the same name, but with the **.cs** extension. You must place all the logic implementation and model references in this **.cs** file, similar to what was done with the **Book** example. Also, it can have multiple methods associated with the page, different from the MVC approach, where there is a strong relationship between the controller action and the views. For that reason, the Razor pages project is considered more flexible, manly in simple contexts.

> Considering that many legacy projects were developed using the obsolete Asp. Net Web Forms project type from the .NET Framework, it is pretty common to read articles and presentations, making a comparison between the old Asp. Net Web Forms and Asp.Net Core Razor Pages. However, they are completely different in their essence. The Razor Pages are not based in the Postback concept and do not keep the view state in the server in all the page life cycles.

The Blazor template to the Web project typeswas introduced in the .NET platform since .NET 3.0, ready for production use. This type of project uses Web Assembly and Razor engine to create powerful client applications running server-side code directly on the browser. Usually, a regular system based on the Web technology renders to the client-side only HTML, CSS, and JavaScript. In a Blazor project, it is possible to run C# code directly on the browser.

Also, among the available project templates in Visual Studio, there are many options for mobile and game development. The first one is based in Xamarin, a framework that allows us to create multi-platform mobile applications for Android and iOS using the only C# language. It is an impressive engine that made possible to create a single app and generates the underlying native code for Android and iOS platform, increasing the productivity and the adoption of the .NET platform by mobile developers who traditionally use Java or Apple technologies to build their apps. For game development, it is possible to use Unity 3D using C#, and reuse all the native libraries from .NET 5.

Conclusion

The .NET 5 platform was created to meet all the necessary cross-platform requirements, being possible to develop enterprise applications to the most popular operation systems, such as Linux, macOS, and Windows. As you could see along with this chapter, it is possible to use Visual Studio IDE and Visual Studio Code to develop and build .NET 5 applications, taking the benefits of all extensions provided by the companies and individual developers that have contributed to open-source projects related to .NET 5.

In this chapter, you learned the essential information on cross-platform concepts and got yourself familiar with the main types of project existent on .NET 5, such as Web and desktop applications, creating practical examples.

In the next chapter, you will learn the best practices related to object-oriented programming. Further more, you will have the opportunity to apply all the associated concepts with practical exercises.

Points to remember

- Visual Studio contains numerous types of projects that facilitate the creation of projects in .NET Core.

- The C# language can be used across all the project types in .NET.

- .NET 5 allows us to create cross-platform applications for Web, desktop, and mobile platforms.

Questions

1. Which are the two tools available to create .NET 5 applications?

2. Explain the best strategy to migrate projects from the .NET Framework to .NET 5.

3. In which version of .NET, the support to Windows Presentation Foundation was added?

CHAPTER 3
Basic Concepts of Object-Oriented Programming

Software development is an abstract process, and correlation with the real world is done by the implementation of business or system requirements, which are represented in the software in a reliable way, in general, using the object-oriented programming paradigm. The concept behind that helped the software industry in creating more stable, readable, and extensible code for enterprise applications. It made more accessible the daily routine for developers in general, bringing a smart design for any use developed with any language that supports that paradigm.

Beyond that, the object-oriented discussion brought to the market many additions and contributions such as the SOLID principles concepts, which increased the quality of software across the world and gave the possibility to build robust and scalable applications, taking the software engineering to the next level in terms of techniques and professionalism. Further more, because of all these facts, it is essential for any developer these days to learn this paradigm properly and to be able to apply its concepts in real and complex scenarios, which is a mandatory requirement for almost all positions in the market for developers.

With this chapter, you will have the opportunity to learn the essential concepts of object-oriented programming, such as classes, constructors, methods, abstract and static classes, inheritance, and interfaces. Additionally, explanations and examples of design patterns and SOLID principles will be introduced.

Structure

In this chapter, we will discuss the following topics:

- Classes, constructors, and methods
- Static classes and methods
- Structs
- Abstract classes, inheritance, and interfaces

Objectives

After studying this unit, you should be able to:

- Understand object-oriented programming concepts
- Discuss essentialaspects of design patterns
- Create fundamental applications using object-oriented programming
- Use the SOLID principles in real projects

Classes, constructors, and methods

Starting from the scratch with **Oriented-Oriented Programming (OOP)** concepts, you must know that any software in the market and any code implementation using a programming language have a target to achieve, an intention based on business or system requirements. There are many ways to solve a single problem in software engineering. Still, in terms of keeping and writing understandable code, it is vital to design a code that represents the real-world situation related to the actual issue that the software is trying to solve. The OOP helps us in abstracting the complexity of software development and in maintaining a good correlation between technical implementations and most of the scenarios we could find in the market.

The C# language supports OOP since its first version, and every application that uses .NET must apply this paradigm, considering all the native libraries of the platform are based on this concept. Additionally, the .NET platform takes the benefitof advanced concepts of design patterns and SOLID principles, which will be explained further in this book, using realscenario examples.

The OOP allows us to organize the implementation of software requirements around objects, which will represent the behavior and state of something that needs to be abstract in the system. An object could contain properties and methods, which will be responsible for keeping and manipulating the state of it and certain operations related to the object itself. In C# language and other ones based on the OOP paradigm, an object is represented by a class that should have similar characteristics to the realworld in a faithful representation.

For better understanding, just imagine a scenario where an online store needs to be developed using C# language and .NET. According to the fictional case, the system should implement the following requirements:

1. Allow users to register products and product types.

2. Every product should have a unique number to identify the product and a title.

3. Users are considered who access the online shop, but who do not necessarily make a purchase.

4. Once a purchase is made in the online shop by a user, the same user should be registered as a customer with additional information.

5. The products could contain different properties based on their type.

Considering the given scenario, if we would start the plan the structure of our code to keep everything well organized, we must create the classes first, with the basic properties that are common to every object of these classes. Starting from the model for the product, the initial implementation of the class would have the implementation as seen in the following screenshot:

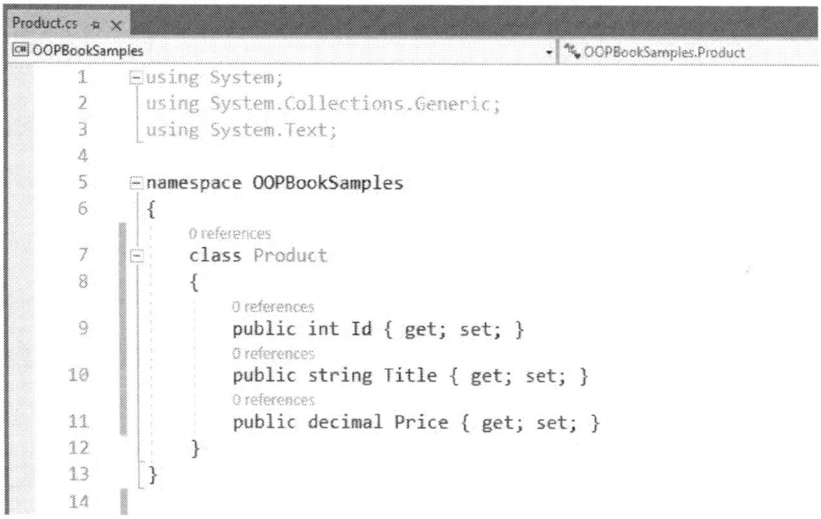

Figure 3.1: Product class

In that case, the fields **Id**, **Title**, and **Price** represent the properties of the **Product** class, and each one hasits own type, such as integer, string, and decimal. You must realize that there is a keyword before each property. The keyword means the access modifier or scope of the property. And, in OOP, there are the following access modifiers:

- **Public:** The class or property can be freely accessed by other classes, even by the ones that are not present in the same assembly.

- **Private:** The property can be accessed only by the same class where the property belongs to.
- **Protected:** The property can be accessed only by the same class or the derived classes.
- **Internal:** The property or class can be accessed by other classes, but with the limitation that the class should belong to the same assembly.
- **Protected internal:** The class or property can be accessed by any other class in the same assembly and for all derived classes, even if they are presented in another assembly.

Depending on the keyword, the access level changed as seen in the representation in the following image:

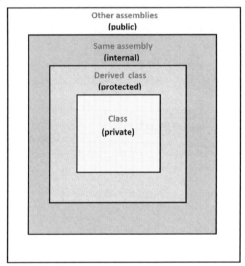

Figure 3.2: Access level

OOP has principles that enforce the best practices of coding using this paradigm and has the purpose to not violate the mechanisms that should be followed in any software that uses these concepts, such as encapsulation, inheritance, polymorphism, and reusability. The following sections have detailed information on each of them.

Encapsulation

This concept has the purpose of avoiding external interference on the object state, protecting the access to the properties of the class and its methods. To meet this objective successfully is essential to understand the access level property, which was explained previously in this chapter. Controlling the access to properties, methods, and classes ensures that only the code that needs to have access to other specific code is under control. In OOP, each class must be independent and contain the necessary code to meet its target.

Inheritance

Following the principle of reusability, it is possible in OOP to use the concept of inheritance, which allows us to share properties and methods that mostly have something in common. A class that inherits from another class is called a derived class, and the base class is called parent class. The C# language allows us to use only one inheritance associated with a class, but it is possible to use interfaces to meet a similar objective. Moving forward with the previous example related to the online store, a store could contain many types of distinct products that would share common properties and methods between them, but other properties might be specific for each one of those. For instance, the class **Movie** is a type of product and shares similar characteristics to other products such as **Id**, **Title**, and **Price**. But, specific properties are only related to the **Movie** class. Considering the class product seen in *figure 3.1* already contains particular properties, the **Movie** class can inherit from the **Product** class, as seen in the following screenshot:

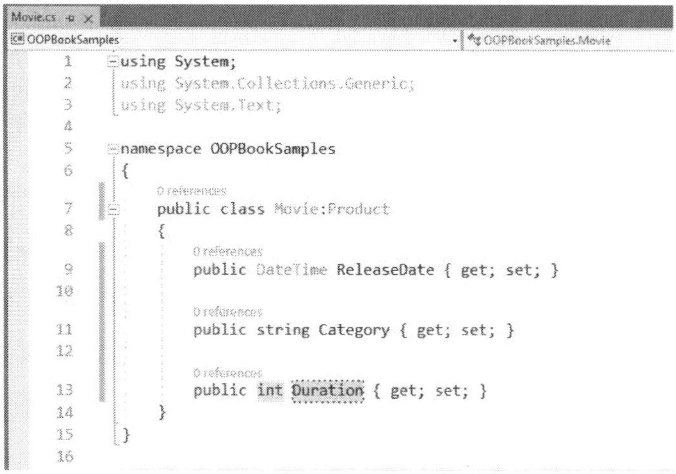

Figure 3.3: Movie class

In the signature of the class, an inheritance is declared from the **Product** class, and that means the **Movie** class will contain all the properties from the **Product** class and the specific fields from its own class: release date, category, and duration. The decision to inherit or not from another class depends on the context and generally is based on business requirements. If different classes have a clear correlation, the inheritance concept could be suitable. This practice helps developers to save time writing code across the system and to keep the consistency of the system architecture.

Reusability

Generally, the costs of any software are measured by the number of hours spent in writing the code, among other activities such as business analyses, software design, and management. Considering the time to develop software represents one of the essential points for a project to succeed, it is necessary to use techniques that allow us to save time in building the software we are working on. Definitely, reusability is one of the essential concepts of OOP because it represents less time to develop systems.

Going back to the online store example, considering it has already implemented a base **Product** class, if the online store had a vast number of products of different types, the use of base class would save a relevant time in implementing the other classes. It applies as well in more complex scenarios where not only simple properties and methods can be reused, but whole libraries and external functionalities.

Polymorphism

This concept in OOP allows us to overwrite a method from a parent class and share among multiple classes a standard interface to give integrity and consistency in the software architecture. As its name suggests, polymorphism is the possibility to have many forms for a common method. In the online store example, imagine that each product could have its way to apply discounts based on custom rules. In that case, the base class (**Product**) would have a standard method to calculate the discount, but all the derived classes can over write its behavior according to the specific situations.

For instance, the parent class (**Product**) could have a specific method applying a 7% discount, as seen in the following screenshot:

```
using System;
using System.Collections.Generic;
using System.Text;

namespace OOPBookSamples
{
    public class Product
    {
        public int Id { get; set; }
        public string Title { get; set; }
        public decimal Price { get; set; }

        public virtual void ApplyDiscount()
        {
            this.Price = Decimal.Multiply(this.Price, (7/100));
        }
    }
}
```

Figure 3.4: Method to apply the discount in the Product class

But, on the other hand, the child class (**Movie**) can overwrite the implementation of the **ApplyDiscount** method, as seen in the following screenshot:

Figure 3.5: *Method to apply the discount in the Movie class*

The **Movie** class is applying a different policy for discount, once the discount value is 10%, there fore distinct from the parent class. It is possible to change the implementation of a method from the parent class, only if the method in the parent class has the modifier **virtual**, as seen in *figure 3.4*.

Partial class

To keep the good practices of coding and project structure, usually, all the classes are presented in the same file, which will have the same name as the class, as highlighted in the following screenshot:

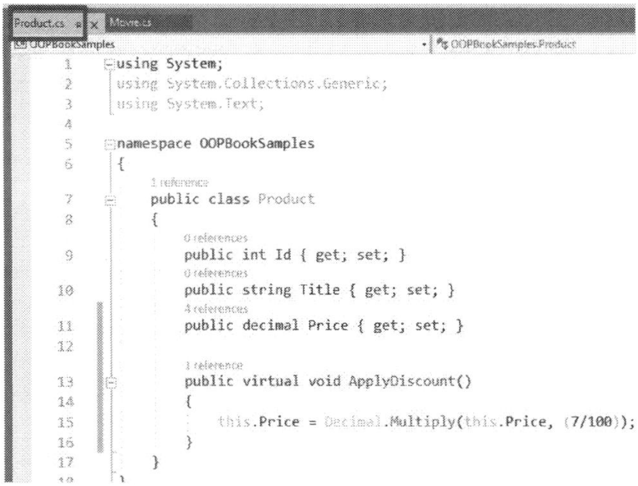

Figure 3.6: *File name pattern for classes*

However, in case of the class containing a great number of code lines and in the situation where many developers need to work at the same time in the same file, it is convenient to split the class into multiple files, to avoid conflicts and to have a logical separation for better understanding. Even though the class is presented in more than one file, the compile will combine all of them as a single class. In the next code example, there are two files regarding the **Product** class, one containing the fields and another one the methods, as seen in the following screenshot:

```
PartialProduct.cs  ⊕ ×
OOPBookSamples                                         OOPBookSamples.Product
1    using System;
2    using System.Collections.Generic;
3    using System.Text;
4
5    namespace OOPBookSamples
6    {
         2 references
7        public partial class Product
8        {
9
             1 reference
10           public virtual void ApplyDiscount()
11           {
12               this.Price = Decimal.Multiply(this.Price, (7/100));
13           }
14       }
15   }
```

Figure 3.7: Product partial class

The keyword **partial** was used to transform the class into a partial class, and it contains only the apply **discount** method. In the opposite, the other file that includes the implementation of the **Product** class will only provide the properties, as seen in the following screenshot:

```
Product.cs  ⊕ ×
OOPBookSamples                                         OOPBookSamples.Product
1    using System;
2    using System.Collections.Generic;
3    using System.Text;
4
5    namespace OOPBookSamples
6    {
         2 references
7        public partial class Product
8        {
             0 references
9            public int Id { get; set; }
             0 references
10           public string Title { get; set; }
             4 references
11           public decimal Price { get; set; }
12
13       }
14   }
15
```

Figure 3.8: Product partial class

The use of partial classes is quite flexible, but it is recommended to do that just in the cases where the class is big enough to be split. Additionally, if a class contains a lot of lines of code, usually, it is a clear indication that the class should be refactored to follow the single responsibility principle, which is a good practice stated by the SOLID principles that will be explained further in this chapter.

Constructor

In OOP, the constructor is the method called when an instance of the object is created. In other words, a class contains the implementation, and every time a class is used, an object is created, having the same type as the class. In the scenario of the online store, considering there is a class called **Product** in the system, every time this class needs to be used, we must create a new instance of an object, referring the class, as seen in the following screenshot:

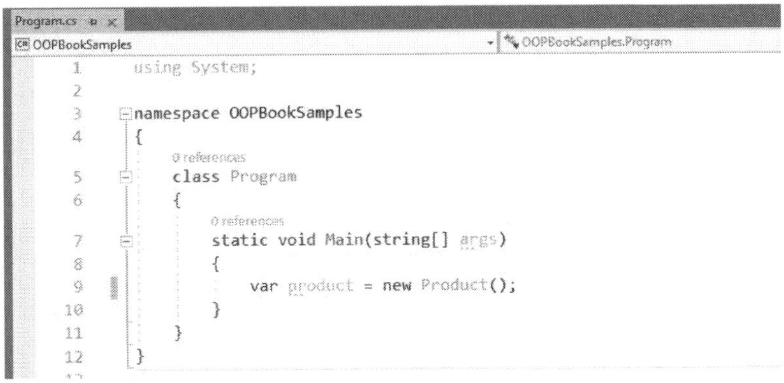

Figure 3.9: *Product object instance*

When the keyword new is used, it indicates to the compile that a new instance of the **Product** class should be created, and this object will be placed in a new space in the memory. Additionally, in this operation, the new object is initialized, and the constructor method is called. You can specify many constructor methods in the class, and all of them should have the same name as the class, as seen in the following screenshot:

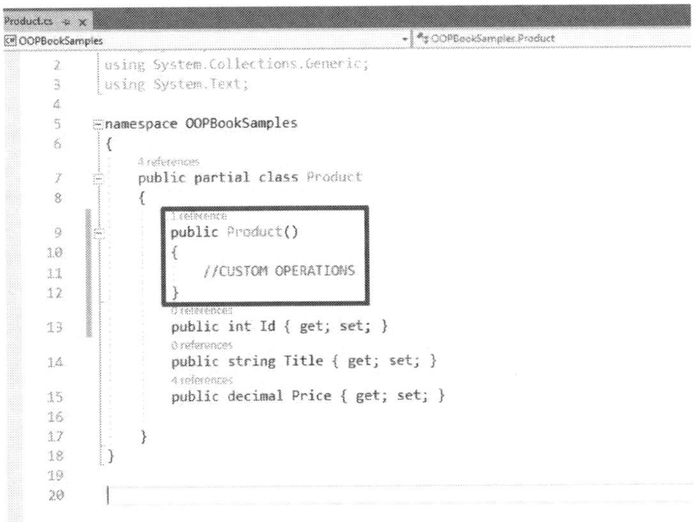

Figure 3.10: *Constructor*

Usually, the constructor methods are used to set the initial state of the object and, if the **constructor** method is not specified, the compile will run the default constructor method, which is an **empty** method. It is essential to understand how constructors work because the state management of the objects is one of the main points to apply the best practices of the OOP paradigm correctly.

It is possible as well to pass parameters in the constructor, which in specific cases are necessary to make operations when an object is initialized, as seen in the following screenshot:

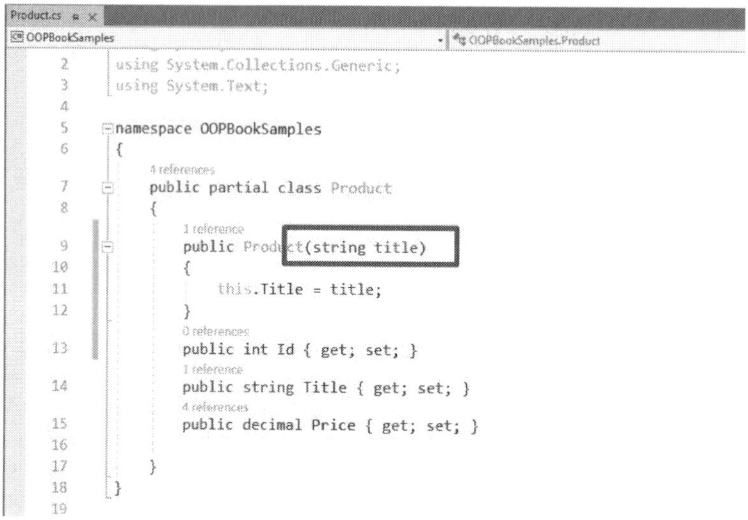

Figure 3.11: Constructor with parameters

A class could have multiple constructors for distinct particular reasons. It depends on the purpose of the class and on the access level defined by properties and methods in the class.

Static classes

In C# language, a static class represents a class that cannot have an instance created. This means the system will keep in the memory a single instance of the class, which will be used for the whole system. Considering that characteristic, it is not possible to use the keyword **new** when there is the intention to use the static class. Usually, the static classes are used in cases where the class does not need to keep its state dynamically. For instance, the online store could have a static class to make certain common operations for the system, such as type conversions, math operations, and others. The following screenshot contains an example of a static class called **Helper**, which has a method that returns a unique identifier:

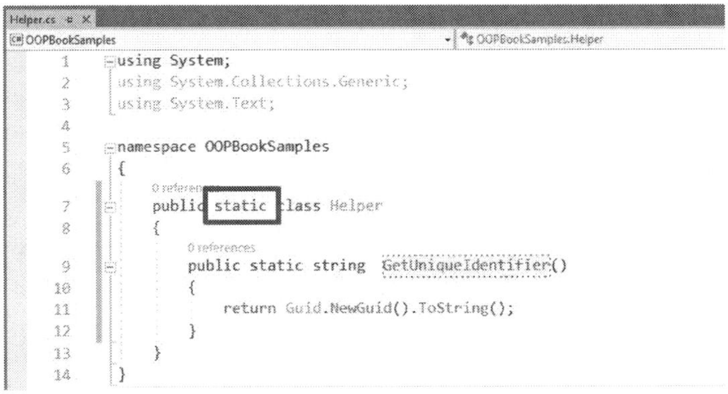

Figure 3.12: Static class

As highlighted in the previous screenshot, a keyword static was used to transform the class **Helper** into a static class. Considering it is not possible to create an instance of static classes, the compile will generate an error if an implementation tries to proceed that, as seen in the following screenshot:

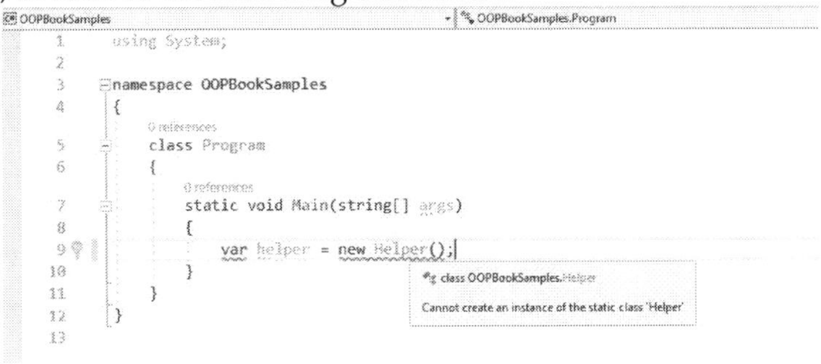

Figure 3.13: Compile error for static class

To use the methods presented in the static class, you must call the methods directly without using the keyword **new**, as seen in the following screenshot:

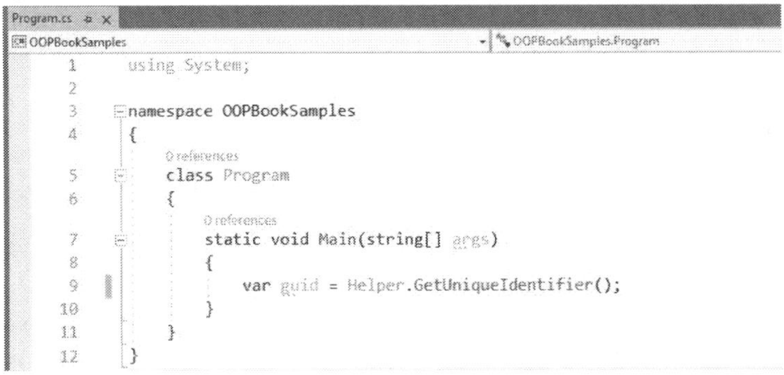

Figure 3.14: Correct use of static class

Usually, when a static class is defined, all its members follow the same signature in terms of being static to keep consistency in the class.

Structs

The structs in C# language have a similar implementation to classes, including properties and methods. However, the main difference between them is the way that they are kept in memory in a program developed in C#. The conventional class is considered a reference type, which means that the type does not store its value in the memory, but only the address where the value will be stored. On the other hand, structs contain their own value, and because of that, access to their values is much faster than reference types. Furthermore, structs have restrictions in comparison to classes, as follows:

- It is not possible to use structs in an inheritance process.

- It is not possible to use an empty constructor. It is mandatory to have a constructor with parameters.

- It is required to set values to local variables when they are created.

- The instance of the object created from a **struct** class is removed from the memory once the method that is using the object has its process completed.

The syntax of the struct is quite similar to the class, as seen in the following screenshot:

```csharp
using System.Text;

namespace OOPBookSamples
{
    0 references
    struct Customer
    {
        0 references
        public int Id { get; set; }
        0 references
        public string FullName { get; set; }
        0 references
        public DateTime BirthDay { get; set; }
    }
}
```

Figure 3.15: Struct class

A struct must have a constructor with parameters, as the following screenshot:

```
Customer.cs + ×
OOPBookSamples                                    OOPBookSamples.Customer
  1    using System;
  2    using System.Collections.Generic;
  3    using System.Text;
  4
  5    namespace OOPBookSamples
  6    {
           1 reference
  7        struct Customer
  8        {
               0 reference
  9            public Customer (int id, string fullName, DateTime birthDay)
 10            {
 11                this.FullName = fullName;
 12                this.BirthDay = birthDay;
 13                this.Id = id;
 14            }
 15
               1 reference
 16            public int Id { get; set; }
               1 reference
 17            public string FullName { get; set; }
               1 reference
 18            public DateTime BirthDay { get; set; }
 19        }
 20    }
 21
 22
```

Figure 3.16: *Constructor for struct*

The use of structs is pretty useful in the cases of a specific part of the system that requires high performance and when the primary purpose of the implementation is to only keep a temporary state of the object, with known endoflife inside the method calls.

Interfaces

In OOP, an interface represents a contract that should be followed for all the class that implements the interface. In other words, an interface contains everything that is mandatory for a class to have, such as properties and methods, following specific signatures. This concept is significant to implement business requirements correctly and to give consistency to the development process.

In C# language, an interface can be created with the interface keyword just before the name of the interface. As a concept, the interfaces do not contain any implementation, which is the responsibility of the classes that will implement those. Going back to the online store example, considering there would be a requirement that all the product types should implement a method reference to delivery; an interface could be created to ensure that all the classes related to product type will implement this method. A basic interface for product would appear as seen in the following screenshot:

```
  1    namespace OOPBookSamples
  2    {
           0 references
  3        public interface IProduct
  4        {
               0 references
  5            void Deliver();
  6        }
  7    }
```

Figure 3.17: *Constructor for struct*

According to this interface, it is mandatory for all the classes that will implement this interface to have a method called **Deliver** with the same signature with out any returning as a result. To enforce the contract between the interface and related classes, in the signature of the class, you must declare after the name one or more interfaces, as seen in the following screenshot:

```csharp
using System;
using System.Collections.Generic;
using System.Text;

namespace OOPBookSamples
{
    public partial class Product: IProduct
    {
        public Product(string title)
        {
            this.Title = title;
        }
        public int Id { get; set; }
        public string Title { get; set; }
        public decimal Price { get; set; }

    }
}
```

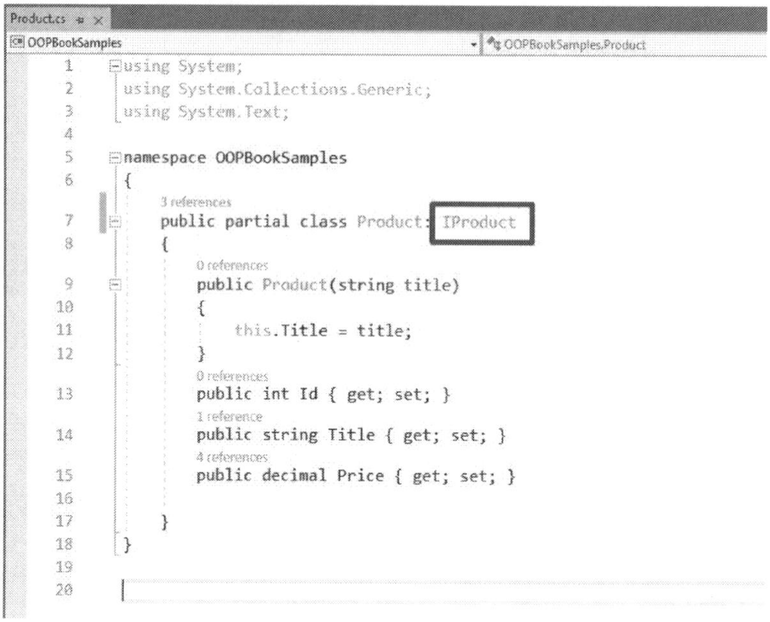

Figure 3.18: Constructor for struct

Considering the implementation of the delivery method is mandatory to the **Product** class from that point, before version 8.0 of C#, the compile would show an error accusing that the underlying implementation is missing. But, since version 8.0 of the C# language, a default implementation can be specified in the interface, and the related classes donot need to implement the method with the same signature. Therefore, it is possible to have default implementation in interfaces, as seen in the following screenshot:

```csharp
using System;
using System.Collections.Generic;
using System.Text;

namespace OOPBookSamples
{
    public interface IProduct
    {
        public void Deliver() { Console.WriteLine("Default implementation"); }
    }
}
```

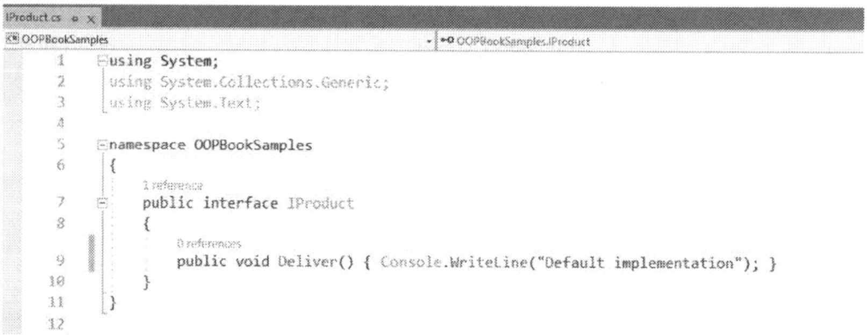

Figure 3.19: Constructor for struct*

Another aspect of interfaces is that you cannot change or specify access levels regarding properties and methods in interfaces because all of them are public by default. This means that it is not possible to use the keywords **private**, **protected**, or **internal** in properties. The methods and properties can be declared with out an access level, as seen in the following screenshot:

```
2     using System.Collections.Generic;
3     using System.Text;
4
5     ⊟namespace OOPBookSamples
6      {
          1 reference
7          public interface IProduct
8          {
              1 reference
9              int Id { get; set; }
              0 references
10             void Deliver() { Console.WriteLine("Default implementation"); }
11         }
12     }
13
```

***Figure 3.20**: Interface without access level*

The use of interfaces can reduce the complexity of the software and can get higher maintainability of the code, once they give consistency to the classes and the possibility to apply a pattern across the system. Additionally, the interfaces are essential to make the tests easier in the code level because the implementation would have a more general construction, and a bunch of different tests can be applied to different parts of the system without spending so much energy covering in a test plan.

Conclusion

As you could see in this chapter, the OOP paradigm is the base of C# language, and it is one of the most important concepts of good practices in software development, representing something that every developer must know about. The correct use of the paradigm allows companies to create testable, scalable, and stable software and help to reduce the costs of the development process, minimizing the risks of issues being introduced to the project. All the logical implementation for business and system requirements are organized in classes, which can be reused, tested, and extended. All the classes must have modifiers that will change the access level of the classes themselves or their properties. Additionally, the C# language contains options to optimize the use of memory (structs) and allows us to give consistency and integrity to the software architecture applying the concept of interfaces and taking all the benefits of the SOLID principles.

With this chapter, you have learned how to create classes, properties, methods, and changing the access level for each of them. Additionally, you had the opportunity to get yourself familiar with interfaces, structures, and other types in C# language, which allows you to create and apply the concepts of the OOP paradigm in real projects. Finally, you learned the basic concepts of SOLID principles and can identify points in a system that could be improved using them.

In the next chapter, you will have the opportunity to learn more complex concepts regarding interfaces and inheritance in OOP, applying those concepts in more advanced scenarios.

Points to remember

- Objects represent an instance of a class in OOP.

- Interfaces are the contracts that become mandatory in the implementation of methods and properties for any class associated with them.

- Inheritance is the best way to reuse code in the OOP paradigm.

Multiple-choice questions

1. **Which type of structure can be used to specify contracts for classes in C#?**

    a. Properties

    b. Interfaces

    c. Inheritance

    d. Protected

2. **How many interfaces can be used associated with a single class?**

    a. One

    b. Two

    c. Five

    d. Unlimited

3. **What is the access level that restricts the access to the assembly of the same assembly?**

    a. Protected

    b. Public

    c. Internal

    d. Private

Answer

1. b
2. d
3. c

Questions

1. Explain the difference between classes and structs.

2. Explain the meaning of SOLID principles briefly.

CHAPTER 4
Interfaces in C#

Interfaces are one of the most important and essential concepts in object-oriented programming and its correct use can bring us the advantage to implement powerful and extensible software architecture, solve real problems regarding complex implementations, and give to any project a good standard to be followed in multiple scenarios. Considering, in C# language, it is possible to use only one inheritance, interfaces represent a good alternative in terms of object definition, extensibility, and identity in object-oriented programming.

With this chapter, you will have the opportunity to learn deeply the implementation of interfaces in C# and understand how to use its concept in distinct scenarios, implementing testable and reusable functional code, always taking the benefits of best practices of object-oriented programming.

Learning advanced concepts of interfaces is important because it gives you the chance to properly apply those in real-life projects and give you a better understanding of legacy, third-party libraries and mainly of the .NET platform in general, as itmassively uses interfaces and related concepts such as dependency injection and inversion of dependency.

Structure

In this chapter, we will discuss the following topics:

- Definition and implementation of interfaces
- Creation of testable classes
- Dependency injection concepts
- Best practices using interfaces

Objectives

After studying this unit, you should be able to:

- Understand interface concepts
- Apply interfaces using C# language
- Create fundamental applications the best practices of interfaces
- Build testable classes

Definition and implementation of interfaces

Interfaces in C# are the most efficient way to simulate the behavior of multiple inheritances considering .NET does not support multiple inheritances, which consists of a single class be derived from more than one class. An interface represents a contract that should be followed by any class that implements it as the same happens in legal contracts. Once a method or property is defined in the interface, the class that is using that interface must implement all the specifications of that interface as mandatory.

Traditionally, an interface contains just signatures and not implementation. However, C# 8.0 brought a new functionality that allows us to specify default implementation for methods, and it represents an alternative to abstract classes in specific scenarios. By definition, an interface is a group of methods and properties that are required for each class that needs to use the interface. It gives consistency and integrity to software development and makes it easier to test, change, and extend functionalities.

There are advantages and clear benefits in the use of interfaces because it adds loose coupling to the design and software architecture, the possibility to create reusable components, helps in maintainability, and decreases the risk to introduce issues in the project, once the implementation is separated from the interface, which contains a single specification.

For instance, imagine the scenario where it is needed to implement a system that allows the users to register different types of products. All the products share similar basic properties and characteristics. Still, they have relevant differences that it is reasonable to use an interface that contains all the properties that are common for all products. A few products could have distinct specifications, such as ideal temperature and expiration date. And, other products could have even new properties, such as legal requirements and roles based on safety. Considering how various the products could be, it is not possible in object-oriented programming to create a single class that would have all the potential properties and methods for all products and would universally represent every specific situation.

Therefore, the following screenshot represents a simple example of the interface for the product:

```csharp
namespace Interfaces
{
    0 references
    public interface IProduct
    {
        0 references
        int Id { get; set; }

        0 references
        string Name { get; set; }
        0 references
        decimal Price { get; set; }

        0 references
        int HeightDimension { get; set; }

        0 references
        int WidthDimension { get; set; }

        0 references
        public int Type { get; set; }

        0 references
        decimal CalculateDiscount();
    }
}
```

Figure 4.1: Product interface

In that case, the interface called **IProduct** has all the methods and properties that would be shared by all the product classes that will implement its contract. In the given scenario, it is mandatory for the classes to define the logical routine for the method responsible for calculating the discount, and the compile will throw an error if the method does not have the same signature and name. The method is a part of the contract and should be followed by every class that refers to that interface. In that way, we guarantee the uniformity between the pieces of code that represent the same context. To use interfaces in C# language, you must refer it after the class name; similarly, it is done for inheritance. In case of the implementation of properties, methods and events are missing in the class, Visual Studio will show a warning indicating which specification of the interface has not being implemented, as seen in the following screenshot:

```
MobilePhone.cs + ×
IntefacesBook                                                    IntefacesBook.MobilePhone
    1       using Interfaces;
    2
    3     namespace IntefacesBook
    4     {
              0 references
    5         public class MobilePhone: IProduct
    6         {
    7         }                          +o interface Interfaces.IProduct
    8     }
    9                                    'MobilePhone' does not implement interface member 'IProduct.Id'
   10                                    'MobilePhone' does not implement interface member 'IProduct.Name'
   11                                    'MobilePhone' does not implement interface member 'IProduct.Price'
   12                                    'MobilePhone' does not implement interface member 'IProduct.HeightDimension'
   13                                    'MobilePhone' does not implement interface member 'IProduct.WidthDimension'
   14                                    'MobilePhone' does not implement interface member 'IProduct.Type'
   15                                    'MobilePhone' does not implement interface member 'IProduct.CalculateDiscount()'
   16
   17                                    Show potential fixes (Alt+Enter or Ctrl+.)
   18
   19
   20
```

Figure 4.2: Interface implementation error

In this example, a class called **MobilePhone** was created, and considering the interface was not implemented, it is not possible to compile the project in Visual Studio until the full interface is implemented. Considering the class could contain properties and methods apart from the required ones defined by the interface, it is possible to give particular behavior for each product. The correct implementation of the **IProduct** interface would be as the following screenshot:

```
MobilePhone.cs + ×
IntefacesBook                                                    IntefacesBook.MobilePhone
    2
    3     namespace IntefacesBook
    4     {
              0 references
    5         public class MobilePhone : IProduct
    6         {
              1 reference
    7             public int Id { get; set; }
              1 reference
    8             public string Name { get; set; }
              1 reference
    9             public decimal Price { get; set; }
              1 reference
   10             public int HeightDimension { get; set; }
              1 reference
   11             public int WidthDimension { get; set; }
              1 reference
   12             public int Type { get; set; }
   13
              0 references
   14             public string InternetPlan { get; set; }
   15
              1 reference
   16             public decimal CalculateDiscount()
   17             {
   18                 return 0.3m;
   19             }
   20         }
   21     }
   22
```

Figure 4.3: Interface implementation

After creating the properties and methods with the same signature as required by the interface, Visual Studio does not show any error message anymore, and whatever further future change in the interface will directly affect all the classes that contain its implementation. As seen in the implementation class, a property called **`InternetPlan`** was created. In that context, it applies only for the **`MobilePhone`** class; therefore, it is possible to extend the classes despite the mandatory implementation defined by the interface. Furthermore, a specific logic for the discount was implemented in the underlying method, and it could be particular for each individual class of product.

In case of most of the products that would share similar discounts, as it was said before, it is practicable to specify default logical statement in interfaces regarding members and methods, as seen in the following screenshot:

```
namespace Interfaces
{
    public interface IProduct
    {
        int Id { get; set; }

        string Name { get; set; }
        decimal Price { get; set; }

        int HeightDimension { get; set; }

        int WidthDimension { get; set; }

        public int Type { get; set; }

        decimal CalculateDiscount()
        {
            return 0.3m;
        }
    }
}
```

***Figure 4.4**: Interface implementation*

In that case, the default value of the discount for all products will be **`0.3`**, and if the method in the interface has a default implementation, it is not mandatory for the class the implementation of it, with the compile not showing any error regarding missing method implementation. That feature is only available since version 8.0 of C#.

In terms of flexibility, the use of interfaces allows us to switch between different classes that implement the same interface, being possible to build generic logical routines that can be easily extended and modified without a significant impact on the software. The interface can be used as a parameter in methods and the creation of variables, as seen in the following screenshot:

```csharp
using Interfaces;
using System;
using System.Collections.Generic;

namespace IntefacesBook
{
    class Program
    {
        static void Main(string[] args)
        {
            List<IProduct> productList = new List<IProduct>();

            IProduct product1 = new WashingMachine();
            product1.Name = "Washing Machine";

            IProduct product2 = new MobilePhone();
            product2.Name = "Mobile Phone";

            productList.Add(product1);
            productList.Add(product2);

            foreach(var product in productList)
            {
                Console.WriteLine(product.Name);
            }

            Console.Read();
        }
    }
}
```

Figure 4.5: Generic objects with interfaces

A generic list of **IProduct** type was created, and the list was populated with two items of different classes: **WashingMachine** and **MobilePhone**. Both of them represent a distinct implementation of **IProduct** class, but for the compile, they are as they were of the same type because they share the same interface. It gives us the possibility to easily extend that functionality referring more classes for other kinds and making joint operations, as they were of the same type, such as loop the list to show results or saving in a database a collection of objects.

Multiple interfaces

Since the first version of the .NET platform, multiple inheritances are not possible for C# language, but a similar result can be achieved using multiple interfaces. In our sample scenario, an online store could have products that will be sold only as online products, such as online books and other info products. For these types of products, the system may have specific characteristics that are valid only for this category of product and other properties for non-online products are not suitable for the online ones, such as the properties regarding product dimension. Pondering this issue, to split the interfaces in specialized ones is recommended, and that will contain the properties and methods related to the particular categories of products, as seen in the following screenshot:

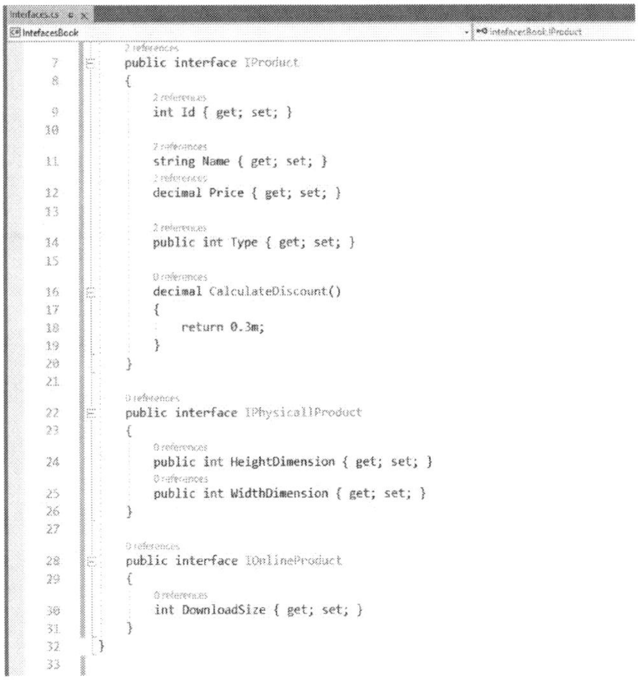

Figure 4.6: Multiple interfaces

Instead of having a single generic interface for products, the system might have multiple interfaces that contain the specific properties that apply to particular scenarios. For instance, the info related to download size exists just for online products and dimensions only for physical products. All the standard specifications for the general products can belong to the **IProduct** interface that has fewer properties than the previous example. Using the multiple interfaces concept, the **WashingMachine** class would refer to two interfaces, as seen in the following screenshot:

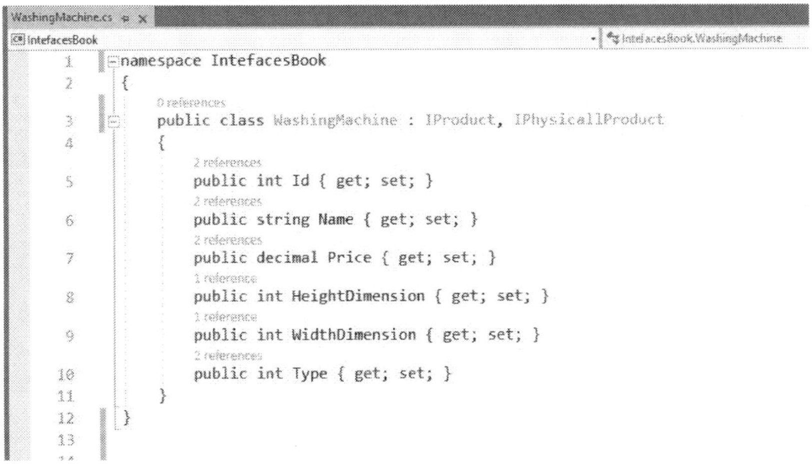

Figure 4.7: Multiple interfaces

The properties **Id**, **Name**, **Price**, and **Type** are being implemented forced by the interface **IProduct**, and the properties **HeightDimension** and **WidthDimension** are specifications of the **IPhysicalProduct**. In case of the system would have an online product such as online books or electronic products, the **IOnlineProduct** interface should be referred to in the underlying class, as seen in the following screenshot:

```
namespace IntefacesBook
{
    0 references
    public class EletronicBook: IProduct, IOnlineProduct
    {
        3 references
        public int Id { get; set; }
        3 references
        public string Name { get; set; }
        3 references
        public decimal Price { get; set; }
        3 references
        public int Type { get; set; }
        1 reference
        public int DownloadSize { get; set; }
    }
}
```

Figure 4.8: *Multiple interfaces*

In that case, the class does not contain any specific reference to dimension, but it is implementing the property regarding download size. There is no limitation in the number of interfaces that can be used in a class, and it gives us flexibility and consistency across the project of software in terms of the same pattern being used by all the classes that are related to products.

Testability of interfaces

One of the significant issues in the market associated with projects of software is the difficulty of testing the functionalities efficiently, and the leading cause of that is the highcoupling between methods and components in the software, which makes the software harder to test. As was explained previously in this book, there are many ways to reduce the dependency between classes in object-oriented programming, such as SOLID principles. Following the best practices of software development allows us to develop systems where the architecture has high flexibility and maintainability in order to increase the quality of software.

With the use of interfaces, it is possible to cover faster more cases of tests and easily mock classes that will simulate the original classes that we are trying to test. As an example, a real case scenario could have a method in a class responsible for making database operations. Regarding the classes that implement the **IProduct** interfaces, even the software could have hundreds of classes that implement the interface; it is possible to cover an appropriate amount of code in the tests if the system contains methods that have the **IProduct** interface as a parameter, instead of the implementation of it, as seen in the following screenshot:

```
namespace IntefacesBook
{
    public class ProductData
    {
        public void Create(IProduct product)
        {

        }

        public void Update(IProduct product)
        {

        }

        public void Delete(IProduct product)
        {

        }
    }
}
```

Figure 4.9: Database operations for products

Considering the system could have a wide variety of product types, all of them share the same database operations in the given scenario. It means that the methods create, update, and delete of the class **ProductData** can be called passing as a parameter any class that implements the **IProduct** interface. This approach facilitates the effort in writing unit tests. Also, it helps in the maintainability of software in all the places where the methods are being called, as seen in the following screenshot:

```
namespace IntefacesBook
{
    class Program
    {
        static void Main(string[] args)
        {
            WashingMachine washingMachine = new WashingMachine()
            {
                Name = "Whasing Machine",
                Price = 150
            };

            MobilePhone mobilePhone = new MobilePhone()
            {
                Name = "Mobile Phone",
                Price = 100,
                InternetPlan = "Unlimited"
            };

            EletronicBook eletronicBook = new EletronicBook()
            {
                Name = "Eletronic Book",
                Price = 25,
                DownloadSize = 2000
            };

            ProductData productData = new ProductData();

            productData.Create(washingMachine);
            productData.Create(mobilePhone);
            productData.Create(eletronicBook);
        }
    }
}
```

Figure 4.10: Testable classes using interfaces

Despite the fact that the example contains instances of objects from three distinct classes, all of them can be passed as a parameter to the **Create** method of the class **ProductData** because the method expects to receive an implementation of the interface **IProduct**.

Dependency injection

One of the most notable and visible characteristics of .NET, in general, is the extensive use of the dependency injection concept, mainly in ASP.Net Core applications. Over time, many concepts of programming, object-oriented paradigm, design patterns, and software architecture become largely widespread in the market, and they are transformed into common sense, considering many companies and developers have attested the benefits of certain practices in software development, and dependency injection is definitely one of those. To understand its concept properly, check out the following screenshot:

```csharp
namespace IntefacesBook
{
    public class Document
    {
        private IDocumentConverter PDFConverter = new PDFConverter();
        private IDocumentConverter ExcelConverter = new ExcelConverter();

        public void ConvertDocumentToPDF(int documentId)
        {
            this.PDFConverter.Converter(documentId);
        }

        public void ConvertDocumentToExcel(int documentId)
        {
            this.ExcelConverter.Converter(documentId);
        }
    }
}
```

Figure 4.11: Dependency inversion example

In this example, there are two explicit dependencies:

- The **Document** class depends on the **PDFConverter** and **ExcelConverter** to fully achieve its objective.
- If the **Document** would have more methods that donot necessarily call any method from external classes, it is possible for the **Document** class to work without the other two associated classes, but the strong dependency still there.

In other words, the document class directly depends on the **PDFCoverter** and **ExcelConverter** classes, and obviously, they represent dependencies of the **Document** class. Considering that, usually, the conversion of the document involves third-party libraries, depending on the way that we implement the **Document** class, its maintainability and testability will be clearly harmed. The associated classes in the example are highly coupling to the document class because this implementation violates the open-close principle, which states that the classes in object-oriented programming should be open for extensions but closed for modifications in their behavior.

There are many good technical ways to reduce the dependency between classes, and in the example, a better design could be achieved passing the parameters in the constructor of the **Document** class as interfaces, instead of creating instances of it as a private at the beginning of class, as demonstrated in the following screenshot:

```
Document.cs + ×
InterfacesBook                                                            InterfacesBook.Document
    2       {
                1 reference
    3           public class Document
    4           {
    5               private IDocumentConverter _pdfConverter;
    6               private IDocumentConverter _excelConverter;
    7
                    0 references
    8               public Document(IDocumentConverter PDFConverter, IDocumentConverter ExcelConverter)
    9               {
   10                   _pdfConverter = PDFConverter;
   11                   _excelConverter = ExcelConverter;
   12               }
   13
                    0 references
   14               public void ConvertDocumentToPDF(int documentId)
   15               {
   16                   this._pdfConverter.Converter(documentId);
   17               }
   18
                    0 references
   19               public void ConvertDocumentToExcel(int documentId)
   20               {
   21                   this._excelConverter.Converter(documentId);
   22               }
   23           }
   24       }
   25
```

Figure 4.12: Document class using dependency injection

With this approach, you can inject an implementation of **PDFConverter** and **ExcelConverter** class in the **Document** class and reducing the coupling between all these classes. Beyond that, it consistently improves the testability and reusability of the **Document** class once it is possible to mock the conversion classes in case of it is necessary to apply tests in the **Document** class, without needing a dependency of the third-party libraries. Another important extra factor is that in case there is a software requirement change that includes the support of conversion to other formats, the modification in the **Document** class would be minimal if the new converter class implements the same **IDocumentConverter** interface.

Conclusion

As you could see in this chapter, the object-oriented programming paradigm in C# language provides interesting and useful features such as interfaces to build robust enterprise applications, applying the best practices of software development regarding reusability and software architecture aspects that allow us to reduce the dependency between components in the projects. The correct use of interfaces is one of the main points to build powerful enterprise applications using the .NET platform. It is mandatory knowledge to create practical and high-quality applications and strongly facilitate the reusability and integrity of the components of the software, reducing the costs of projects, and minimizing the risks regarding software maintenance.

With this chapter, you have learned how to create interfaces, applying its concept in different scenarios and how to take the benefits for building testable, reusable, and extensible applications using the C# language. Also, you had the opportunity to learn about dependency injection, which allows you to reduce the dependency between components and give you the chance to extend the software functionality, avoiding huge risks.

In the next chapter, you will have the chance to learn the basic concepts of encapsulation and polymorphism in .NET 5 applications using C# 9.0 and how to apply them in different scenarios, in order to build high-standard enterprise applications and solve distinct problems that you could face in many projects.

Points to remember

- The C# language does not support multiple inheritances, but it is possible to use multiple interfaces instead.

- Interfaces give consistency to the software architecture and increase aspects of the testability of the classes.

- Dependency injection is largely used in .NET projects, and its concept helps us to reduce the dependency between classes and components.

Multiple-choice questions

1. **Which version of C# introduced the possibility to have default implementation in interfaces?**

   a. 8.0

   b. 7.2

   c. 1.0

   d. C# does not support this feature

2. **How many interfaces can a class implement?**

    a. Two

    b. Unlimited

    c. None

    d. One

3. **Which term better represent the purpose of interfaces?**

    a. Polymorphism

    b. Inheritance

    c. Contracts

    d. Accessibility

Answer

1. a
2. b
3. c

Questions

1. Explain the difference between inheritance and interface in C# language.

2. Explain the concept of dependency injection.

3. Why do the interfaces help the software development in terms of testability?

4. According to what you have learned in this chapter; list the benefits of the use of interfaces.

CHAPTER 5

Encapsulation and Polymorphism in C#

The C# language provides features that help in the implementation of routines that protect the classes in the object-oriented programming from unexpected changes in their members, or even violation of the good practices using this vital paradigm using the encapsulation and polymorphism concepts in .NET applications, with the purpose of having a reliable and robust software architecture.

With this chapter, you will have the opportunity to learn the concept of encapsulation and polymorphism using the C# language deeply and to understand the benefits of their applicability in real projects.

Learning the advanced concepts of the object-oriented programming paradigm such as encapsulation and polymorphism is important because it gives you the chance to safely scale and extend functionalities in existent software and build applications from scratch, applying mechanisms that keep the components correctly isolated. The knowledge of fundamental object-oriented programming is fundamental to understand the design patterns and other essential-related subjects properly.

Structure

In this chapter, we will discuss the following topics:

- Concept of encapsulation
- Examples in C# and .NET 5 applications

- Concept of polymorphism
- Examples and good practices of polymorphism

Objectives

After studying this unit, you should be able to:

- Understand the encapsulation and polymorphism concepts
- Apply encapsulation and polymorphism using the C# language
- Identity the use of encapsulation and polymorphism in existent projects

Definition of encapsulation

Every class implemented in the C# language should not be dependent on other classes as much as possible, and a single class must have a clear and unique purpose to facilitate its reusability, maintainability, and also to increase the possibility to extend the functionalities properly in the software as long as there are new requirements to implement. The high mutability is an intrinsic aspect to any project of software, and for that reason, is in escapable the use of mechanism in the C# language that helps in making changes in the software in the same time as the consistency of the classes is preserved from external effects from other classes or components in the software.

In that context, encapsulation conveniently protects the members and methods from a class, avoiding the possibility of other classes changing their behavior unexpectedly, and modifying the value of members that should be used only in the context of the class itself. This target can be achieved by using the access-level modifiers available in the C# language correctly, which allows modifying the visibility of properties and methods that are involved in sensitive or critical operations to keep the integrity of the class as a single unit.

As was previously explained in this book, the C# language provides the following access-level modifiers:

- Public
- Private
- Protected
- Internal

Each one of those modifiers determines the visibility of methods and properties to other classes, and the decision of which modifier should be used is an essential part of the software development based on the object-oriented programming, once the expected behavior of classes, methods, and even components could be compromised if the suitable restriction is not being applied at the correct level.

There are two main ways to implement encapsulation in the C# language: one of them is using the methods that manipulate the variables in a class, and another one is the use of properties, keeping their primary purpose.

The first one that will be demonstrated in this section is the possibility to implement the encapsulation using methods, despite its limitation. As an example, imagine that we have a class called **Product**, and each product has specific business requirements regarding the product price and discount, such as limitation of the discount to a 10% for all products or evena validation related to a product price, which cannot have a value smaller than a certain number. It is possible to build the class as shown in the following screenshot:

```csharp
namespace DesignPatternsEncapsulation
{
    public class Product
    {

        public Product(decimal discount, decimal price)
        {
            this.Discount = CheckDiscount(discount);
            this.Price = CheckDiscount(price);
        }
        public int Id { get; set; }
        public string Name { get; set; }
        public int Type { get; set; }

        public decimal Price { get; set; }

        public decimal Discount { get; set; }

        private static decimal CheckDiscount(decimal discount)
        {
            if(discount < 0 || discount > 10)
            {
                throw new ArgumentOutOfRangeException();
            }

            return discount;
        }

        private static decimal CheckPrice(decimal price)
        {
            if (price < 100)
            {
                throw new ArgumentOutOfRangeException();
            }

            return price;
        }
    }
}
```

***Figure 5.1**: Product class*

The class has a private method called **CheckPrice** to validate the price that is being passed in the constructor of the class. The price in this example should not be smaller than 100. Additionally, there is another private method called **CheckDiscount**, which is validating the discount value that is being passed in the constructor. The value must be greater than zero and smaller than 10. In the two methods, if the value is invalid, respecting the business requirements, the system will throw an exception.

This approach partially protects the **Product** class from violation of the requirements, because private methods are handling and populating the properties discount and price accordingly. However, there is a clear limitation in this implementation, and it is not fully following the best practices of encapsulation. The reason is the access level specified for the properties price and discount, as highlighted in the following screenshot:

```
}
0 references
public int Id { get; set; }
0 references
public string Name { get; set; }
0 references
public int Type { get; set; }

1 reference
public decimal Price { get; set; }
▄▄▄▄▄▄▄

1 reference
public decimal Discount { get; set; }
▄▄▄▄▄▄▄

2 references
```

Figure 5.2: Product class access level

Both of them are marked as public, which means that the values passed in the constructor of the class are not the only way to update these two properties because they can be accessed by external classes, violating its expected behavior. In the creation of the instance, a specific value could be passed, and a completely different one can be passed after that, and the methods responsible for the validation will not be used in that case, as shown in the following screenshot:

```
Program.cs  ↔ ✕
[C#] DesignPatternsEncapsulation
1    namespace DesignPatternsEncapsulation
2    {
     0 references
3        class Program
4        {
         0 references
5            static void Main(string[] args )
6            {
7                Product product = new Product(5, 200);
8                product.Discount = 15;
9                product.Price = 50;
10           }
11       }
12   }
13
```

Figure 5.3: Class access-level violation

In the example, the values 5 and 200 were passed regarding **Discount** and **Price**, and after the creation of the method, a value of 15 was passed as **Discount** and 50 for the **Price** property, which was different from what is determined by the check methods. Considering that possibility, it is not recommended to use methods for the encapsulation of properties, but it is necessary to protect the properties through their access level. Therefore, however, the class partially meets its purpose; there is a big issue that must be avoided while following the best practices of object-oriented programming and encapsulation principles. The properties that are being changed by the validation methods need to have their access level specified as private, and new properties that only get the values from the private properties must be created, as shown in the following screenshot:

```
         1 reference
10       public Product(decimal discount, decimal price)
11       {
12           this.Discount = CheckDiscount(discount);
13           this.Price = CheckDiscount(price);
14       }
         0 references
15       public int Id { get; set; }
         0 references
16       public string Name { get; set; }
         0 references
17       public int Type { get; set; }
18
         3 references
19       private decimal Price
20       {
21           get; set;
22       }
23
         3 references
24       private decimal Discount
25       {
26           get;set;
27       }
28
         0 references
29       public decimal GetDiscount()
30       {
31           return this.Discount;
32       }
         0 references
33       public decimal GetPrice()
34       {
35           return this.Price;
36       }
37
         2 references
38       private static decimal CheckDiscount(decimal discount)
39       {
40           if(discount < 0 || discount > 10)
41           {
42               throw new ArgumentOutOfRangeException();
43           }
44
45           return discount;
46       }
47
```

Figure 5.4: Product class with private properties

With that implementation, the direct assignment to the **Price** and **Discount** properties will not be possible anymore, protecting the class of external violation. The methods **GetDiscount** and **GetPrice** were created to achieve the objective of reading the values of discount and price values, respectively. In that way, the purpose of the encapsulation was fully implemented once it is not possible to violate the business requirements defined by the class.

In terms of performance, there is another efficient way to meet the same objective as the previous example using only the properties of the class, instead of methods, to get the price and discount values. Properties are important resources in object-oriented programming, and their correct use represents a huge benefit in terms of clean code and good practices of software development, even if they are the most basic part of the classes. In the C# language, properties work in the same way as methods. All the properties count on two blocks of code: **get** and **set**. The get block statement is the place where it is possible to implement routines when the property is read, and the set block statement is used when the property has its value modified, as shownin the following screenshot:

```
1 reference
public Product(decimal discount, decimal price)
{
    this.Discount = CheckDiscount(discount);
    this.Price = CheckDiscount(price);
}
0 references
public int Id { get; set; }
2 references
public string Name {
    get { return Name.ToUpper(); }
    set { this.Name = value; }
}

}
0 references
```

Figure 5.5: Product name property

The get statement of the **Name** property was modified to use the method **Upper** every time the property is accessed or read. It allows us to specify a general implementation that will be used by all the instances of the class and conveniently centralize the necessary operations regarding the property. There fore, it is not needed to explicitly repeat this operation when an instance of an object is created, saving relevant time in the development process. As it is possible to make operations in the **get** and **set** statements, they can be used to fully and safely implement the validation methods for the discount and price properties. In that way, we guarantee that the properties will always be validated, and the intrinsic properties of the class will be visible and specified as public fields. In addition, the **GetDiscount** and **GetPrice** methods can be removed, as shownin the following screenshot:

```
Product.cs ✦ ✕
⬚ DesignPatternsEncapsulation                                              ▾  ⬚ DesignPatternsEncapsulation.Product
    8
    9              private decimal _discount;
   10              private decimal _price;
                   1 reference
   11              public Product(decimal discount, decimal price)
   12              {
   13                  this._discount = CheckDiscount(discount);
   14                  this._price = CheckDiscount(price);
   15              }
                   0 references
   16              public int Id { get; set; }
                   2 references
   17              public string Name
   18              {
   19                  get { return Name.ToUpper(); }
   20                  set { this.Name = value; }
   21
   22              }
                   0 references
   23              public int Type { get; set; }
   24
                   2 references
   25              public decimal Price
   26              {
   27                  get { return this._price;  }
   28                  set { this._price = CheckPrice(Price); }
   29              }
   30
                   2 references
   31              public decimal Discount
   32              {
   33                  get { return this._discount; }
   34                  set { this._discount = CheckPrice(Discount); }
   35              }
```

Figure 5.6: *Use of the get and set statements*

In the preceding example, the **set** statement is used for applying the validation for the discount and price properties, even the possibility of the assignment of those values directly from external operations considering the access level is specified as public.

Definition of polymorphism

The C# language fully supports the concept of polymorphism, which consists of the implementation of different methods with the same name, but with different parameters or distinct behavior. As its name suggests, it is possible to have multiple forms of the same routine that was defined in a class for many reasons: reusability, specialization, consistency, and integrity.

As an example, continuing with the **Product** class given in the previous section, in a real scenario, an online store could have a wide variety of types of products, and each one must have distinct and special business requirements, which technically would require different methods, but keeping the same class. The following two screenshots represent the base **Product** class and another class called **Television,** which inherits from the base class, but has a distinct implementation of the **Discount** method, as follows:

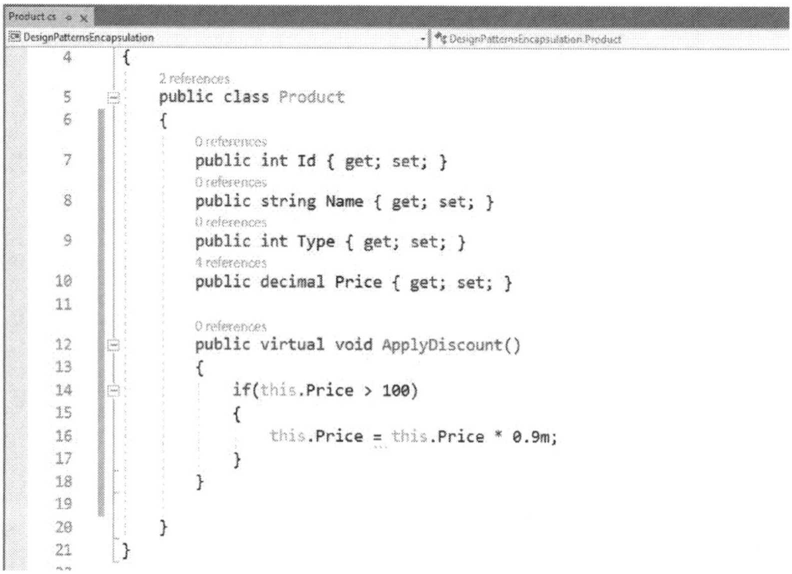

```
{
    2 references
    public class Product
    {
        0 references
        public int Id { get; set; }
        0 references
        public string Name { get; set; }
        0 references
        public int Type { get; set; }
        4 references
        public decimal Price { get; set; }

        0 references
        public virtual void ApplyDiscount()
        {
            if(this.Price > 100)
            {
                this.Price = this.Price * 0.9m;
            }
        }

    }
}
```

Figure 5.7: Base Product class

In this example, the keyword **virtual** was specified in the **ApplyDiscount** method, which means that it is allowed to the other class that inherits from the **Product** class to change the default implementation of the method if it is needed. The child class could have another rule regarding discount, but the same name of the method would be kept, and the **override** keyword must be used in that case to indicate for the compile that this class is not taking the method from the base class, as shownin the following screenshot:

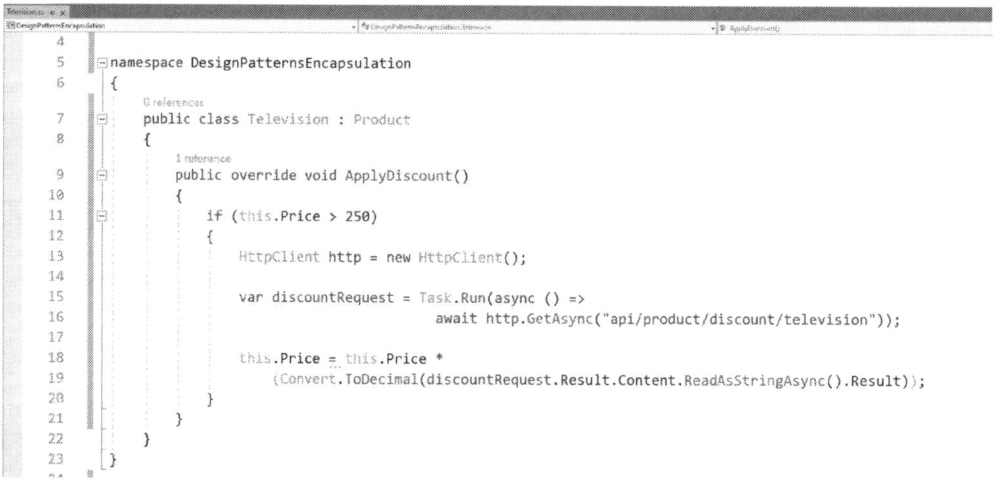

```
namespace DesignPatternsEncapsulation
{
    0 references
    public class Television : Product
    {
        1 reference
        public override void ApplyDiscount()
        {
            if (this.Price > 250)
            {
                HttpClient http = new HttpClient();

                var discountRequest = Task.Run(async () =>
                                await http.GetAsync("api/product/discount/television"));

                this.Price = this.Price *
                    (Convert.ToDecimal(discountRequest.Result.Content.ReadAsStringAsync().Result));
            }
        }
    }
}
```

Figure 5.8: Television class

The **ApplyDiscount** method contains a completely different implementation. It is getting the discount from an external resource via an HTTP request, and the condition presented in the method is slightly different from the base class. As seen in the line number 7, the television class inherits from **Product**, and for that reason, all the properties from the base class donot need to be again specified in the class once they already exist in the parent one.

Therefore, the **Television** class has identical methods and properties as the parent class, but with a different behavior, once the discount is distinctly calculated, applying the concept of polymorphism with the possibility to extend the implementation across the system in many other specialized classes. This type of polymorphism is called runtime polymorphism, considering the different behavior of the method is being explicitly defined using the keywords **virtual** and **override**. Further more, it is possible to apply polymorphism in compile time using different parameters for the methods of the same class. Although that has limitations compared to the runtime polymorphism, considering it needs to be done in a single class, it allows us to give a meaningful objective to a single class. One of the good principles of object-oriented programming is that a class should have a single reason to exist and change, following the single responsibility principle. Considering those important concepts, runtime polymorphism allows us to keep the integrity and consistency of the class, at the same time, as many methods with a tiny variation on their behavior can be created. One of the native examples that exist in the .NET Core and C# language is the conversion methods. A single class called **Convert** contains many methods that have the same name, but different parameters. Therefore, the purpose of the methods is the same, but the input is quite different, as shownin the following screenshot:

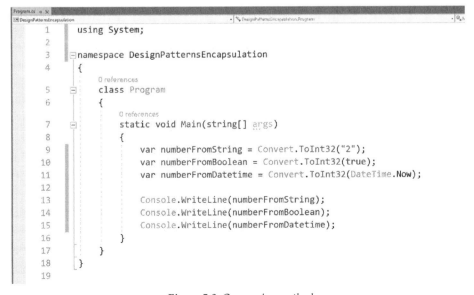

Figure 5.9: Conversion method

Belonging to the **System** name space, the **Convert** class has many methods available with the same name, but with a different signature. In the example, the method **ToInt32** receives distinct parameters from different types. It means that all of them have the same purpose, which consists of converting the input to an integer value. Only that method contains 19 options, and it is a good example of how we can use the compile-time polymorphism concept to maintain the integrity and meaning of a class.

Conclusion

As you saw in this chapter, the object-oriented programming paradigm in the C# language is fully supported, proving interesting and useful features such as encapsulation and polymorphism to build and consistently implement the best practices of software development in enterprise applications, giving the software architecture a possibility to overload the methods and protect the classes from an external or unexpected behavior. The correct use of encapsulation and polymorphism is one of the main points of object-oriented programming, and they are essential to building high-standard applications using the .NET Core platform and C# language, being mandatory knowledge for developers and software architectures.

With this chapter, you have learned how to use polymorphism and encapsulation in the C# language, apply its concept in different scenarios, and how to take the benefits for building consistent, reusable, and extensible classes and methods.

In the next chapter, you will have the chance to learn the SOLID principles using the C# language and .NET 5 platforms, getting familiar with the best practices of reusable and maintainable software.

Points to remember

- The C# language fully supports encapsulation and polymorphism.
- Encapsulation protects the members of the classes from an external violation.
- The .NET platform and C# language widely use the polymorphism concept across the framework.

Multiple-choice questions

1. **Which alternative does not represent an access modifier for C# language?**
   a. Private
   b. Protected
   c. Public
   d. Interface

2. **Which keywords can be used to allow runtime polymorphism?**

   a. Virtual and override

   b. Public and private

   c. Runtime and compile

3. **Which keyword can be used to allow a different method implementation from a parent class keeping the same name and signature?**

   a. Public

   b. Virtual

   c. Overloading

   d. Protected

Answer

1. d

2. a

3. b

Questions

1. Explain the difference between polymorphism in runtime and compile time.

2. What are the main benefits of encapsulation in object-oriented programming?

3. According to what you have learned in this chapter, explain the purpose of the virtual keyword in inheritance presented in the C# language.

CHAPTER 6
SOLID Principles in C#

With this chapter, we are starting our journey into the best practices of object-oriented programming using the C# language. Any project of software could face similar challenges, such as scalability, maintenance, regression issues, and to make easier the software development process, it is highly recommended to follow the five most famous principles of object-oriented design: **Single-Responsibility Principle (SRP)**, **Open–Closed Principle (OCP)**, **Liskov Substitution Principle (LSP)**, **Interface Segregation Principle (ISP)**, and **Dependency Inversion Principle (DIP)**. You will learn how to apply all these common practices in real projects using the C# language, a mandatory knowledge to get started with design patterns. Considering the high complexity that the software development might have in terms of coding, it is essential and extremely important to understand the SOLID principles and be able to identify those inexistent projects and third-party libraries.

Structure

In this chapter, we will discuss the following topics:

- The single-responsibility principle
- The open–closed principle
- The Liskov substitution principle
- The interface segregation principle

- The dependency inversion principle

Objectives

After studying this unit, you should be able to:

- Understanding the SOLID principles
- Identify the principles in existent projects
- Apply the principles in basic projects in .NET 5 using C#

6.1 The single-responsibility principle (SRP)

The SOLID principles represent good practices that should be followed by all software developers who build systems using the OOP pattern. The principles contribute to having a well-written code, providing maintainability, and extensibility. Considering software development is a logical and intellectual process, the same software requirement could be implemented distinctly by different developers, and different approaches could be applied to get the same result.

Good software development is not only about visible software functionalities, but beyond that, it is about to have high standards in terms of software architecture and engineering. It is not hard to find projects of software that have failed because of technical problems and limitations regarding maintenance and extensibility. In any software development life cycle, the costs of changes get higher when changes are made after production releases. The changes in existent functionalities will likely introduce new issues in the project, and, in the meantime, new features are being released, becoming a great challenge for any software development team to keep the project moving forward with high quality.

For that reason, keeping the code clean as much as possible and following the good practices of software development is essential to maintain a long-term solution project that supports relevant changes over time and is ready to absorb constantly new requirements.

The SRP is the first of the list defined by the SOLID acronym, and this is frequently applied to software development using OOP, considering it is highly recommended that a class in this paradigm should have a single responsibility. Therefore, the implementation of any part of the software should have a clear and unique objective, being much easier to make changes to that and to extend its functionality.

As an example, imagine a scenario in which a commercial system contains a specific routine that consists of converting a document to PDF; send it by email to customers after a financial transaction, and finally, recording logs in the database regarding this operation. In this short case, there are four different requirements and targets to meet. First of all, we must create a class in the C# language that implements the necessary code for all these requirements and does not follow the SRP. The implementation would be like the class represented in the following screenshot:

```csharp
using Microsoft.Office.Interop.Word;
using System;
using System.Net.Mail;

namespace SOLIDPrinciplesBook
{
    0 references
    public class CommercialTransaction
    {
        0 references
        private void CompleteTransaction()
        {

            //CONVERTING A WORD TO PDF
            Microsoft.Office.Interop.Word.Document wordDocument;
            Microsoft.Office.Interop.Word.Application appWord =
                new Microsoft.Office.Interop.Word.Application();

            wordDocument = appWord.Documents.Open(@"C:\desktop\myDocument.docx");
            wordDocument.ExportAsFixedFormat(@"C:\desktop\myConvertedDocument.pdf",
                WdExportFormat.wdExportFormatPDF);

            //SENDING EMAIL
            System.Net.Mail.MailMessage mail = new System.Net.Mail.MailMessage();
            SmtpClient SmtpServer = new SmtpClient("smtp.companyexample.com");

            mail.From = new MailAddress("dotnotreply@companyexample.com");
            mail.To.Add("customerexample@gmail.com");
            mail.Subject = "Transaction confirmed";
            mail.Body = "This is a transaction confirmation";

            SmtpServer.Port = 587;
            SmtpServer.Credentials = new System.Net.NetworkCredential("username", "password");
            SmtpServer.EnableSsl = true;

            SmtpServer.Send(mail);

            //RECORDING LOG
            new LogTransaction()
                .RecordTransaction("Transaction finished at " + DateTime.UtcNow.ToString());
        }
    }
}
```

Figure 6.1: Single responsibility example

The implementation presented in the previous screenshot contains three distinct responsibilities:

1. Convert a document to PDF format.

2. Send an email to a user.

3. Record the transaction in a log file.

According to the method name (**CompleteTransaction**), the main purpose of this routine would be the transaction completion, but the code has detailed implementation for sending emails and for PDF conversion as well. That means it is not following the single responsibility principle, and there is a great possibility to introduce bugs in this code, considering a change in one of the multiple responsibilities could easily affect the other related existent routines in the same method. Additionally, the actual approach as it is becoming harder to reuse the same method in different parts of the project, considering the routine to send emails and convert documents to PDF, is inside the method itself.

An alternative would be refactoring this code, hiding the implementation of everything secondary to the method, and keeping only the code associated with transaction completion, as shown in the following screenshot:

```csharp
using System;

namespace SOLIDPrinciplesBook
{
    public class CommercialTransaction
    {
        private void CompleteTransaction()
        {

            new Document().ConverToPDF(@"C:\desktop\myDocument.docx");
            new Email().Send();
            new LogTransaction()
                .RecordTransaction("Transaction finished at " + DateTime.UtcNow.ToString());
        }
    }
}
```

Figure 6.2: Single responsibility refactor

This new version of the same implementation has significant improvements in terms of coding. The complexity related to emails and conversion to PDF was moved to other classes and can be reused in the parts of the software. Further more, the method **CompleteTransaction** contains fewer code lines, and it is easier to understand their purpose. The most important point of the SRP is that a class should have only one reason to change. After the refactor process, the code is split into three different classes, and they can be distinctly changed, without affecting the others. Therefore, the primary class is not violating the principle anymore.

6.2 The open–closed principle (OCP)

The OCP is the second of the SOLID acronym, and the idea behind this principle is that an object should be open to an extension, but closed for changes in its behavior. Any software has a huge amount of business requirements converted into code, and the requirements can frequently change because of business requests, new regulations, or simply because of a better understanding of the purpose of the software. However, many requirement changes should not represent or require modifications to the code every time. If a specific routine in the code is being changed several times, it probably means that the design or pattern used for developing this part of code is not clear enough, and it is not following the best practices of software development. Further more, each change in the software could cause an impact in production environments for adding errors to an existent functionality, which should be extremely avoided as much as possible. Following the OCP, if a new requirement is requested and it requires to change an existent class or method in the code, the class should be extended to contemplate this new request and not changed. Therefore, adding new requirements should be considered as new functionalities and should represent extensions instead of modifications.

For instance, imagine the following scenario. There is a system that allows users to create accounts and have access to online movies on a streaming platform. At the first moment, there is a single account type that has the same behavior and requirements for every user. The following represents a simple implementation of that:

```csharp
using System.Collections.Generic;

namespace SOLIDPrinciplesBook
{
    class Program
    {
        static void Main(string[] args)
        {
            List<User> users = new List<User>
            {
                new User { FullName = "Elon", Active = true, Email = "elon@example.com" },
                new User { FullName = "Martin", Active = true, Email = "martin@example.com" },
                new User { FullName = "Mary", Active = true, Email = "mary@example.com" },
                new User { FullName = "John", Active = true, Email = "john@example.com" }
            };

            List<Customer> customers = new List<Customer>();
            PlatformAccount platformAccount = new PlatformAccount();

            foreach (var user in users)
            {
                customers.Add(platformAccount.Generate(user));
            }
        }
    }
}
```

Figure 6.3: Open–closed example

As seen in the previous screenshot, the routine is creating a list of four users, and for each item, a method **Generate** is being from the class **PlatformAccount**. This class contains a mapping between user and customer account, as shown in the following screenshot:

```
PlatformAccount.cs  ⊸ ×
SOLIDPrinciplesBook                    ▾  SOLIDPrinciplesBook.PlatformAccount   ▾  Generate(User user)
    4
    5      namespace SOLIDPrinciplesBook
    6      {
               2 references
    7          public class PlatformAccount
    8          {
                   1 reference
    9              public Customer Generate(User user)
   10              {
   11                  Customer customer = new Customer();
   12
   13                  customer.FullName = user.FullName;
   14                  customer.Email = user.Email;
   15                  customer.Active = user.Active;
   16                  customer.Password = user.Password;
   17
   18                  return customer;
   19              }
   20          }
   21      }
   22
```

Figure 6.4: Platform account class

The **Customer** and **User** classes in this example have the same fields, as it is shown in the following two screenshots:

```
User.cs  ⊸ ×
SOLIDPrinciplesBook                                        ▾  SOLIDPrinciplesBook.User
    1      using System;
    2      using System.Collections.Generic;
    3      using System.Text;
    4
    5      namespace SOLIDPrinciplesBook
    6      {
               7 references
    7          public class User
    8          {
                   5 references
    9              public string FullName { get; set; }
                   5 references
   10              public string Email { get; set; }
                   1 reference
   11              public string Password { get; set; }
                   5 references
   12              public bool Active { get; set; }
   13          }
   14      }
```

Figure 6.5: User class

The **Customer** class has the representation as shown in the following screenshot:

```
Customer.cs  -þ X
SOLIDPrinciplesBook                                                    SOLIDPrinciplesBook.Customer
   1      using System;
   2      using System.Collections.Generic;
   3      using System.Text;
   4
   5      namespace SOLIDPrinciplesBook
   6      {
              5 references
   7          public class Customer
   8          {
                  1 reference
   9              public string FullName { get; set; }
                  1 reference
  10              public string Email { get; set; }
                  1 reference
  11              public string Password { get; set; }
                  1 reference
  12              public bool Active { get; set; }
  13          }
  14      }
  15
```

Figure 6.6: Customer class

In real scenarios, the platform account class would use in its implementation amethod that would insert the customer in the database and could contain extra code, but as the objective is just to demonstrate the OCP, the complexity was hidden to facilitate the comprehension. Considering that a requirement can change anytime in that part of software because of business requirement modifications imagine that there is a requirement that the streaming company will start having other types of accounts for customers, such as premium accounts with different logic in comparison to the standard account. In that scenario, there are two main options: changing the implementation of the platform account class to check if the customer has a premium account, and if yes, the method would run different code, as shown in the following screenshot:

```csharp
using System.Collections.Generic;
using System.Text;

namespace SOLIDPrinciplesBook
{
    public class PlatformAccount
    {
        public Customer Generate(User user)
        {
            Customer customer = new Customer();

            customer.FullName = user.FullName;
            customer.Email = user.Email;
            customer.Active = user.Active;
            customer.Password = user.Password;

            if(customer.IsPremiumAccount)
            {
                GeneratePremiumAccount(customer);
            }

            return customer;
        }

        private void GeneratePremiumAccount(Customer customer)
        {
            //Custom implementation for premium account
        }
    }
}
```

Figure 6.7: Premium account implementation

The implementation, as shown in the previous screenshot, violates the OCP because the platform account class was modified instead of being just extended. It now contains an **if** statement in case the customer has a premium account, and it is calling a different method. There are a couple of limitations andrisks using this approach:

- All the methods that have to call the **create** method must set the property **isPremiumAccount** correctly. It is easy to make mistakes in coding and forget to set the property value to **true**.

- In the case this class would have a complex implementation, adding code to the method could easily affect the behavior for other types of accounts, such as the standard one that should remain as it is.

- If in the future, new account types are included, such as bronze, silver, and gold, it would add extra conditions on the platform account class, and it would get a higher complexity of the code.

An alternative implementation that follows the recommendations of the OCP would extend the functionality to provide the premium account option instead of changing the existing class used to create the standard account. To meet this target, it is possible to use interfaces to abstract the **User** and **PlatformAccount** classes. In that way, the standard and the premium account would do separated classes, and the implementation of the first original class will not be modified, as shown in the following screenshot:

```csharp
using System.Collections.Generic;

namespace SOLIDPrinciplesBook
{
    class Program
    {
        static void Main(string[] args)
        {
            List<IUser> users = new List<IUser>
            {
                new User { FullName = "Elon", Active = true, Email = "elon@example.com" },
                new User { FullName = "Martin", Active = true, Email = "martin@example.com" },
                new User { FullName = "Mary", Active = true, Email = "mary@example.com" },

                new PremiumUser { FullName = "John", Active = true, Email = "john@example.com" }
            };

            List<Customer> customers = new List<Customer>();

            foreach (var user in users)
            {
                customers.Add(user.PlatformAccount.Generate(user));
            }
        }
    }
}
```

Figure 6.8: Premium account implementation

A premium user class was created and shared the same interface as the **User** class, as shown in the next two screenshots:

```csharp
using System;
using System.Collections.Generic;
using System.Text;

namespace SOLIDPrinciplesBook
{
    public class User : IUser
    {
        public string FullName { get; set; }
        public string Email { get; set; }
        public string Password { get; set; }
        public bool Active { get; set; }

        public IPlatformAccount PlatformAccount { get; set; } = new PlatformAccount();
    }
}
```

Figure 6.9: Standard user class

Both of the user classes (**User** and **PremiumUser**) have a property called **PlatformAccount**, and it refers to an interface and creates an instance of different classes for the user and user premium objects, as shown in the following screenshot:

```csharp
using System;
using System.Collections.Generic;
using System.Text;

namespace SOLIDPrinciplesBook
{
    1 reference
    public class PremiumUser : IUser
    {
        8 references
        public string FullName { get; set; }
        8 references
        public string Email { get; set; }
        4 references
        public string Password { get; set; }
        8 references
        public bool Active { get; set; }

        3 references
        public IPlatformAccount PlatformAccount { get; set; } = new PremiumPlatformAccount();
    }
}
```

Figure 6.10: Standard user class

The OCP is highly recommended if the software is already being used in a production environment and new requirements need to be added in the existent functionalities. The principle helps to keep an understandable code and voids issues in legacy projects.

6.3 The Liskov substitution principle (LSP)

This principle was defined and created by *Barbara Liskov*, and the main point and objective of this good practice are to avoid throwing exceptions in a system when inheritance is not used in a recommended way. Inheritance allows to reuse the implementation from a parent and common class across the software, but when a specific method or property from the parent class does not apply to all the possible children classes, it indicates that the model does not perfectly reflect the business requirement, and it could generate issues in production environments with unhandled exceptions.

To demonstrate this principle, we will create a scenario that represents the same conditions that the principle tries to solve. For example, imagine a system that allows the creation of user accounts in an online book service, and there are two different types of accounts: premium and standard. The standard account has access to a limited number of titles, and the premium account has unlimited access to the titles and can share access with family members. Both have things in common, and it is natural to create a base class that would be a parent of each one, as shown in the following screenshot:

```
BaseUser.cs + X
SOLIDPrinciplesBook                                          ▼  SOLIDPrinciplesBook.BaseUser
      1    Eusing System;
      2     using System.Collections.Generic;
      3     using System.Text;
      4
      5    Enamespace SOLIDPrinciplesBook
      6     {
                 9 references
      7            public class BaseUser
      8            {
                       0 references
      9                public string FullName { get; set; }
                       0 references
     10                public string Email { get; set; }
                       0 references
     11                public string Password { get; set; }
     12
                       0 references
     13                public virtual void GiveAccessFamilyMembers()
     14                {
     15                    Console.WriteLine("Access granted to family members");
     16                }
     17
                       0 references
     18                public virtual void AccessToLimitedTitles()
     19                {
     20                    Console.WriteLine("Access to limited titles");
     21                }
     22
                       0 references
     23                public virtual void AccessToUnlimitedTitles()
     24                {
     25                    Console.WriteLine("Access to unlimited titles");
     26                }
     27
     28
     29            }
     30     }
     31
```

Figure 6.11: User base class

As seen in the previous screenshot, there are, in the **BaseUser** class, properties related to the state of the object, such as full name, email, and password. But, the class also contains methods responsible for giving access to book titles and family members. Considering the standard and premium user classes are derived from the base class, the implementation of both is as shown in the following screenshot:

```
StandardUser.cs + X
SOLIDPrinciplesBook                                    ▼  SOLIDPrinciplesBook.StandardUser              ▼  GiveAccessFamilyMembers()
      1    Eusing System;
      2     using System.Collections.Generic;
      3     using System.Text;
      4
      5    Enamespace SOLIDPrinciplesBook
      6     {
                 0 references
      7            public class StandardUser: BaseUser
      8            {
                       2 references
      9                public override void AccessToLimitedTitles()
     10                {
     11                    base.AccessToLimitedTitles();
     12                }
     13
                       1 reference
     14                public override void AccessToUnlimitedTitles()
     15                {
     16                    throw new InvalidOperationException("This type of account does not have unlimited access");
     17                }
     18
                       1 reference
     19                public override void GiveAccessFamilyMembers()
     20                {
     21                    throw new InvalidOperationException("This type of account does have access to family members");
     22                }
     23            }
     24     }
     25
```

Figure 6.12: User standard class

The class contains methods that donot necessarily apply to the standard user class, but the premium user class, such as family member access and access to unlimited titles. The problem with this implementation is that if an instance of **StandardUser** class is created and by mistake, amethod that should only belong to the premium user class is called, the system will throw an exception, and the functionality would miss its integrity. Further more, the proposed model does not reflect the business requirements that have specific rules for the premium account.

There are two ways to solve this problem: one is to remove the methods related to the premium account from the base class and the other one is to use interfaces. The following screenshot represents the first solution:

```csharp
1   using System;
2   using System.Collections.Generic;
3   using System.Text;
4
5   namespace SOLIDPrinciplesBook
6   {
        2 references
7       public class BaseUser
8       {
            0 references
9           public string FullName { get; set; }
            0 references
10          public string Email { get; set; }
            0 references
11          public string Password { get; set; }
12
13      }
14  }
15
```

Figure 6.13: Refactored user base class

The methods were removed from the class because they were not generic to be used by every child class, according to the requirements stated for this example. On the other hand, the methods were accordingly placed in the standard and premium user classes, as shown in the following screenshot:

```
SOLIDPrinciplesBook                                    ▾  SOLIDPrinciplesBook.StandardUser
   1    ⊟using System;
   2     using System.Collections.Generic;
   3     using System.Text;
   4
   5    ⊟namespace SOLIDPrinciplesBook
   6      {
                0 references
   7    ⊟       public class StandardUser: BaseUser
   8            {
                    0 references
   9    ⊟           public void AccessToLimitedTitles()
  10                {
  11                    Console.WriteLine("Access to limited titles");
  12                }
  13            }
  14
                0 references
  15    ⊟       public class PremiumUser: BaseUser
  16            {
                    0 references
  17    ⊟           public void AccessToUnlimitedTitles()
  18                {
  19                    Console.WriteLine("Access to unlimited titles");
  20                }
  21
                    0 references
  22    ⊟           public void GiveAccessFamilyMembers()
  23                {
  24                    Console.WriteLine("Access granted to family members");
  25                }
  26            }
  27      }
  28
```

Figure 6.14: *Refactored user child classes*

The main point of good practices of inheritance in OOP is that the parent class should contain only the generic and common implementation for the child class. The LSP states that the parent class should be replaceable by the child class and vice-versa. Although the concept of the LSP is slightly different from the OCP, they have similar purposes, which avoid introducing issues in the system when a change is applied based on new requirement requests.

6.4 The interface segregation principle (ISP)

This principle helps the developers to avoid making mistakes using interfaces that do not represent the business requirements. Similar to the LSP, where there is a recommendation of using in a parent class only the properties and method that appliesto all child classes, the interface segregation principle applies the same concept, but regarding interfaces. To clearly understand the principle, refer to the following screenshot that contains an interface for the product:

```
IProduct.cs
SOLIDPrinciplesBook                         SOLIDPrinciplesBook.IProduct

using System;
using System.Collections.Generic;
using System.Text;

namespace SOLIDPrinciplesBook
{
    public interface IProduct
    {
        public string ProductId { get; set; }
        public string Title { get; set; }
        public decimal Price { get; set; }

        public decimal Weight { get; set; }
        public decimal Width { get; set; }
        public decimal Height { get; set; }

    }
}
```

***Figure 6.15**: Product interface*

In a really common scenario like an online store, the system could easily contain various types of products, and they could have different properties. For instance, the following screenshot represents the implementation of two different classes: **`Television`** and **`OnlineBook`**:

```
using System;
using System.Collections.Generic;
using System.Text;

namespace SOLIDPrinciplesBook
{
    public class OnlineBook : IProduct
    {
        public string ProductId { get ; set;  }
        public string Title { get  ; set  ; }
        public decimal Price { get  ; set  ; }
        public decimal Weight { get  ; set  ; }
        public decimal Width { get  ; set  ; }
        public decimal Height { get  ; set  ; }
    }

    public class Television : IProduct
    {
        public string ProductId { get; set; }
        public string Title { get; set; }
        public decimal Price { get; set; }
        public decimal Weight { get; set; }
        public decimal Width { get; set; }
        public decimal Height { get; set; }
    }
}
```

***Figure 6.16**: Online book and television classes*

As shown in the previous screenshot, considering the two classes are implementing the same **IProduct** interface, both have the same properties. The problem with this implementation is that not all the types of products share the same properties or the same methods. For example, the fields related to product dimension (**Width** and **Height**) make sense only for **Television** and not for **OnlineBook**. To have a more clear code definition, the interface segregation principle states that it would be better to create a distinct interface for each product type, as shown in the following screenshot:

```
SOLIDPrinciplesBook                                          •○ SOLIDPrinciplesBook.ITelevision
1    using System;
2    using System.Collections.Generic;
3    using System.Text;
4
5    namespace SOLIDPrinciplesBook
6    {
         0 references
7        public interface IOnlineBooks
8        {
             0 references
9            public int MinutesDuration {get; set; }
10
11       }
12
         0 references
13       public interface ITelevision
14       {
             0 references
15           public decimal Weight { get; set; }
             0 references
16           public decimal Width { get; set; }
             0 references
17           public decimal Height { get; set; }
18
19       }
20   }
21
```

Figure 6.17: Interface segregation

Each specific class must use its underlying interface, which contains the correct fields that should be used in the class. The same concept applies to methods, and it is one of the most important best practices in terms of the OOP paradigm.

6.5 The dependency inversion principle (DIP)

The last one of the SOLID principles, the DIP, has the purpose of enforcing the good practice of hiding the implementation between classes in the cases where there are dependencies between them. To avoid risks in the development process, each class should contain only the implementation related to the class itself and keep low-level loosely coupled in the relation between them.

For example, a class called **Document** might have a method that has the responsibility of converting a document to a PDF or other formats. In real-case scenarios, the implementation of the conversion document would be placed in a different class, and it would be referred in the document class, as shown in the following screenshot:

```csharp
1   using System;
2   using System.Collections.Generic;
3   using System.Text;
4
5   namespace SOLIDPrinciplesBook
6   {
        3 references
7       public class Document
8       {
9           private IDocumentConversion PdfConverter = new PdfConverter();
10          private IDocumentConversion ExcelConverter = new ExcelConverter();
11
            0 references
12          public void GetPdfFormat()
13          {
14              var pdf = this.PdfConverter.Convert(this);
15          }
16
            0 references
17          public void GetExcelFormat()
18          {
19              var excel = this.ExcelConverter.Convert(this);
20          }
21      }
22  }
23
```

Figure 6.18: Document class

In this example, there are two obvious dependencies:

1. The document class depends on the classes **ExcelConverter** and **PdfConverter**.

2. For certain operations, it is possible for the document class to keep its original functionality without direct association with the converter classes.

Therefore, the document class depends on the other two classes, and the converter classes are dependencies of the **Document** class. Considering that, usually, the document conversion process uses third-party libraries in case there is a requirement that needs to change the third-party library, the high dependency between the document conversion classes and other parts of the software could be problematic.

An alternative to reduce the dependency between classes and to follow the DIP is to pass interfaces as parameters in the constructor of the class that depends on other classes, as shown in the following screenshot:

```
Document.cs ⊕ ×
[C#] SOLIDPrinciplesBook                              ▼ ◀ SOLIDPrinciplesBook.Document                    ▼ ◆ pdfConverter
     1      ☐using System;
     2       using System.Collections.Generic;
     3       using System.Text;
     4
     5      ☐namespace SOLIDPrinciplesBook
     6       {
                 4 references
     7      ☐    public class Document
     8           {
     9               private IDocumentConversion pdfConverter;
    10               private IDocumentConversion excelConverter;
    11
                     0 references
    12      ☐        public Document (IDocumentConversion PdfConverter, IDocumentConversion ExcelConverter)
    13               {
    14                   this.pdfConverter = PdfConverter;
    15                   this.excelConverter = ExcelConverter;
    16               }
    17
                     0 references
    18      ☐        public void GetPdfFormat()
    19               {
    20                   var pdf = this.pdfConverter.Convert(this);
    21               }
    22
                     0 references
    23      ☐        public void GetExcelFormat()
    24               {
    25                   var excel = this.excelConverter.Convert(this);
    26               }
    27           }
    28       }
    29
```

Figure 6.19: *Dependency inversion principle*

Implementing in that way, you can inject the implementation of the converter classes in to the **Document** class, once they share the same interface. Further more, it improves the testability of the classes, because it is easier to create mock classes to simulate the behavior of the converter classes.

Conclusion

The SOLID principles were created to help write better code, and it applies perfectly to the C# language, considering it is an OOP language. All the principles have the purpose of minimizing the impact of changes in existing software and help us to write cleaner code. The SRP can be used not only in class and method level but even in an architecture design to reduce the dependency between components and to have more a reusable functionality. The main point related to OCP and LSP is that it is safer to extend the functionality in the software than change the existing implementation. It avoids break-changes and turns the code more readable. The same benefits apply to the ISP and DIP.

In this chapter, you learned the essential information on SOLID principles and became familiar with the main advantages of using those principles in different scenarios of software development in your .NET Core projects, creating practical examples.

In the next chapter, you will start the journey across the design pattern with practical examples of the abstract factory pattern, using the .NET 5 and C# 9.0 language.

Points to remember

- The OCP is more recommended when changes are required in an existent project.

- All the principles have common objective, which is to reduce the impact of changes in the software.

- The SOLID principles perfectly apply to the C# language and for projects developed in .NET.

Questions

1. Explain the main advantages of the LSP.

2. Which SOLID principle helps us to reduce the dependency between classes?

3. Explain the risks of changes in existent projects.

CHAPTER 7
Abstract Factory

The design of robust software architecture represents a considerable challenge in terms of applying the advanced object-oriented programming concepts and a correct definition of abstractions that faithfully represent the complex business requirements presented in real scenarios. There are numerous solutions for distinct levels of complexity, and in this chapter, you will start your journey through the most used design patterns seen in .NET applications, beginning withthe abstract factory.

Learning the abstract factory pattern provides you the chance to elegantly apply the best practices of the object-oriented programming paradigm regarding polymorphism and encapsulation while developing a stable structure to extend and scale the complexity of a project that quickly supports requirement changes. The knowledge of this design pattern is crucial to get familiar with the other patterns available and hugely used in the market.

With this chapter, you will have the opportunity to understand the abstract factory pattern using the C# language, applying its concept in a step-by-step sample.

Structure

In this chapter, we will discuss the following topics:

- Abstract factory concept

- Examples in the C# and .NET Core

Objectives

After studying this unit, you should be able to:

- Understand the abstract factory pattern

- Applythe abstract factory in real-world projects

- Identify the use of encapsulation, polymorphism, and another object-oriented programming

Abstract factory definition

Any design pattern in software development represents a general solution for common situations that frequently happen in real scenarios, being a robust alternative to build a software architecture that follows the most recognized approaches largely used in the market. All the projects of software vary in business requirements and context, but many of them have a similar technical purpose in terms of implementation and code challenges.

For instance, imagine the scenario where a system has, as the main functionality, the intention of register products and services for an online store. Even the companies sell different types of products; the infrastructure behind the implementation of this kind of system is quite similar in terms of classes, business logic implementation, data models, database structure, and technical requirements, such as the necessity of control transactions and supports the record of a huge amount of entities that contain distinct properties and characteristics. Therefore, it is possible to say that there is a pattern followed by any online store, which requires to build and support the creation and management of complex records, many families of products, and the ability to provide a particular behavior of the system in terms of business requirements and work flow based on the product type.

In that context, among the list of all the available design patterns, there is the abstract factory pattern, which allows us to create families of related objects, abstracting the complexity of the building of those from the part of the software that is primary consuming and creating the objects. In summary, in case the system needs to create complex objects that contain distinct ways to create the related properties based on rules, the abstract factory pattern encapsulates the implementation and logic behind the factory of the concrete classes, giving us the possibility to extend the architecture by inserting more types of objects of the same family, with out compromising the integrity of the implementation.

As was demonstrated previously in this book, the correct use of interfaces in software based on the object-oriented programming paradigm is one of the most important characteristics to have a testable, extensible, and reliable project of software, which represents one of the key points of the abstract factory pattern.

Abstract factory scenario

Considering the abstract factory consists of reducing the complexity of object families'creation, it is fundamental to apply its concepts by implementing projects that have requirements similar to the problems that the abstract factory tries to solve. Therefore, in this section, you will have the opportunity to implement the base structure of a mobile company that sells distinct plans to customers regarding text messages, mobile data, and other services, which represents a scenario solvable by the abstract factory pattern with the following business requirements:

- The company will offer two types of plans for the customers: prepaid and postpaid.

- Both plans must have different conditions for text messages, internet connection speed, and mobile data limits.

- The prepaid option has a limited plan for text messages, up to 1,000 messages monthly.

- The prepaid option has a maximum speed of 10 megabytes per second.

- The prepaid plan has a 10 gigabytes limit for data transfer with in the month.

- The postpaid option offers unlimited data transfer and text messages.

- The postpaid plan has a high-speed internet connection, such as 500 megabytes per second.

The requirements clearly show that the mobile plans have the same structure in terms of properties for the objects, but the type and state of the objects are slightly distinct, as shown in the following representation:

Mobile plan	Text message limit	Mobile data transfer	Connection speed
Prepaid	1,000/month	10 gigabytes/month	10 megabytes/sec
Postpaid	Unlimited	Unlimited	500 megabytes/sec

Table 7.1: Mobile plans

Given that scenario, the use of the abstract factory allows us to build this complex objects by abstracting their implementation of the highest level in the application, which, in this pattern, is conventionally called **Client**, as shown in *figure 7.1*:

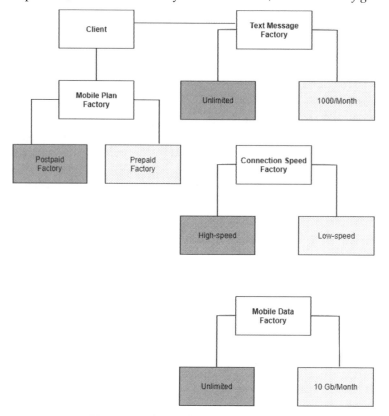

Figure 7.1: *Abstract factory implementation*

The correlation between the mobile plan and the type of compound objects is high lighted in the previous image by the color blue for the postpaid plan and by the color yellow for the prepaid plan. The abstract factory is known in the market as the *factory of factories* pattern, once the subset of objects created by the main factory is other factories as well.

Abstract factory implementation

Considering the requirements are already established, and the model structure is defined with the proper correlations, the first step in the coding process would be the creation of the individual classes and interfaces. In the entire example of this chapter, a .NET Core Console application is used as the client, and the interaction with the database is not present to keep the focus on the C# implementation. Following the diagram demonstrated in *figure 7.1*, we must create the first class in the project for each factory, starting by the **Text Message Factory**, including the underlying interface, with the scope limited to the representation shownin the following figure:

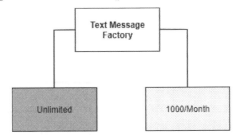

Figure 7.2: *Text Message Factory representation*

The implementation of the **Text Message Factory** requires an interface that includes properties related to the concrete type (unlimited and 1,000/month), using interfaces as shownin the following screenshot:

```csharp
using System;
using System.Collections.Generic;
using System.Text;

namespace AbstractFactory
{
    public interface ITextMessageFactory
    {
        string Name { get; set; }
        string QuantityPerMonth { get; set; }
    }

}
```

Figure 7.3: *Text Message Factory interface*

The interface contains only two properties in that example, which have the purpose of identifying the difference between the objects when they are going to be consumed by other classes in the given scenario. Starting the abstract factory creating interfaces is a good practice in terms of future test ability and extensibility of the entire solution. The next step is to create the concrete class that implements the interface for *Text Message Factory*, as shown in the following screenshot:

```csharp
namespace AbstractFactory
{
    public class ThousandTextMessage : ITextMessageFactory
    {
        public string Name { get; set; } = "A thousand text messages";
        public string QuantityPerMonth { get; set; } = "1000";
    }
}
```

Figure 7.4: *Thousand Text Message class*

As the given scenario contemplates the two types of text message plan (unlimited and thousand messages), we must create the second class regarding the **unlimited** type, implementing the same interface **ITextMessageFactory**, as shown in the following screenshot:

```
namespace AbstractFactory
{
    1 reference
    public class UnlimitedTextMessage : ITextMessageFactory
    {
        3 references
        public string Name { get; set; } = "Unlimited Text Message";
        2 references
        public string QuantityPerMonth { get; set; } = "Unlimited";
    }
}
```

Figure 7.5: Unlimited Text Message class

Considering both of the types implement the same interface, they have mandatorily the same members and methods, but each of them can implement a distinct behavior based on each specification. This approach allows us to consistently create unit and mock tests, inject the data, and give us the possibility to extend to other types consistently with out breaking the existing implementation.

A mobile plan in this context must contain information on text messages, internet connection, and mobile data plan, as shown in the list of requirements at the beginning of this section. Considering the infrastructure for the text message is already created, the next step is the creation of **Internet Connection Factory**, which should follow the structure presented in *figure 7.6*:

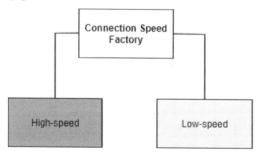

Figure 7.6: Connection Speed Factory representation

The implementation of the **Connection Speed Factory** requires an interface that includes properties related to the concrete type (high speed and low speed), using interfaces as shownin the following screenshot:

```
namespace AbstractFactory
{
    5 references
    public interface IConnectionSpeedFactory
    {
        4 references
        string Name { get; set; }
        2 references
        string Velocity { get; set; }
    }
}
```

Figure 7.7: Connection Speed Factory interface

The interface contains only two properties in that example (**Name** and **Velocity**), which have the purpose of identifying the difference between the objects when will be consumed by the implementation class. The next step is to create the concrete class that implements the interface for *Connection Speed Factory*, as shown in the following screenshot:

```
namespace AbstractFactory
{
    1 reference
    public class LowSpeed : IConnectionSpeedFactory
    {
        4 references
        public string Name { get; set; } = "Low Speed";

        2 references
        public string Velocity { get; set; } = "50 Mb/Sec";
    }
}
```

Figure 7.8: Low-Speed Factory class

As the given scenario contemplates the two types of connection speed (high speed and low speed), we must create the second class regarding the high-speed type, implementing the same interface **IConnectionSpeedFactory**, as shown in the following screenshot:

```
namespace AbstractFactory
{
    1 reference
    public class HighSpeed : IConnectionSpeedFactory
    {
        4 references
        public string Name { get; set; } = "High Speed";

        2 references
        public string Velocity { get; set; } = "500 Mb/Sec";
    }
}
```

Figure 7.9: High-speed class

Considering both of the types share the exact same interface, it is mandatory for the implementation of members and methods with similar signature, but each of them might implement a distinct behavior based on their specification. The mobile plan requires the creation of an extra and last factory class responsible for handling the creation of mobile data transfer information, which must have two different types, as shown in the following figure:

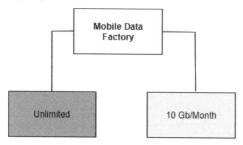

Figure 7.10: Mobile Data Factory representation

The implementation of the *Mobile Data Factory* requires the creation of an interface that includes the properties related to the future concrete types (unlimited and 10 Gb/month), sharing the same interface, as shownin the following screenshot:

```
namespace AbstractFactory
{
    public interface IMobileDataFactory
    {
        string Name { get; set; }
        string Limit { get; set; }
    }
}
```

Figure 7.11: Mobile Data Factory interface

The interface has two main properties in that example (**Name** and **Limit**), which have the purpose of identifying the difference between the objects. The next step is to specify the concrete class that implements the interface for *Mobile Data Factory*, as shownin the following screenshot:

```
namespace AbstractFactory
{
    public class UnlimitedMobileData : IMobileDataFactory
    {
        public string Name { get; set; } = "Unlimited";
        public string Limit { get; set; } = "Unlimited";
    }
}
```

Figure 7.12: Unlimited Mobile Data class

Considering the case scenario requires two types of unlimited mobile data (unlimited and 10 Gb), we must create the second class regarding the limit to 10 Gb limit for the prepaid option, implementing the same interface **IMobileDataFactory**, as shown in the following screenshot:

```
namespace AbstractFactory
{
    1 reference
    public class TenGigabytes : IMobileDataFactory
    {
        2 references
        public string Name { get; set; } = "10 Gb/sec";
        2 references
        public string Limit { get; set; } = "10 Gb/sec";
    }
}
```

Figure 7.13: *Ten Gigabytes Mobile Data class*

At this point, all the necessary sub-classes regarding the properties for the main factory are already created, making possible the implementation of the prepaid and postpaid options, which will be responsible for handling the custom creation of each mobile plan obeying all the requirements determined in the beginning of this section. The abstract factory pattern allows us to create complex objects for abstracting and encapsulating details of their implementation, making the code easier to read and understand for the developers. In a real-case scenario, the mobile plan factory must be responsible for creating any extra type apart from the two plans following the fast business requirement changes coming from the stake holders and from the new demands on the market. Because of that, in case new types need to be added, the main class responsible for the creation will hide the complexity of the creation of the new types, and the functionality can be extended safely without a huge concern of adding issues to the software architecture.

Similar to what was done with the factories for the sub-classes (text message, mobile data, and connection speed), the next step in the process of abstract factory pattern implementation is to create the infrastructure responsible for creating the compound object related to the prepaid and postpaid options for mobile plans represented in *figure 7.14*:

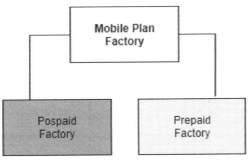

Figure 7.14: *Mobile plan factory representation*

To facilitate tests and increase the aspects of reusability, it always recommended to use the interfaces and the main abstract factory, which must refer to other interfaces instead of concrete classes in the definition of its properties, as shown in the following screenshot:

```
using System;
using System.Collections.Generic;
using System.Text;

namespace AbstractFactory
{
    public interface IMobilePlanFactory
    {
        ITextMessageFactory CreateTextMessage();

        IConnectionSpeedFactory CreateConnectionSpeed();

        IMobileDataFactory CreateMobileData();
    }
}
```

Figure 7.15: Mobile Plan Factory interface

The interface contains three properties, one for each characteristic determined by the requirements regarding text message, connection speed, and mobile data. As a convention, the abstract factory pattern uses the prefix **Create** related to the generation of each property. It helps in the identification of the pattern by other developers who know how the design pattern works. Also, it is recommended to use the suffix **Factory** in the name of the classes to indicate the design pattern as well. The use of meaningful names in software development is one of the most important good practices of coding because it allows us to reduce the amount of software documentation and decrease the time spent in analyzing the work flow implemented on the code.

Once the interface for the mobile plan factory is already created, the next step is the creation of the two mobile plans available, according to the requirements, following their individual specification strictly. First of all, we must create the **PrepaidFactory** class, implementing the underlying interface, as shown in the following screenshot:

```
namespace AbstractFactory
{
    public class PrepaidFactory : IMobilePlanFactory
    {
        public IConnectionSpeedFactory CreateConnectionSpeed()
        {
            return new LowSpeed();
        }

        public IMobileDataFactory CreateMobileData()
        {
            return new TenGigabytes();
        }

        public ITextMessageFactory CreateTextMessage()
        {
            return new ThousandTextMessage();
        }
    }
}
```

Figure 7.16: Prepaid Mobile Plan Factory class

The **PrepaidFactory** class creates the instances of related properties following the specific requirements, such as **LowSpeed** class instance in the method **CreateConnectionSpeed,** and the same for the other two creation methods regarding other properties, which also refer to the interfaces. On the other hand, the **PostpaidFactory** class automatically populates its properties with different types according to its own specification, as shown in the following screenshot:

```csharp
using System;
using System.Collections.Generic;
using System.Text;

namespace AbstractFactory
{
    1 reference
    public class PostpaidFactory : IMobilePlanFactory
    {
        4 references
        public IConnectionSpeedFactory CreateConnectionSpeed()
        {
            return new HighSpeed();
        }

        2 references
        public IMobileDataFactory CreateMobileData()
        {
            return new  UnlimitedMobileData();
        }

        3 references
        public ITextMessageFactory CreateTextMessage()
        {
            return new UnlimitedTextMessage();
        }
    }
}
```

Figure 7.17: Postpaid Mobile Plan Factory class

This approach helps to make the interpretation of the code quite easy to make, considering that each factory class is explicitly creating its own instances of different objects, and even, they share a similar interface. The very last step in the implementation is the specification of a client class, the highest level in the hierarchical structure of the pattern, which does not need to know details on the deeper levels because the sub-factory classes handle the complexity of each object creation by respecting the requirements for the **Prepaid** and **Postpaid** mobile plans. In the given scenario, the client class must implement the logical statement with the necessary rules to create the correct instance of the factory class based on the mobile plan type. In order to clarify the purpose of the code, it is possible to create an **enum** in this context, referring the two types of mobile plans, as shown in the following screenshot:

```csharp
using System;
using System.Collections.Generic;
using System.Text;

namespace AbstractFactory
{
    public enum MobilePlan
    {
        Prepaid = 1,
        Postpaid = 2
    }
}
```

Figure 7.18: Mobile plan enum

Further more, the client class could receive in the constructor a specific type and also contain the logical statement to create the underlying mobile plan factory, as demonstrated in the following screenshot:

```csharp
namespace AbstractFactory
{
    public class MobilePlanClient
    {

        private IMobilePlanFactory _mobilePlanFactory;
        public MobilePlanClient(MobilePlan mobilePlan)
        {
            if(mobilePlan == MobilePlan.Prepaid)
            {
                _mobilePlanFactory = new PrepaidFactory();
            }
            else
            {
                _mobilePlanFactory = new PostpaidFactory();
            }
        }

        public string Describe()
        {
            return @$"Mobile Plan: {_mobilePlanFactory.CreateConnectionSpeed().Name}.
                    Text Message: {_mobilePlanFactory.CreateTextMessage().Name}.
                    Internet Connection: {_mobilePlanFactory.CreateConnectionSpeed().Name}";
        }
    }
}
```

Figure 7.19: Mobile plan enum

In this example, the constructor of the class receives a mobile plan type referring to the **enum** previously created, and there is an **if** statement on this method that checks the type. There fore, based on its value, a distinct instance of a mobile plan factory will be created, being the **Prepaid** or **Postpaid** factory. Additionally, a method called **Describe** is specified for showing the difference between the objects in this example, only for demonstration.

In a .NET Core Console application, we can create one or multiple instances of the **MobilePlan** class and show the result of the **Describe** method, as shown in the following screenshot:

```
using System;

namespace AbstractFactory
{
    0 references
    class Program
    {
        0 references
        static void Main(string[] args)
        {
            var mobilePlanClient = new MobilePlanClient(MobilePlan.Prepaid);
            Console.WriteLine(mobilePlanClient.Describe());

            mobilePlanClient = new MobilePlanClient(MobilePlan.Postpaid);
            Console.WriteLine(mobilePlanClient.Describe());

            Console.ReadLine();
        }
    }
}
```

Figure 7.20: Console application program

The Console application creates two instances of the **MobilePlanClient**, each one of different type (**Prepaid** and **Postpaid**) and shows on the screen the description of the mobile plan. After running the application, you will obtain the specification for each type of mobile plan, as shown in the following screenshot:

```
Mobile Plan: Low Speed.
                Text Message: A thousand text messages.
                Internet Connection: Low Speed
Mobile Plan: High Speed.
                Text Message: Unlimited Text Message.
                Internet Connection: High Speed
```

Figure 7.21: Console application result

The use of the abstract factory classes by the client class is quite simple because it hides the implementation of each mobile plan type from the highest level of the application, delegating all the responsibility to the specialized class. It allows developers to focus on the interpretation of what better represents the business requirement and encapsulate unnecessary details at this point.

Conclusion

As you learned in this chapter, the abstract factory pattern is helpful in managing the creation of object families, keeping an elegant and sophisticated software architecture that allows us to extend, test, and maintain the related functionality with out compromising the aspects of readability of the code. Considering that the pattern extensively uses interfaces, it is possible to have a consistent structure and reap all the benefits of object-oriented programming practices by following the highest recommended approaches in scenarios similar to the one demonstrated during this chapter.

With this chapter, you have learned how to implement in a real scenario the abstract factory pattern using the C# language and are able to understand the central point of design patterns in general, which is the possibility of using general solutions for common problems in software development in terms of implementation and software architecture.

In the next chapter, you will have the chance to continue your journey into the design patterns using the C# language and .NET Core platform, learnthe singleton pattern, and apply all the general knowledge you have got in the first chapters of this book.

Points to remember

- The abstract factory is conventionally considered as the factory of other factories.

- The main purpose of the pattern is to build complex objects with out exposing their implementation.

- The C# language fully supports the abstract factory pattern once it is based on the interfaces and might use abstract classes as well, which are common types in the object-oriented programming paradigm.

Multiple-choice questions

1. **Which is the recommended suffix to be used in a class name using anabstract factory pattern?**

    a. Interface

    b. Factory

    c. Abstract

    d. Create

2. **What definition better represents the abstract factory pattern?**

    a. It is a design pattern that allows us to create a single instance of an object for the entire application.

    b. The pattern represents a way to create multiple objects of the same type.

    c. This pattern allows us to create multiple object families by encapsulating the implementation of each family of objects in other sub-factories.

3. **Which alternative contains some benefits of the abstract factory pattern?**

   a. Testability, extensibility, and easy maintenance

   b. An abstraction of database operations

   c. Performance and scalability

Answer

1. b
2. c
3. a

Questions

1. Explain the main purpose of the abstract factory pattern.

2. Why is the use of interfaces important in the abstract factory pattern?

3. According to what you have learned in this chapter, create a hypothetical scenario where the abstract factory could be applied, apart from the example given in this chapter.

CHAPTER 8
Singleton

Many scenarios in software development require keeping a single instance of a certain object across the system for distinct purposes such as sharing database connections, in-memory cache objects, or even an instance of a class that is responsible for keeping the same business requirements in all the parts of the application. The single pattern allows us to achieve this objective, being one of the most used and known patterns in applications built using the .NET platform with the C# language.

Learning the singleton pattern gives you the chance to understand in which scenarios that use of this pattern could be useful and helps you to recognize the pattern in legacy projects and third-party libraries.

With this chapter, you will have the opportunity to apply the single pattern concept in projects based on the .NET Core and C# language through a step-by-step sample.

Structure

In this chapter, we will discuss the following topics:

- Singleton pattern concept
- Examples in C# and .NET Core

Objectives

After studying this unit, you should be able to:

- Understand the Singleton pattern
- Apply the Singleton pattern in real-world projects
- Identify the use of the pattern in legacy projects and third-party libraries

8.1 Singleton pattern definition

The singleton pattern, as its name suggests, has the main target to guarantee that only one instance of a certain class is available in the system, sharing the same state globally to other classes across the software. With this pattern, the structure of the underlying class restricts the creation of other instances using the same class, usually using the static modifier. The .NET Core introduced many improvements regarding the use of the singleton pattern combined with the concept of dependency injection, becoming easier to manage and create a single point of access to a specific instance without the need to explicitly specify the singleton implementation in the class level.

Similar to theother patterns, the singleton pattern has advantages and disadvantages depending on the scenarios where it is applied. One of the benefits is the unsureness that the system will keep the same instance of a class for the entire system safely, managing concurrence issues correctly. Following the best practices of object-oriented programming, this approach restricts the specification of all the class constructors as private regarding their visibility, which avoids the possibility of violation and inappropriate creation of multiple instances with distinct states.

Regarding the negative points of the singleton pattern used in certain scenarios, it is possible to say that in general, it makes the unit tests more complicated to make once the singleton class is marked with the static modifier, being a challenge to get the state our desire behavior correctly. And, considering the pattern has the clear purpose of keeping a global access point to its state, concurrent and parallel threads accessing the class needs to use the concept of lock to guarantee that all the calls will receive the same result, which situation might cause performance issues in critical scenarios where any extra nano seconds in the response is critical.

Once you have learned the theoretical concepts of the singleton pattern, the next section will teach how to apply it in distinct scenarios practically and will give you the opportunity to see how this is used natively in distinct project types in the .NET Core and C# language.

8.2 Singleton implementation

Considering each design pattern has the purpose of solving a specific problem in software development using standard approaches of OOP, it is essential to build a scenario where the problems happen after that applying the solution using the singleton pattern.

Imagine the hypothetical scenario where a system requires to keep globally the same instance of a class responsible for using an external resource, such as a third-party Web service that converts documents to a PDF format. One of the requirements in the scenario would be to restrict the quantity of authentication to the external resource to a single one, avoiding extra costs and performance issues in the authentication process. Therefore, a single session in the **PDFConverter** system should remain open as much as possible and should be shared between all the routines in the system that calls the **PDFConverter** service. If a standard class is used, the class would have an implementation similar to that shown inthe following screenshot:

```
public class PDFConverter
{
    private Session _session;
    private PDFService _pdfService;

    0 references
    public PDFConverter()
    {
        _pdfService = new PDFService();
        _session = _pdfService.StartSession();
    }

    0 references
    public void ConvertToPDF(string filePath)
    {
        _pdfService.Convert(filePath, _session);
    }
}
```

Figure 8.1: PDF converter class

Once the PDF service class requires a **Session** object in the converter method as seen in the **ConvertToPdf** method body, a new **Session** object is being created each time a new instance of the class **PDFConverter** is created. Considering there is a requirement in the given scenario states that a single **Session** should be used as much as possible for multiple calls to the external service, the current implementation does not perfectly satisfy this requirement, because multiple instances of the class can be created. To easily see the result, a new method called **GetSessionInfo** was implemented in the class, as shown in the following screenshot:

```
21      0 references
22      public void GetSessionInfo()
23      {
24          Console.WriteLine("Session Info: " + _session.Id);
        }
```

Figure 8.2: Get session info method

The information given by the method allows us to follow the work flow being executed in run time by the code in order to understand that the entire system is using the different instances of the session object for each request.

8.2.1 Multiple instances

In this scenario, if the system tries to create multiple instances of the **PDFConverter** class and calls the **GetSessionInfo** method, completely different session info will be shown because each instance the class is creating a new instance of the **Session** class, as shown in the following screenshot:

```
7           static void Main(string[] args)
8           {
9               string filePathDocumentOne = @"C:\Temp\file1.docx";
10              PDFConverter pDFConverterFirstDocument = new PDFConverter();
11              pDFConverterFirstDocument.ConvertToPDF(filePathDocumentOne);
12
13              pDFConverterFirstDocument.GetSessionInfo();
14
15              string filePathDocumentTwo = @"C:\Temp\file2.docx";
16              PDFConverter pDFConverterSecondDocument = new PDFConverter();
17              pDFConverterSecondDocument.ConvertToPDF(filePathDocumentTwo);
18
19              pDFConverterSecondDocument.GetSessionInfo();
20
21              Console.ReadLine();
22
23          }
```

Figure 8.3: Multiple PDF converter instances

Between lines nine and eleven, the first document is converted to PDF using a specific instance of the **PDF Converter** class, and between lines fifteen and seventeen, the second document is converted using a new instance of the converter. As the program is calling the method **GetSessionInfo** two times (lines number thirteen and nineteen), when the Console application runs, the system shows on the screen the session information for the two document conversions, as shown in the following screenshot:

```
Session Info: b214c57e-1f2c-471b-b952-bbaeb1dc8796
Session Info: 7ac45c62-0b22-45c0-b5a6-bb58846ab992
```

Figure 8.4: Session information

As shown, two distinct sessions were generated, which means that the implementation does not meet the desired requirement. Despite this is just an example of creating multiple instances in the same method in the **Program.cs** file in a Console Application, the idea behind the requirement is to create an infrastructure and global access to the **PDFConverter** with the purpose of avoiding the possibility of making mistakes in the development process. Therefore, the software architecture should have a structure that restricts the creation of multiple instances of the

PDFConverter class explicitly. That represents a real and common problem in software development once it is not conceivable to totally restrict the violation of the requirement without using a mechanism that denies the creation of multiple instances of the class.

8.2.2 Modifications for the singleton pattern

The singleton pattern is a simple and suitable solution for the given scenario, and its implementation requires significant changes in the **PDFConverter** class to prevent the creation of multiple instances and guarantee that the system would not face any issue in concurrent access to the external resource responsible for convertingthe documents to PDF. First of all, all the class constructors in the singleton pattern should use the **private** modifier, and the class should use the **sealed** modifier, as highlighted in the following screenshot:

```
5    public sealed class PDFConverter
6    {
7        private Session _session;
8        private PDFService _pdfService;
9
     2 references
10       private  PDFConverter()
11       {
12           _pdfService = new PDFService();
13           _session = _pdfService.StartSession();
14       }
15
     2 references
16       public void ConvertToPDF(string filePath)...
20
     2 references
21       public void GetSessionInfo()...
25   }
26 }
```

Figure 8.5: First modifications of the PDF Converter class

The **sealed** modifier prevents other classes to inherit from the **PDFConverter** class, a necessary condition to avoid the creation of multiple instances of the class by inheritance. However, after these small changes, the routine in the **Program.cs** file shows an expected error, considering it is not allowed to create an instance of the **PDFConverter** class after changing the constructor visibility to **private**, as shown in the following screenshot:

```
string filePathDocumentOne = @"C:\Temp\file1.docx";
PDFConverter pDFConverterFirstDocument = new PDFConverter();
pDFConverterFirstDocument.ConvertToPDF(filePathDocumer   class SingletonPattern.PDFConverter (+ 1 overload)

                                                         'PDFConverter.PDFConverter()' is inaccessible due to its protection level
pDFConverterFirstDocument.GetSessionInfo();
```

Figure 8.6: Compile error

The actual objective is to avoid the creation of multiple instances, but after the changes, it is not possible anymore to create an instance of the **PDFConverter** class, which means that the implementation of singleton was not achieved yet. By convention, the singleton pattern requires to use a **GetInstance** static property, which handles the creation of a new instance of the class only if the state of the instance is null, as highlighted in the following screenshot:

```csharp
8 references
public sealed class PDFConverter
{
    private Session _session;
    private PDFService _pdfService;

    private static PDFConverter instance;

    0 references
    public static PDFConverter GetInstance
    {
        get
        {
            if(instance == null)
            {
                instance = new PDFConverter();
            }

            return instance;
        }
    }

    3 references
    private PDFConverter()...

    2 references
    public void ConvertToPDF(string filePath)...

    2 references
    public void GetSessionInfo()...
}
```

Figure 8.7: Get Instance method

In that case, the class constructor method still as private and the class now has a static method that always returns the same instance of the class, except in the case when the instance is null. That implementation guarantees that the exact same instance will be used across the system, even if the class is referred to in several distinct places in the program.

After these changes, the principal requirement is satisfied in terms of infrastructure and implementation, being required extra small changes in the **Program.cs** file in the context of this example. Considering a static property is being used by the **PDFConverter** class, the program keeps only one reference in the memory regarding the class, preventing the possibility of new instances to be created. Despite the result being completely different; visually, the code remains quite similar, as shown in the following screenshot:

```
 7          static void Main(string[] args)
 8          {
 9              string filePathDocumentOne = @"C:\Temp\file1.docx";
10              PDFConverter pDFConverterFirstDocument = PDFConverter.GetInstance;
11              pDFConverterFirstDocument.ConvertToPDF(filePathDocumentOne);
12
13              pDFConverterFirstDocument.GetSessionInfo();
14
15              string filePathDocumentTwo = @"C:\Temp\file2.docx";
16              PDFConverter pDFConverterSecondDocument = PDFConverter.GetInstance;
17              pDFConverterSecondDocument.ConvertToPDF(filePathDocumentTwo);
18
19              pDFConverterSecondDocument.GetSessionInfo();
20
21              Console.ReadLine();
22
23          }
```

Figure 8.8: Get Instance method

Instead of calling the class constructor method, the static property is being called for the object responsible for converting the documents one and two. Therefore, the routine had a tiny impact in terms of implementation. If the Console application runs, both conversion processes are sharing the same session, as shown in the following screenshot:

```
Session Info: d5494576-dcf8-4c26-af15-3d27bfc401dd
Session Info: d5494576-dcf8-4c26-af15-3d27bfc401dd
```

Figure 8.9: Session result

The current singleton implementation presents a limitation in scenarios in which there is a huge amount of simultaneous access to the **PDFConverter** class in case many concurrent attempts to the class may happen. To avoid the occurrence of exception, it is safer to use the lock feature in the C# language, which will prevent that more than one call be made regarding the block of the code responsible for creating a new instance of the **PDFConverter** class in case of it is null. With the lock statement, all the other threads need to wait to access the resource. The following code represents the change for thread-safe implementation:

```
12          private static readonly object _lockThreadSafe = new object();
13
            2 references
14          public static PDFConverter GetInstance
15          {
16              get
17              {
18                  if(instance == null)
19                  {
20                      lock (_lockThreadSafe)
21                      {
22                          instance = new PDFConverter();
23                      }
24                  }
25
26                  return instance;
27              }
28          }
```

Figure 8.10: Lock statement

The use of a lock is highly recommended in high-demanded scenarios, and this feature needs to be carefully used in case of the routine protected by it represents a relevant time to run.

8.2.3 Thread-safe implementation

A private property called **lockThreadSafe** was specified, and the **GetInstance** static property locks that property before creating a new instance of the **PDFConverter** class in case if it is null. Usually, this implementation in the singleton pattern is nominated as thread safety singleton and represents a good alternative when the intense concurrent access to a specific routine might be problem atic and could cause exceptions.

An extra approach that can be taken regarding the singleton pattern is the use of **Lazy** type, structure available in the C# language to use the concept of thread-safe implementation implicitly with out adding the extra lock statement code. If we refactor the previous code to use **Lazy** type, the implementation looks like the code presented in the following screenshot:

```csharp
public sealed class PDFConverter
{
    private Session _session;
    private PDFService _pdfService;

    private static readonly Lazy<PDFConverter> lazy = new Lazy<PDFConverter>(() => new PDFConverter());
    public static PDFConverter GetInstance => lazy.Value;

    private PDFConverter(){...}

    public void ConvertToPDF(string filePath){...}

    public void GetSessionInfo(){...}
}
```

Figure 8.11: Lock statement

The use of **Lazy** type reduces the amount of code needed to implement the singleton pattern and produces the exact same result, being a good alternative to have a more legible code.

The .NET Core platform provides extra options to handle the singleton pattern in Asp. Net Core applications, encapsulating the process of explicitly creating a singleton class, as was done previously in this section. To check how it works, the next scenario is to move or refer the **PDFConverter** class in an Asp.Net Core MVC project and add to the application configuration specifications regarding the singleton pattern. Considering the service configuration will handle the creation of a single instance of the **PDFConverter** class across the system, the previous implementation of the class is not necessary anymore, and a standard non-static can be used in the scenario, as shown in the following screenshot:

```
 5      public class PDFConverter : IPDFConverter
 6      {
 7          private Session _session;
 8          private PDFService _pdfService;
             0 references
 9          public PDFConverter()
10          {
11              _pdfService = new PDFService();
12              _session = _pdfService.StartSession();
13          }
14
            3 references
15          public void ConvertToPDF(string filePath)[...]
19
            3 references
20          public string GetSessionInfo()
21          {
22              return "Session Info: " + _session.Id;
23          }
24      }
```

Figure 8.12: Refactor in the PDF Converter class

Considering the Asp.Net Core uses the concept of dependency injection good practice to handle services inside the Controllers in Asp.Net MVC and Asp.Net Web API projects, a new interface **IPDFConverter** was created and associated with the **PDFConverter** class in order to facilitate the injection of the singleton class in the Controllers and in other parts of the software that needs to use the same resource.

The services configuration in the Asp.Net Core applications is usually done in the **Startup** class inside the method **ConfigureServices** where it is possible to register classes and give them a singleton state, referring the interface and concrete class, as shown in the following screenshot:

```
15      public class Startup
16      {
            0 references
17          public Startup(IConfiguration configuration)
18          {
19              Configuration = configuration;
20          }
21
            1 reference
22          public IConfiguration Configuration { get; }
23
24
            0 references
25          public void ConfigureServices(IServiceCollection services)
26          {
27              services.AddControllersWithViews();
28
29
30              services.AddSingleton<IPDFConverter, PDFConverter>();
31          }
32
            0 references
33          public void Configure(IApplicationBuilder app, IWebHostEnvironment env)[...]
```

Figure 8.13: Add singleton service

Once a Singleton class is registered in the **Startup** class, the Asp.Net Core application recognizes automatically that a single instance of the class must be created across the application, but only in the places where the dependency injection of the **IPDFConverter** interface is being specified in the class constructor. To use the **PDFConverter** class in an Asp.Net Core project, it is possible to have a similar structure as the one specified previously in the Console application, but inside a Controller action instead. The method in the **PDFConverter** class responsible for returning the session information was changed to return a string value instead of the previous implementation with the purpose of showing the session information in the View layer of the Asp.Net Core application.

For demonstration purposes, it is possible to include the necessary code inside the Index action in the **HomeController**, very similar towhat was previously done in the Console application. The main difference, in that case, would be the reference to the **PDFConverter** class, which requires to use the instance provided by the dependency injection associated with the **HomeController**, once the Asp. Net Core application becomes, in that case, responsible for managing the creation of the **PDFConverter** instance and to guarantee that the aspects of concurrence global access to the underlying resource is always providing the same instance of the class every time the class is used. After the applicability of the necessary changes in the **HomeController**, the class would be like the following screenshot:

```csharp
13      public class HomeController : Controller
14      {
15          private readonly IPDFConverter _pdfConverter;
16
17          public HomeController(IPDFConverter pdfConverter)
18          {
19              _pdfConverter = pdfConverter;
20          }
21
22          public IActionResult Index()
23          {
24              List<string> sessionInfoList = new List<string>();
25
26              string filePathDocumentOne = @"C:\Temp\file1.docx";
27              _pdfConverter.ConvertToPDF(filePathDocumentOne);
28
29              sessionInfoList.Add(_pdfConverter.GetSessionInfo());
30
31              string filePathDocumentTwo = @"C:\Temp\file2.docx";
32              _pdfConverter.ConvertToPDF(filePathDocumentTwo);
33
34              sessionInfoList.Add(_pdfConverter.GetSessionInfo());
35
36              return View(sessionInfoList);
37          }
38      }
39  }
```

Figure 8.14: Home controller changes

As highlighted in the previous screenshot, the class constructor receives a **PDFConverter** interface, and the application automatically injects an instance of the **PDFConverter** class to be used in the context. The **IndexController** action has a similar implementation, as was done in the Console application. Still, it is storing in a list of string objects the session information for the two calls of the **PDFConverter** class. If the application runs multiple times, the system will keep the same session ID for every call, even if the page is refreshed multiple times. After changing the Index view to show the session information list is returned by the action controller, the result is similar to the previous version of the Singleton class, but it is on that time being handled by the application globally, as shown in the following screenshot:

Figure 8.15: Session information in the webpage

Even the **PDFConverter** class does not implement the singleton pattern explicitly, considering the class is registered in the **Startup** class to behave as Singleton, the result satisfies the requirement to keep a single instance of the class across the application, in every place where the class is being injected in the constructor. As shown in the previous screenshot, the session is shared between the two calls, even if the page is refreshed. A new session ID will be generated only when the application restarts in the server or if, for some reason, the state of the object is recycled in the server memory.

Conclusion

As you learned in this chapter, the singleton pattern is helpful in maintenance of the same instance of a class across the system, solving a common problem in software development in the cases where a system needs to provide global access to a certain resource with the exact same state. This pattern is largely used in .NET applications, and the .NET Core version of the platform introduced a non-invasive way to work with the singleton pattern with out the need to create static class, allowing us to write unit tests and to keep the original classes safe from technical changes.

With this chapter, you have learned how to implement in a real scenario the singleton pattern using the C# language and became able to understand in which scenarios the pattern can be used. Additionally, you have learned how to apply the singleton pattern in the Asp.Net Core applications and how to implement thread-safe singleton classes.

In the next chapter, you will have the chance to continue your journey into the design patterns using the C# language and .NET Core platform, learning the prototype pattern and applying all the general knowledge you have gained in the first chapters of this book.

Points to remember

- The singleton pattern can be manually implemented using a private constructor and static properties in the class.

- The **lock** statement can be used to prevent concurrence issues in the singleton implementation.

- The .NET Core platform for Asp.Net Core applications allows us to use the singleton pattern registering the class in the **Startup** class to behave as a unique instance combined with the concept of dependency injection.

Multiple-choice questions

1. **Which feature in the C# language can be used to avoid issues in concurrent access to a resource?**

   a. Lock statement

   b. Factory

   c. Static

   d. Private

2. **In which class, a singleton class can be registered in the Asp.Net Core applications?**

   a. Program class

   b. Global.asax

   c. Controllers

   d. Startup

3. **What is the alternative to the lock statement for singleton classes?**

   a. Tasks

   b. Lazy type

   c. Parallel loops

   d. None of the alternatives

Answer

1. a
2. d
3. b

Questions

1. Explain the main purpose of the singleton pattern.

2. What are the main benefits of registering the class as singleton in the services of the Asp.Net applications?

3. According to what you have learned in this chapter, create a hypothetical scenario where the singleton pattern could be applied apart from the example given in this chapter.

CHAPTER 9
Prototype

Many real-scenarios require software development to create new instances of complex objects, multiple times, which may cause performance issues and extra challenges such as excessive memory consumption and extra processing time, representing a limitation for scalation and other desired characteristics of modern applications. The prototype pattern allows us to create copies of complex objects, which is one of the most used and known patterns in applications built using the .NET platform with the C# language. Additionally, the concept behind this pattern is largely applied by many libraries, not only in the C# language but in other languages equally based on the OOP paradigm.

Learning the prototype pattern gives you the chance to understand in which scenarios that use of this pattern could be useful and helps you to recognize the pattern in legacy projects and third-party libraries.

With this chapter, you will have the opportunity to apply the single pattern concept in projects based on the .NET Core and C# language through a step-by-step sample.

Structure

In this chapter, we will discuss the following topics:

- Prototype pattern concept
- Examples in C# and .NET Core

Objectives

After studying this unit, you should be able to:

- Understand the prototype pattern
- Apply the prototype pattern in real-world projects
- Identify the use of the pattern in legacy projects and third-party libraries

9.1 Prototype pattern definition

The prototype pattern has the primary purpose of allowing the efficient copy of complex objects, thus saving time and resources in the creation of new instances of a certain object. With this pattern, the full hard process behind the creation of a complex object is essentially hidden from the client once the high-cost creation process occurs just one time and any other extra instances of the object are made using an approach that allows us to create a full copy of an object when is possible to change the individual properties after the creation as needed. There fore, the first object works as a model for the new instances, keeping the correct initial state to used and accordingly modified by the other instances.

This pattern is part of the creational patterns once it helps in the generation of objects them selves, and, in specific scenarios, it can be used combined with other patterns, such as abstract factory and builder. Any factory pattern represents a complex structure in many cases in order to achieve the correct creation of complex objects. On the other hand, the prototype pattern is much more straight forward than the others, considering it does not require extra classes, inheritance, and multiple interfaces to achieve its purpose. However, all the complexity behind the creation of the first object would require additional implementation logic. There fore, each scenario states a custom analysis on how the approach would be better, always thinking in terms of simplicity, maintenance, extensibility, and development costs.

In a software developed using the OOP paradigm, sometimes, it is not allowed to copy specific properties because they are marked as private, or they might require extra logic to be correctly populated. In that case, the prototype pattern represents an excellent option to achieve the target of copying all the properties, keeping the desired object state. This approach is mostly taken by packages and libraries that manage the copy of complex structures such as XML objects, ORM database contexts, among many other examples.

Once you have learned the theoretical concepts and purpose of the prototype pattern, the next section will teach out how to apply it in a real scenario with a practical example and will allow you to see how the pattern is used natively in distinct project types in the .NET Core and C# language.

9.2 Prototype implementation

Considering the prototype pattern is about the object copy facilitation strategy before we start to code a real-scenario prototype pattern example, you must understand the difference between a shallow copy and deep copy in the C# language, which will help you to make the right decisions in terms of architecture implementation and will allow you to prevent unexpected software behavior, manly in production environments. Usually, in the scenario where it is necessary to copy an object to another one, both of the objects will share the same address in the memory. There fore, if a particular routine makes changes in the original instance of the object, all the copies will be affected and will have their properties changed at the same time. Although they apparently are different instances, they are in the exact same address in the memory, and physically, they are the same. That process is called shallow copying C# language, and it can be achieved using the operator = for assignment.

The following code sample represents the **Customer** class and the creation of two instances of that type, one creating an entirely new instance and the second instance is created as a copy from the first object, as shown in the following screenshot:

```
using System;

namespace BPB_Prototype_Pattern
{
    class Program
    {
        static void Main(string[] args)
        {
            Customer customer1 = new Customer() { Name = "Customer 1" };
            Customer customer2 = customer1;

            customer2.Name = "Customer 2";

            Console.WriteLine("Instance One:" + customer1.Name);
            Console.WriteLine("Instance Two:" + customer2.Name);

            Console.WriteLine();
        }
    }

    public class Customer
    {
        public int Id { get; set; }
        public string Name { get; set; }
        public string Phone { get; set; }
        public string Address { get; set; }
    }
}
```

Figure 9.1: Shallow copy example

Considering the second instance is being created as a copy from the first instance using the equal operator, all the changes made in the first instance automatically reflects into the second instance and vice-versa. If we run the Console Application exemplified in the screenshot, the console will print the **name** property of the two instances, and once the name of **Customer 2** is changed in Line 12, the change affects directly **Customer 1**, as shown in the following screenshot:

Figure 9.2: Shallow copy result

As was said before, both of the objects are sharing the same address in the memory. There fore, they do not really are programmatically distinct objects. This behavior may cause a few issues for developers who are not familiar with the C# language, and it is not hard to introduce bugs in projects of any kind if the correct approach is not taken regarding object copies in real projects. Additionally, there is another way to make a shallow copy, which consists of implementing the **ICloenable** interface. This interface forces the implementation of the **Clone** method, and it is possible to use a native method called **MemberwiseClone** to make the shallow copy. For reference-type properties, the clone method keeps the same reference. For testing that behavior, you can implement the code as shown in the following screenshot:

```
class Program
{
    0 references
    static void Main(string[] args)
    {
        Customer customer1 = new Customer() { Name = "Customer 1", Address = new Address() { Street = "Address 1" } };
        Customer customer2 = (Customer) customer1.Clone();
        customer2.Address.Street = "Address 2";

        Console.WriteLine("Address - Instance One:" + customer1.Name);
        Console.WriteLine("Address - Instance Two:" + customer2.Name);

        Console.WriteLine();
    }
}

4 references
public class Customer: ICloneable
{
    0 references
    public int Id { get; set; }
    3 references
    public string Name { get; set; }
    0 references
    public string Phone { get; set; }
    2 references
    public Address Address { get; set; }

    1 reference
    public object Clone()
    {
        return this.MemberwiseClone();
    }
}
```

Figure 9.3: MemberwiseClone method

In that case, the property **Address** is not a primitive type in the C# language, and when a copy is created using the standard **MemberwiseClone** method, all the properties can be normally changed in the copy, but the **Address** property shares the same memory location as the original instance, in this context, **Customer 1**.

As an alternative to the shallow copy option, the C# language allows us to use the concept of **DeepCopy**, which consists of the creation of actual copies that do not share the same place in the memory, and a change in one object does not affect the other ones. In the majority of cases, it is the expected behavior of object copies, but for using that efficiently, it is imperative to understand and learn how to create deep copies in the correct way. After changing the clone method of the previous example, the source object needs to be serialized in a memory stream object, and the return must be de deserialization of the same object, as shown in the following screenshot:

```csharp
[Serializable]
5 references
public class Customer: ICloneable
{
    0 references
    public int Id { get; set; }
    1 reference
    public string Name { get; set; }
    0 references
    public string Phone { get; set; }

    4 references
    public Address Address { get; set; }

    1 reference
    public object Clone()
    {
        using (var memoryStream = new MemoryStream())
        {
            var binaryFormatter = new BinaryFormatter();
            binaryFormatter.Serialize(memoryStream, this);
            memoryStream.Position = 0;

            return (Customer)binaryFormatter.Deserialize(memoryStream);
        }
    }
}
```

Figure 9.4: Deep copy

The clone method will guarantee that a new reference in the memory will be created for the copy. There fore, any changes made in the original object will not affect any copy because they are completely independent of each other at this point. The code demonstrates how to make copies of an object without requiring to specify property by property individually, which could cause performance problems for large objects and takes more time to code, potentially causing extra issues in the case new properties are added to the involved classes.

Considering that you already learned the difference between deep and shallow copy in the C# language, it is time to get familiar with the prototype pattern by following a real practical example. Imagine a hypothetical scenario where you are working on a project related to a streaming platform, which gives the customers opportunity to buy monthly plans. Each plan has its own specifications, and they represent, technically, a complex class to be populated in runtime, implementing many business requirements. In the case the company upgrades the policies for a specific plan, only the plan version and price will change, but the rest of the properties remain the same.

Considering that context, it would be an advantage to create a copy of the first version of the customer's plan and change only the properties we need to change effectively. It allows us to save memory in the application server and increases the performance for the user, mainly for complex operations. Each design pattern has the purpose of solving a particular problem in software development, and there is always a good reason to use some of them in real scenarios. In the scope of this example, the requirements clearly state that the customer plan is still the same, except for the version number and price. If it has this exact behavior, depends on the costs of the creation of new objects, the use of the prototype pattern is fairlyapplicable, considering the pattern has the purpose of making efficient copies of objects.

The given scenario must have two classes that represent the plan for customers, as shown in the following screenshot:

```csharp
namespace BPB_Prototype_Pattern
{
    0 references
    public class CustomerPlan
    {
        0 references
        public PlanVersion Version { get; set; }
        0 references
        public decimal Price { get; set; }
        0 references
        public string Name { get; set; }
        0 references
        public List<string> CompanyPolicies { get; set; }

        0 references
        public List<string> Regulations { get; set; }

        0 references
        public List<string> Languages { get; set; }
    }

    1 reference
    public class PlanVersion
    {
        0 references
        public int Version { get; set; }

        0 references
        public DateTime Creation { get; set; }
        0 references
        public DateTime Expiration { get; set; }
    }
}
```

Figure 9.5: Customer plan class

As shown in the preceding screenshot, the **CustomerPlan** class contains properties regarding company policies, regulations, and other information. According to the requirements, always these properties must have the same values for all customer plans the system could have with only the price and version being changeable on each upgrade. Considering the given explanation regarding the shallow copy, if a developer does not implement the copies correctly in the system, it will have incorrect behavior once it would share the same address in the memory, as shown in the following screenshot:

```csharp
0 references
static void Main(string[] args)
{
    CustomerPlan planVersionOne = new CustomerPlan()
    {
        Name = "Plan Version 1",
        Price = 100,
        Version = new PlanVersion() { Version = 1 }
    };

    CustomerPlan planVersionTwo = planVersionOne;
    planVersionTwo.Price = 200;
    planVersionTwo.Name = "Plan Version 2";
    planVersionTwo.Version = new PlanVersion() { Version = 2 };

    Console.WriteLine("Plan 1 - Price:" + planVersionOne.Price);
    Console.WriteLine("Plan 2 - Price:" + planVersionTwo.Price);

    Console.WriteLine(planVersionTwo);
}
```

Figure 9.6: Second shallow copy example

The precedingcode creates two distinct instances of the **CustomerPlan** class assigning different values for the name, price, and version properties. What is the problem with this code? Considering that there is a requirement of keeping the same value for the company policies and regulation properties, the routine copies the first plan to create the second customer plan. After the copy, the rest of the code changes the exclusive values for the second plan (name, price, and version). If this code is run in a Console application, the change made in the second customer plan reflects in the first object created in the code, as shown in the following screenshot:

```
C:\Users\Alexandre Malavasi\source\repos\BPB-Prototype-Pattern\b
Plan 1 - Price:200
Plan 2 - Price:200
```

Figure 9.7: Second shallow copy result

As shown, both of the customer plans have the same price, because the two objects share the same location in the memory. In that case, the result is not matching to the business requirements. For solving this problem, at the same time as we keep an excellent performance, it is possible to apply the prototype pattern using the **DeepCopy** approach shown previously in this section. There is the option of using the **IClonable** interface; however, considering by default the clone method is more recommended for shallow copies, it always better to explicitly create a **DeepCopy** method with that specific name, as shown in the following screenshot:

```
public class CustomerPlan
{
    2 references
    public PlanVersion Version { get; set; }
    4 references
    public decimal Price { get; set; }
    2 references
    public string Name { get; set; }
    0 references
    public List<string> CompanyPolicies { get; set; }

    0 references
    public List<string> Regulations { get; set; }

    0 references
    public List<string> Languages { get; set; }

    1 reference
    public object DeepCopy()
    {
        using (var memoryStream = new MemoryStream())
        {
            var binaryFormatter = new BinaryFormatter();
            binaryFormatter.Serialize(memoryStream, this);
            memoryStream.Position = 0;

            return (CustomerPlan)binaryFormatter.Deserialize(memoryStream);
        }
    }
}
```

Figure 9.8: Clone method for the Customer Plan class

The class properties remain the same, but a new method called **DeepCopy** is presented on the class structure, which allows us to create actual copies of the instances without sharing the same memory address. Considering the **DeepCopy** method is using serialization, all the classes involved in the copy must be marked with the proper serialization annotation. If this is not done, once the project runs, it throws an exception if there is an attempt to use the **copy** method, as shown thefollowing screenshot:

```
1 reference
public object DeepCopy()
{
    using (var memoryStream = new MemoryStream())
    {
        var binaryFormatter = new BinaryFormatter();
        binaryFormatter.Serialize(memoryStream, this);  ⊗
        memoryStream.Position = 0;

        return (Customer)binaryFormatter.Deserialize(me
    }
}
```

Exception Unhandled   ⤢ ✕

System.Runtime.Serialization.SerializationException: 'Type
'BPB_Prototype_Pattern.CustomerPlan' in Assembly 'BPB-Prototype-
Pattern, Version=1.0.0.0, Culture=neutral, PublicKeyToken=null' is not
marked as serializable.'

Figure 9.9: Clone method for the Customer Plan class

For solving this issue regarding serialization, it is necessary to mark all the class and sub classes as serializable, as shown in the following screenshot:

```
1    using System;
2    using System.Collections.Generic;
3    using System.IO;
4    using System.Runtime.Serialization.Formatters.Binary;
5
6    namespace BPB_Prototype_Pattern
7    {
8
9        [Serializable]
         4 references
10       public class CustomerPlan...
33
34
35       [Serializable]
         3 references
36       public class PlanVersion...
43   }
```

Figure 9.10: Serializable annotation

The classes are totally ready to be used without any runtime exceptions. Considering the previous code sample in the Console application, it is necessary now to change the creation of the second customer plan, which has to use now the new **DeepCopy** method just created. You can change only the line responsible for creating the second customer plan instance. In that case, the system does not keep the same reference in the memory anymore, and any changes made in one of the plans do not affect any other potential copies. With the required changes in the code, the final version that meets the requirements is presented in thefollowing screenshot:

```
10       static void Main(string[] args)
11       {
12           CustomerPlan planVersionOne = new CustomerPlan()
13           {
14               Name = "Plan Version 1",
15               Price = 100,
16               Version = new PlanVersion() { Version = 1 }
17           };
18
19           CustomerPlan planVersionTwo = (CustomerPlan)planVersionOne.DeepCopy();
20
21
22           planVersionTwo.Price = 200;
23           planVersionTwo.Name = "Plan Version 2";
24           planVersionTwo.Version = new PlanVersion() { Version = 2 };
25
26           Console.WriteLine("Plan 1 - Price:" + planVersionOne.Price);
27           Console.WriteLine("Plan 2 - Price:" + planVersionTwo.Price);
28
29           Console.ReadLine();
30       }
```

Figure 9.11: Second plan copy

As you can see in line 19, the second instance of the customer plan is created as a copy of the first one, but it is using the deep copy method, which guarantees that they will not share the same memory address, and the changes can be safely made in both of the objects. If you run the Console application after these changes, you get the result shown in the following screenshot:

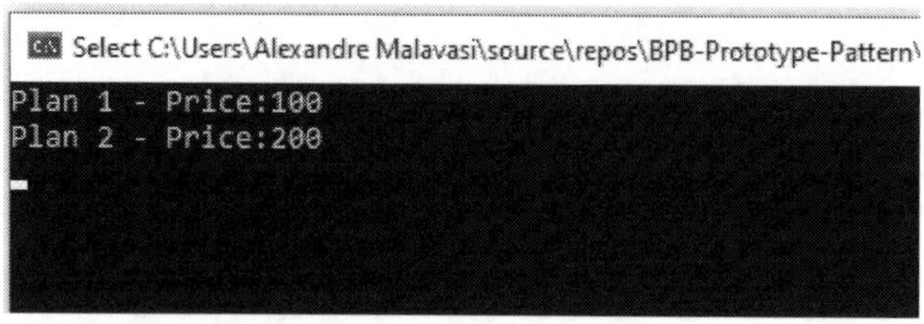

Figure 9.12: *Final deep copy result*

The two objects have different values on the properties that had distinct values being assigned in the routine. In a more complex scenario in which many multiple objects would be created, the gain in performance is much more significant once a copy of a complex object has much less cost than the creation of new instances from scratch.

The prototype pattern allows us to make copies of objectives, applying a better approach to create new objects rather than create new instances manually, assigning each property individually. It is really important to understand the risk in production environments when the memory resource is over-used, which means that any performance improvement in this regard is very welcome.

Conclusion

As you learned in this chapter, the prototype pattern is helpful and useful in all the scenarios that require the creation of multiple instances of a certain class with a similar state, but distinct values in some of their properties. As was demonstrated in the first chapters of this book, the .NET Core platform has highper formance as one of the main improvements, and, because of that, any approach to use the C# language efficiently is highly recommended once it follows the best practices of the .NET platform. The prototype pattern is largely used in .NET applications, and its use is important to manage memory with a proper approach and to give the users an excellent experience through the development of fast and efficient routines.

With this chapter, you have learned how to implement in a real scenario the prototype pattern usingthe C# language and became able to understand in which situations the pattern can be used. Additionally, you have learned the difference between shallow and deep copies using the C# language and understood in which scenario each one is more recommended.

In the next chapter, you will have the chance to continue your journey into the design patterns using the C# language and .NET Core platform, learning the factory method pattern and applying all the general knowledge you have got in the first chapters of this book.

Points to remember

- The prototype pattern allows us to efficiently create copies of objects, save memory resources, and increase the performance of the software in complex operations that require the creation of multiple similar objects.
- The shallow copy keeps the same reference in the memory for all the object instances.
- The deep copy gives us the possibility to create copies of an object, keeping distinct references in the memory.

Multiple-choice questions

1. Which interface can be used in the C# language to force the implementation of a clone method?

   a. `IEnumerable`

   b. `Interface`

   c. `ICopy`

   d. `IClonable`

2. Which method can be used to achieve the shallow copy behavior natively in the C# language?

   a. `MemberwiseClone`

   b. `ObjectClone`

   c. `Copy`

   d. `Clone`

Answer

1. d
2. a

Questions

1. Explain the main purpose of the prototype pattern.
2. Why is the use of prototype pattern important?

3. According to what you have learned in this chapter, create a hypothetical scenario where the prototype pattern could be applied apart from the example given during this chapter.

4. What are the differences between a shallow copy and deep copy in the C# language?

Key terms

- **Shallow copy**: In the C# language, the shallow copy process maintains in the memory the same address reference to all the objects created using a copy method. Therefore, a change in one object affects all the other copies.

- **Deep copy**: In the C# language, the deep copy represents the creation of an object from another one, keeping both of objects in different references in the memory, being the objects totally independent on each other in terms of state changes.

CHAPTER 10

Factory Method

The correct use of design patterns in software development is crucial in keeping the architecture extensible while simplicity still being applied in order to achieve all the good practices stated by the SOLID principles shown before in this book.

Considering the vast list of available design patterns, the concept implemented on each of them may be similar. In some cases, a quick interpretation between them may result in the inability to observe the real difference between them. This may be the case between the abstract factory pattern, already explained in Chapter 7 of this book, and the factory method pattern, which is explained in this chapter.

Learning the factory method pattern gives the programmer the chance to build a more simple architecture and allow the creation of complex objects while applying the best practices, including polymorphism and encapsulation, while developing an alternative to the abstract factory structure. This may be prevalent in all the scenarios where multiple distinct objects need to be created, but without having a substantial amount of subclasses. The knowledge of this design pattern is essential to become familiar with the difference between this factory pattern and other similar creational patterns that have an analogous purpose.

With this chapter, you will have the opportunity to understand the factory method pattern using the C# language and also applying its concept in a step-by-step sample.

Structure

In this chapter, we will discuss the following topics:

- Factory method concept

- Examples in C# and .NET Core

Objectives

After studying this unit, you should be able to:

- Understand the factory method pattern

- Apply the factory method in real-world projects

- Understand the difference between abstract factory and factory method patterns.

10.1 Factory method definition

The factory method represents a simpler alternative to the abstract factory pattern. It allows us to use the concept of the factory to create complex objects in the case where it is not necessary to create many subclasses or an extra family of classes related the main object.

The abstract factory pattern exemplified in *Chapter 7* of this book contains the main factory that creates other factories, being significantly more complex than the factory method pattern. There fore, its use is more recommended when the software architecture is proportionally more complex as well. It is possible to say that the factory method pattern has a similar definition to that of the abstract factory, with the difference that the first is responsible for creating a factory and the other is responsible for creating a factory of factories at multiple levels.

The factory method defines a base class responsible for creating a complex object but delegates to the sub classes the responsibility of creating the new instance of the object. For example, imagine a scenario where the application needs to register products and services for an online store. The use of the factory method is recommended if the product type is known at the beginning of the sell implementation routine and if the objects, in general, do not belong to the same family of products with multiple subtypes and the creation of the complex object does not involve cascade factories or anything unusual in the implementation of its members.

In that context, among the list of all the available design patterns, there is the factory method pattern. This pattern allows us to create complex objects that encapsulate the complexity of the building of those from the part of the software that is primarily consuming and creating the objects. In summary, in the case the system needs to create complex objects that do not contain complex requirements in terms of the creation of their properties, the factory method represents a good alternative. The factory method hides the implementation and logic behind the factory of the main concrete class, which will allow the ability to extend the architecture by inserting new types of objects while keeping architectural consistency.

As was demonstrated in *Chapter 4* of this book, the correct use of interfaces and abstract classes in software based on the object-oriented programming paradigm is one of the most important characteristics to have testable, extensible, and reliable software. This is representative of one of the key points of the factory method pattern. Therefore, if you are not familiar with those concepts, it is recommended to review the first chapters of this book, which contain a basic overview of the interfaces and good practices regarding the object-oriented programming paradigm.

10.2 Factory method implementation

Considering the factory method consists of a simpler alternative to the abstract factory pattern, it is fundamental to apply its concepts in implementing a project that has requirements similar to those in the scenarios specified previously in **Chapter 7**, refactoring the architecture to be compliant with this pattern. There fore, in this section, you will have the opportunity to implement the base structure of a mobile company that sells distinct plans to customers regarding text messages, mobile data, and other services, but with small differences in terms of requirements:

- The company will offer two types of plans for the customers: prepaid and postpaid.

- Both plans must have different conditions for text messages, internet connection speed, and mobile data limits. Only the number of messages and the connection speed are changeable.

- The prepaid option has a limited plan for text messages, up to 2,000 messages monthly.

- The postpaid option has a limited plan for text messages, up to 5,000 messages monthly.

- The prepaid option has a maximum speed of 50 megabytes per second.

- The postpaid option has a maximum speed of 100 megabytes per second.

The requirements clearly show that the mobile plans have the same structure in terms of properties for the objects, but the value of the objects is different, as shown in the following representation:

Mobile plan	Text message limit	Connection speed
Prepaid	2,000/month	50 megabytes/sec
Postpaid	5,000/month	100 megabytes/sec

Table 10.1: Mobile plans

Given that scenario, the use of the factory method pattern allows us to build these complex objects by abstracting their implementation of the highest level in the client application, as shown in *figure 10.1*:

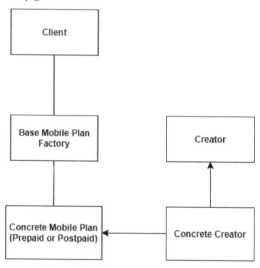

Figure 10.1: Factory method diagram

As you can see in the previous figure, the structure of the factory method pattern is much simpler than that of the abstract factory, considering that the creation of subfactories is not mandatory. Once the requirements are already established in this section, and the model structure is defined, with the proper correlations, coding may commence. The first step in the coding process is the creation of the individual classes and interfaces. For the example in this chapter, a client application architected as .NET Core Console application is used. For this application, the interaction with the database is not present to keep the focus on the C# implementation.

Following the screenshot in *figure 10.1*, we must create the first classes and interfaces to represent the base factory and related classes. We start by creating the **TextMessage** class, including the underlying interface, with the scope limited to the representation shown in the following screenshot:

Figure 10.2: *ITextMessage interface*

The interface contains only two properties in that example, which have the purpose of identifying the difference between the objects when they are going to be consumed by other classes in the given scenario. Beginning the coding process by utilizing the factory method pattern should start by creating interfaces. This is a good practice in terms of future test ability and extensibility of the entire solution.

The next step is to create the concrete class that implements the **TextMessage** interface, as shown in the following screenshot:

Figure 10.3: *TextMessage class*

The implementation of the **TextMessage** class does not contain any specification regarding the requirements, such as a specific value for the **Name** or maximum text messages (**QuantityPerMonth**). The full implementation is the responsibility of the factory, which will abstract the logic behind the text message creation for the parent concrete classes.

A **MobilePlan** in this context must contain information on **TextMessages**, **InternetConnection**, and **MobileDataPlan**, as shown in the list of requirements at the beginning of this section. Considering that the infrastructure for the text message is already created, the next step is the creation of the **InternetConnection** class, including the related interface. The implementation of the **ConnectionSpeed** structure requires an interface (**IConnectionSpeed**) that includes properties related to the future concrete class, as shown in the following screenshot:

```
IConnectionSpeed.cs ⊕ ×
BPB-FactoryMethodPattern                                                    •o BPB_FactoryMethodPattern.IConnectionSpeed
    1      ⊟namespace BPB_FactoryMethodPattern
    2       {
               0 references
    3      ⊟     public interface IConnectionSpeed
    4           {
                   0 references
    5               string Name { get; set; }
                   0 references
    6               int Velocity { get; set; }
    7           }
    8       }
    9
```

Figure 10.4: IConnectionSpeed interface

The interface above contains only two properties **Name** and **Velocity**, which have the purpose of identifying the difference between the objects when they are going to be consumed by the implementation class. The next step is to create the **ConnectionSpeed** concrete class that implements the **IConnectionSpeed** interface, as shown in the following screenshot:

```
ConnectionSpeed.cs ⊕ ×
BPB-FactoryMethodPattern                                                    •s BPB_FactoryMethodPattern.ConnectionSpeed
    1      ⊟namespace BPB_FactoryMethodPattern
    2       {
               0 references
    3      ⊟     public class ConnectionSpeed: IConnectionSpeed
    4           {
                   1 reference
    5               public string Name { get; set; }
                   1 reference
    6               public int Velocity { get; set; }
    7           }
    8       }
    9
```

Figure 10.5: ConnectionSpeed class

As the given scenario contemplates two types of connection speeds (high speed and low speed), the factory will have the responsibility for populating the connection speed properties according to the requirements for each one of the mobile plans. It represents a considerable difference if the abstract factory pattern is used where a concrete class for distinct sub-types needs to be created. There are pros and cons to each approach. The best decision must consider the requirements of the project.

The compound properties of the mobile plan class have been created at this point. The next step is the creation of the mobile plan structure that involves the specification of a common interface **IMobilePlan**, which will be implemented for the two available mobile plan types (postpaid and prepaid), as shown in the following screenshot:

```
IMobilePlan.cs  ♦ ×
[C#] BPB-FactoryMethodPattern                                                    ▾  •O BPB_FactoryMethodPattern.IMobilePlan
    1     ⊟namespace BPB_FactoryMethodPattern
    2      {
              0 references
    3     ⊟     public interface IMobilePlan
    4          {
                  0 references
    5             IConnectionSpeed ConnectionSpeed { get; set; }
                  0 references
    6             ITextMessage TextMessage { get; set; }
    7          }
    8      }
    9
```

Figure 10.6: *IMobilePlan interface*

As was said regarding the connection speed and text message classes, all the classes that implement the **IMobilePlan** interface are not responsible for specifying any values to the compound properties because it is the responsibility of the future factory class. Considering the requirements include two distinct mobile plans, it is necessary to create the concrete class for each type, implementing the underlying interface for the **IMobilePlan** to the **PostPaidMobilePlan** concrete class as shown in the following screenshot:

```
              0 references
    3     ⊟     public class PostpaidMobilePlan: IMobilePlan
    4          {
                  2 references
    5             public IConnectionSpeed ConnectionSpeed { get; set; }
                  2 references
    6             public ITextMessage TextMessage { get; set; }
    7
                  0 references
    8     ⊟         public void PostPaidIntegration()
    9             {
   10
   11             }
   12          }
```

Figure 10.7: *PostpaidMobilePlan class*

Once each mobile plan has its own class, it is possible to specify additional custom methods that can be used, if necessary for each class. With the approach, even though there is a factory for creating each type, each class is still not dependent on each other. This follows a good object-oriented programming practice.

The next step is to create the **PrepaidMobilePlan** class for the prepaid mobile plan, which is achieved by the code demonstrated in the following screenshot:

```
              0 references
   14     ⊟     public class PrepaidMobilePlan : IMobilePlan
   15          {
                  2 references
   16             public IConnectionSpeed ConnectionSpeed { get; set; }
                  2 references
   17             public ITextMessage TextMessage { get; set; }
   18
                  0 references
   19     ⊟         public void PrepaidIntegration()
   20             {
   21
   22             }
   23          }
   24
```

Figure 10.8: *PrepaidMobilePlan class*

As you can realize in *figure 10.8*, the prepaid mobile data class contains a method called **PrepaidIntegration**, which is exclusive to that class. This is an advantage of using the factory method pattern rather than the abstract factory method pattern in certain scenarios. However, the current pattern still requires the creation of factories, one for each mobile plan type, in order to achieve the purpose of encapsulating the creation of the object from the client application. In that case, you need to create a base factory class that will be shared for all the factories, as shown in the following screenshot:

```csharp
namespace BPB_FactoryMethodPattern
{
    public abstract class BaseMobilePlanFactory
    {
        public IMobilePlan GetMobilePlan()
        {
            IMobilePlan mobilePlan = this.CreateMobilePlan();

            return mobilePlan;
        }

        public abstract IMobilePlan CreateMobilePlan();
    }
}
```

Figure 10.9: BaseMobilePlanFactory class

Following the best practices that the factory method pattern states, the base factory class must use the abstract modifier and the **GetMobilePlan** method must refer to a method responsible for creating the mobile plan instance. You may see that pattern in legacy projects or external libraries. If so, this is an indicator of an intention to delegate the creation of the instances to the subclasses in the factory, being the main difference between the current pattern to the abstract factory one.

Once you have the base factory created, it is time to create the individual factories. The individual factories will inherit from the base class, making all the necessary custom operations required for the individual types, as demonstrated in the code illustrated in the following screenshot regarding the prepaid mobile plan:

```
16    public class PrepaidMobilePlanFactory: BaseMobilePlanFactory
17    {
18        public override IMobilePlan CreateMobilePlan()
19        {
20            PrepaidMobilePlan prepaidMobilePlan = new PrepaidMobilePlan();
21
22            prepaidMobilePlan.ConnectionSpeed = new ConnectionSpeed()
23            {
24                Name = "Low Connection Speed",
25                Velocity = 50
26            };
27
28            prepaidMobilePlan.TextMessage = new TextMessage()
29            {
30                Name = "Prepaid Text Message",
31                QuantityPerMonth = 2000
32
33            };
34
35            prepaidMobilePlan.PrepaidIntegration();
36
37            return prepaidMobilePlan;
38        }
39    }
```

Figure 10.10: *PrepaidMobilePlanFactory class*

The **PrepaidMobilePlanFactory** class inherits from the base factory abstract class and overwrites the method responsible for creating the mobile plan, specifying the custom values for the connection speed and text message properties, according to the requirements. Additionally, the method is calls the **PrepaidIntegration** method for running custom operations regarding the creation of the instance. For demonstration purposes, the integration method does not have any implementation, but real scenarios may require extra operations associated with each factory.

Finally, as the requirements state, the next step is to create the underlying factory class for the postpaid mobile plan **PostpaidMobilePlanFactory**, following the same pattern as the previous code, as shown in the following screenshot:

```
44    public class PostpaidMobilePlanFactory : BaseMobilePlanFactory
45    {
46        public override IMobilePlan CreateMobilePlan()
47        {
48            PostpaidMobilePlan postpaidMobilePlan = new PostpaidMobilePlan();
49
50            postpaidMobilePlan.ConnectionSpeed = new ConnectionSpeed()
51            {
52                Name = "High Connection Speed",
53                Velocity = 100
54            };
55
56            postpaidMobilePlan.TextMessage = new TextMessage()
57            {
58                Name = "Postpaid Text Message",
59                QuantityPerMonth = 5000
60
61            };
62
63            postpaidMobilePlan.PostPaidIntegration();
64
65            return postpaidMobilePlan;
66        }
67    }
```

Figure 10.11: *PostpaidMobilePlanFactory class*

With this class, the factory method pattern is fully implemented by strictly following the business requirements specified at the beginning of this section. The last thing that needs to be done is to call the factory classes in a client application and see the results. In a Console application, an instance of each factory class is created, as shown in the following screenshot:

```
3    namespace BPB_FactoryMethodPattern
4    {
         0 references
5        class Program
6        {
             0 references
7            static void Main(string[] args)
8            {
9                BaseMobilePlanFactory prepaidFactory = new PrepaidMobilePlanFactory();
10               IMobilePlan prepaidMobilePlan = prepaidFactory.GetMobilePlan();

12               BaseMobilePlanFactory postpaidFactory = new PostpaidMobilePlanFactory();
13               IMobilePlan postpaidMobilePlan = postpaidFactory.GetMobilePlan();
14           }
15       }
16   }
```

Figure 10.12: Factory class instances

An instance of the mobile plan is retrieved by using the **GetMobilePlan** method provided by each individual factory class, hiding all the aspects of the implementation from the client application, reaching the main purpose of the factory method pattern. As a final step, print the properties of each plan in the Console application, as shown in the following screenshot:

```
BaseMobilePlanFactory prepaidFactory = new PrepaidMobilePlanFactory();
IMobilePlan prepaidMobilePlan = prepaidFactory.GetMobilePlan();

BaseMobilePlanFactory postpaidFactory = new PostpaidMobilePlanFactory();
IMobilePlan postpaidMobilePlan = postpaidFactory.GetMobilePlan();

Console.WriteLine("**************PREPAID MOBILE PLAN**************");
Console.WriteLine("Prepaid Mobile plan speed:" + prepaidMobilePlan.ConnectionSpeed.Velocity);
Console.WriteLine("Prepaid Mobile plan text message:" + prepaidMobilePlan.TextMessage.QuantityPerMonth);


Console.WriteLine("**************POSTPAID MOBILE PLAN**************");
Console.WriteLine("Postpaid Mobile plan speed:" + postpaidMobilePlan.ConnectionSpeed.Velocity);
Console.WriteLine("Postpaid Mobile plan text message:" + postpaidMobilePlan.TextMessage.QuantityPerMonth);

Console.WriteLine();
```

Figure 10.13: Factory method print

If you run the client application with the given implementation, the console shows the difference between the prepaid and postpaid mobile objects, demonstrating that the implementation works as expected and keeps the all the complexity of the object creation to the factory method, as shown in the following screenshot:

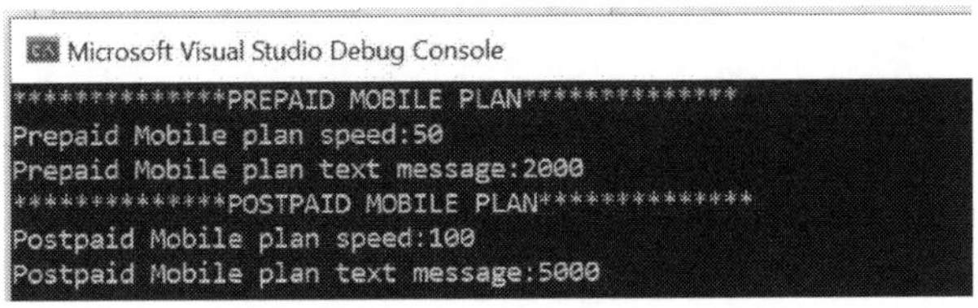

Figure 10.14: *Factory method result*

As illustrated in this chapter, the implementation of the factory method pattern requires less effort than the abstract factory pattern, being possible to combine simplicity with an excellent architecture that allows encapsulating the full implementation of complex operations in abstract classes, avoiding access violation and unexpected behavior in real scenarios.

Conclusion

As you learned in this chapter, the factory method pattern is extremely useful for managing the creation of complex objects with simplicity and efficiency, using the best practices regarding encapsulation and polymorphism. Considering that the pattern extensively uses interfaces and abstract classes, it is possible to have a consistent architecture across the project taking all the benefits of mocking objects for testing and other purposes. This pattern reduces the dependence between classes and gives us the potential to extend functionality without causing any impact to legacy code.

Within this chapter, you have learned how to implement the factory method pattern using the C# language in a real scenario, and the ability to understand the central point of design patterns in general is demonstrated. This supports the ability to use general solutions for common problems in software development in terms of implementation and software architecture.

In the next chapter, you will have the chance to continue your journey into the design patterns using the C# language and .NET Core platform, learn the adapter pattern, and apply all the general knowledge you have received in the first chapters of this book.

Points to remember

- The factory method pattern is much more straightforward to use and implement than the abstract factory one as it has the primary purpose of creating a single object as a factory.

- The C# language fully supports the factory method pattern because it is based on interfaces and abstract classes, which are standard features available in the object-oriented programming paradigm.

Multiple-choice questions

1. **What is the main difference between the abstract factory and factory method patterns?**

   a. The abstract factory creates factories for the subclasses and the factory method only for the main class.

   b. There is no difference between them

   c. The abstract factory creates more simple objects than the factory method pattern.

   d. None of them

2. **Which class is responsible for creating the subclasses' instances in the factory method pattern?**

   a. The main factory.

   b. The underlying subclasses.

   c. The client application.

Answer

1. a
2. b

Questions

1. Explain the main purpose of the factory method pattern.

2. Why is the use of interfaces important in the factory method pattern?

3. According to what you have learned in this chapter, create a hypothetical scenario where the factory method could be applied, apart from the example given in this chapter.

Key terms

- **Factory**: Logical implementation with the purpose of helping in the construction of complex objects.

- **Inheritance**: It allows us to create a correlation between classes, being possible to create a parent class that contains generic implementation to be used by other child classes.

CHAPTER 11
Adapter

Integration between systems is one of the most common scenarios for modern applications. Often, a single company must use multiple systems to meet all the needs to support their business processes. Commonly, they use different applications to support their processes, and it is very likely that the software utilized do not follow the same interface specifications and protocols. Because of this, the use of the adapter pattern helps us to create a friendly interface that allows the correct communication between systems that do not share compatible input and outputs. This problem may not only exist for systems developed by different companies but between legacy and new projects in the same company.

Learning the adapterpattern gives you the chance to build an elegant and efficient architecture to create interfaces between incompatible systems, applying the best practices of SOLID principles, such as the open–close principle, in order to extend the integration between components without changing the original implementation of all the parts involved in the process. The knowledge of the adapter design pattern gives you the opportunity to demonstrate the object-oriented programming practices when developing or modifying software, or in creating theapplication architecture.

With this chapter, you will have the opportunity to understand the adapter pattern using the C# language, applying its concept in a step-by-step sample.

Structure

In this chapter, we will discuss the following topics:

- Adapter pattern concept
- Examples in C# and .NET Core

Objectives

After studying this unit, you should be able to:

- Understand the adapter pattern
- Applythe adapter pattern to real-world projects
- Identify the use of the adapter pattern in existing libraries and legacy projects

11.1 Adapter pattern definition

The adapter pattern is one of the most important patterns used in software development. It supports the simplification of integration between disparate systems. Often, one faces problems in terms of compatibility between the components involved. Additionally, often times, a component is created for a specific purpose, and integration with other components can generate additional requirements that must be met in order to make the integration work while keeping the original systems as they are, avoiding breaking changes to the source and the target.

If a system containsintegration with any other external resource, essentially, this system is already using the adapter pattern implicitly. The data format or method signature between the source and target may be completely different, including the cases where a connection with databases is made. Each database has its particular way to store data, but usually, there is a library in C# or other languages to facilitate the communication between the database and the application. Because the database interprets the data using specific protocols and formats, and the C# language expects to receive the output as classes, objects, or primitive types.

An adapter must be created to allow the use of natively incompatible interfaces that provide useful functionalities, keeping the original implementation of the two or more parts as they initially are. For instance, if a system is required to handle data in the JSON format and a legacy project returns data in the XML format, it is strongly recommended to keep the XML format in the original legacy system, that is, do not break the current interface, and create an adapter to translate the XML returned by the old system into the JSON format. In many cases, integration with other systems is accomplished using third-party software, and their system is not open for modification or any changes in the original source code. In this case, the costs of software development significantly increases considering any changes in legacy code may represent a massive challenge in terms of code interpretation, adaptability, and the probability that the legacy technology is unfamiliar to the development team.

Considering the adapter needs to be made without affecting the parts involved, the pattern requires one to create an adapter class responsible for converting the source format into the format expected by the target class, and visa-versa. This is a critical point in the integration and follows the open–closed principle stated by the SOLID principles. Generally, the adapter pattern must have the structure represented in the following diagram:

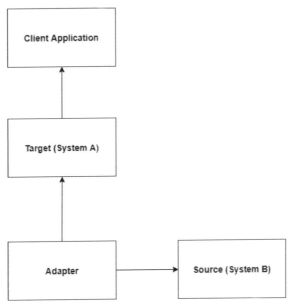

Figure 11.1: *Adapter pattern diagram*

The integration between systems may have different levels in terms of complexity, but in general, the adapter pattern structure retains with the same logic; however, it extends the interface for the purpose of allowing the communication between the target and source, usually because of incompatible formats of inputs and outputs. This structure gives us the opportunity of having many connectors and multiple adapters, all of them being independentof each other. This avoids the possibility of incompatibility errors in production environments.

11.2 Adapter pattern implementation

As was done in the previous chapters regarding the other design patterns, the proper understanding of the adapter pattern requires the implementation of a project similar to the situation that a realscenario would demand. Imagine the scenario in which an online store has a legacy system developed 20 years ago that returns the customer information in the XML format. The XML format was very common two decades ago. The company decided to keep the system as is because the software is stable, and the company has a lifetime contract with another provider regarding the license of the software. There fore, the old system needs to keep all of its current interfaces intact to allow continued functionality with its current providers.

The other systems currently in use by the company were developed using modern technologies such as .NET Core and the C# language. All the APIs exposed by the new systems are based on the JSON format and are based onthe REST technology. Thismeans that any output provided by the legacy system is not directly compatible in terms of format that the newer using JSON-formatted messages.

There are several options to solve this problem. One of them is to replace the old system by a newer one, giving the possibility to maintain the same technology across all the systems used by the company. However, it would demand a considerable time for the development team to migrate to another technology, and the resources must be involved in other projects. Therefore, the first option suggested is likely going to be rejected by the upper management who isresponsible for making decisions in terms of deadlines, costs, and projects in general, in this hypothetical situation.

The second alternative isto modify the legacy system to respond in the JSON format, being compatible with the other systems. However, in the given scenario, the system is not open for modification, there is no access to the source code, and the provider company does not allow alteration in the core of the product.

The last option in that context is to create an adapter to manage appropriately the difference between the format that the newer system expects and the format provided by the legacy system. This approach would allow us to create a wrapper to handle the XML format and transform the response into JSON with out modification of any of the systems involved in the process.

Following the structure proposed by the adapter pattern and for meeting the requirements stated by the sample scenario, the implementation of the solution must specify an adapter responsible for converting the response from the legacy system into a format that the new system is able the interpret. This approach allows us to connect the application with other systems in case different systems need to have their data translated into an understandable format by the target application. As it is possible to realize in this type of solution, it is pretty common to find a similar approach in any library that provides integration with databases, such as Entity Frame work and Hibernate. Actually, these libraries create a wrapper to connect two distinct systems (application and database), and the standard ADO.NET technology provides common interfaces that allow any database providers to develop their own wrappers for the C# language. As you probably realized, some classes in the ADO. NET have the suffix **adapter**, which means it uses the exact same concept as the adapter design pattern. Considering our sample scenario, the architecture of the adapter pattern would have the structure demonstrated in the following diagram:

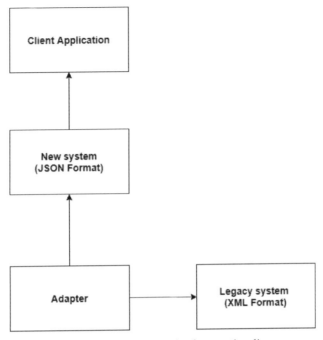

Figure 11.2: Adapter pattern implementation diagram

This diagram is similar to the one given in *figure 11.1*, with the difference that the components are now properly named according to the business requirements. Every time software architecture needs to be defined, it is recommended to specify first the details of the pattern that are intended to be used before the final version of the architecture. The use of any design pattern in any programming language must be easily recognized by the developers who are working on the project and the future developers who will be responsible for maintaining the software. For that reason, usually, all the classes and interfaces related to the design patterns have references on their names regarding the design patterns that they intend to implement.

In real scenarios, the uses of design patterns can be tough to keep and identify if they are used combined with other patterns and are not correctly named. Another reason for the extra difficulties in design pattern implementation is when the wrong pattern is used to solve a specific problem. It is pretty common to find projects where a certain design pattern is used, not because the project required it, but because a developer wanted to use the pattern for learning purposes. However the decision to use any design pattern must be based on the problem that the business requirements state that needs to be solved.

Considering the hypothetical scenario using the adapter pattern, the next step is to create the code necessary to implement the pattern. Once the scenarios define that a legacy system provides the customer information, we must develop classes to simulate its behavior. The first class to be created is the **Customer** class used by the legacy project, as shown in the following screenshot:

```
Customer.cs ⊕ X
[C#] BPBAdapterDesignPattern                                              ▾  ⚙ BPBAdapterDesignPattern.Customer
     1        using System;
     2        using System.Xml.Serialization;
     3
     4        namespace BPBAdapterDesignPattern
     5        {
     6            [Serializable]
                 0 references
     7            public class Customer
     8            {
     9                [XmlAttribute]
                     0 references
    10                public int Id { get; set; }
    11                [XmlAttribute]
                     0 references
    12                public string Name { get; set; }
    13                [XmlAttribute]
                     0 references
    14                public string Address { get; set; }
    15                [XmlAttribute]
                     0 references
    16                public string City { get; set; }
    17                [XmlAttribute]
                     0 references
    18                public string Country { get; set; }
    19                [XmlAttribute]
                     0 references
    20                public string DocumentNumber { get; set; }
    21                [XmlAttribute]
                     0 references
    22                public DateTime BirthDay { get; set; }
    23            }
    24        }
```

Figure 11.3: Customer class

As shown in the previous screenshot, all the class properties are marked as XML attributes in order to serialize to the XML format and accurately simulate the behavior of the legacy system. The next step is to create the logical class responsible for returning the list of customers in the XML format for demonstration purposes. In a real scenario, this implementation would not be necessary once the legacy project would return the data. However, in case you want to implement the adapter pattern example in this chapter fully, you must create these classes as well. It can be done in a standard Console application, which is the approach taken in this section. The logical customer class would have the implementation shown in the following screenshot:

```
C# BPBAdapterDesignPattern                                          ▼  ⚙ BPBAdapterDesignPattern.Cust
    1     ⊟using System.Collections.Generic;
    2      using System.IO;
    3      using System.Xml;
    4      using System.Xml.Serialization;
    5
    6     ⊟namespace BPBAdapterDesignPattern
    7      {
              1 reference
    8          public class CustomerLogic
    9          {
   10              private List<Customer> customers;
                  0 references
   11              public CustomerLogic()
   12              {
   13                  customers = new List<Customer>();
   14                  customers.Add(new Customer() { Id = 1, Name = "Customer 1", City = "New York" });
   15                  customers.Add(new Customer() { Id = 2, Name = "Customer 2", City = "Los Angeles" });
   16                  customers.Add(new Customer() { Id = 3, Name = "Customer 3", City = "Las Vegas" });
   17                  customers.Add(new Customer() { Id = 4, Name = "Customer 4", City = "Sao Paulo" });
   18                  customers.Add(new Customer() { Id = 5, Name = "Customer 5", City = "Dublin" });
   19              }
   20
                  0 references
   21              public virtual string GetCustomers()
   22              {
   23                  var xmlSerializer = new XmlSerializer(customers.GetType());
   24                  using (var stream = new StringWriter())
   25                  {
   26                      using (var xmlWriter = XmlWriter.Create(stream))
   27                      {
   28                          xmlSerializer.Serialize(xmlWriter, customers);
   29                          return stream.ToString();
   30                      }
   31                  }
   32              }
   33          }
   34      }
```

Figure 11.4: Customer logic class

The class constructor creates a list of five customers, and the **GetCustomers** method is using the **virtual** modifier, being possible to overwrite their implementation if it is needed. Initially, the method is serializing the customer list to the XML format, which is perfect for simulating the behavior of the legacy project in our scenario. Considering all the classes regarding the legacy software are already created, the next step is to specify the interfaces and classes necessary to implement the adapter pattern. The first one that you must create is the **ICustomer** interface to abstract the operations made by the **CustomerLogic** class, as shown in the following screenshot:

```
C# BPBAdapterDesignPattern                                    ▼
    1     ⊟namespace BPBAdapterDesignPattern
    2      {
              0 references
    3          public interface ICustomer
    4          {
                  0 references
    5              string GetCustomers();
    6          }
    7      }
```

Figure 11.5: Customer interface

After that, the principal class of the pattern needs to be created, referring the legacy customer logic class and the new **ICustomer** interface, as shown in the following screenshot:

```csharp
using Newtonsoft.Json;
using System.Xml;

namespace BPBAdapterDesignPattern
{
    0 references
    public class CustomerAdapter : CustomerLogic, ICustomer
    {
        3 references
        public override string GetCustomers()
        {
            string originalXml = base.GetCustomers();
            XmlDocument xmlDoc = new XmlDocument();
            xmlDoc.LoadXml(originalXml);

            JsonSerializerSettings jsonSettings = new JsonSerializerSettings();
            jsonSettings.Formatting = Newtonsoft.Json.Formatting.Indented;

            var customers = JsonConvert.SerializeObject(xmlDoc, jsonSettings);

            return customers;
        }
    }
}
```

Figure 11.6: Customer adapter class

As shown in the previous screenshot, the customer adapter class in herits from the customer logic class and overwrites the **GetCustomers** method with the necessary implementation responsible for converting the XML content into the JSON format regarding the customer list information. For the implementation of the above code, it is mandatory to install the **Newtonsoft.Json** package in order to have extra options in terms of JSON serialization. In the NuGet package window, search by the package and install it as shown in the following screenshot:

Figure 11.7: NewtonsoftNuGet package

Considering the full adapter pattern example is already implemented, it is possible already to use and verify if the entire structure is working as expected. For validating the **adapter** class, you can create a new in stance in the Console application and call the **GetCustomers** method, as shown in the following screenshot:

```
Program.cs  ⊕ ×
BPBAdapterDesignPattern                                                    BPBAdapterDesignPattern.Program
 1         using System;
 2
 3       namespace BPBAdapterDesignPattern
 4         {
              0 references
 5           class Program
 6           {
                 0 references
 7               static void Main(string[] args)
 8               {
 9                   CustomerAdapter customerAdapter = new CustomerAdapter();
10                   var customers = customerAdapter.GetCustomers();
11
12                   Console.WriteLine(customers);
13
14                   Console.ReadLine();
15               }
16           }
17         }
18
```

Figure 11.8: Adapter pattern client

The adapter pattern is quite simple compared with the other ones because it does not require the creation of multiple classes and interfaces. Only one class is responsible for intermediating the communication between two different systems. Although it is simple, the use of the adapter pattern represents a powerful and safe way to integrate systems and components that do not share similar interfaces. This makes it possible to extend the functionality with out changing the source code. Every single design pattern was defined with the purpose of solving a common problem in software development. By convention, this means that a vast amount of companies and projects share the same problem in their projects. Considering what you have learned in this chapter, it is recommended that you apply the concept of the adapter pattern in real projects. Use the adapter pattern with responsibility, making decisions based on what each project requires.

Conclusion

As learned in this chapter, the adapter pattern is a powerful solution for integrating systems that require communication and interaction but do not share similar input and output formats, but that need communication and interaction.

This pattern is one of the most commonly implemented design patterns. Once implemented, the adapter pattern facilitates the communication between software applications based on the object-oriented programming paradigm. Under the hood, this pattern uses the open–closed principle stated by the SOLID principles, which represent a good practice of extending the functionality of a particular routine with out changing the behavior of any component involved in the interaction. In that case, the source and target classes or components will retain their current interfaces while allowing extensibility of these interfaces to allow for passing of data that has differing content and format. The adapter pattern maintains the responsibility of converting data between two components though a single adapter class.

In this chapter, you have learned how to implement in a real scenario the adapter pattern using the C# language and became able to understand the central purpose of design patterns in general, which consists in solving problems in software development following the best practices of the object-oriented programming and applying solutions that are largely used by many companies in the market.

In the next chapter, you will have the chance to continue your journey into the design patterns using the C# language and .NET Core platform, learn the composite pattern, and apply all the general knowledge you have got in the first chapters of this book.

Points to remember

- The adapter pattern is one of the most simple design patterns, but its use represents a powerful way to integrate systems.

- The adapter pattern does not require the creation of multiple classes and various levels, being necessary only the creation of the adapter class.

- The same pattern is hugely used in libraries responsible for database interactions and manipulation of external resources.

Multiple-choice questions

1. **Which alternative does not represent a characteristic of the adapter pattern?**

   a. The adapter pattern helps in the integration between systems.

   b. The adapter pattern is complex and hard to implement.

   c. Database integrations widely use the pattern.

   d. None of them.

2. **In which class should the logic of the integration between systems be placed?**

   a. Adapter class

   b. Client application

   c. Abstract class in the system

   d. Source class

Answer

1. b
2. a

Questions

1. Explain the primary purpose of the adapter pattern.

2. According to what you have learned in this chapter, create a hypothetical scenario in which the adapter pattern could be applied apart from the example given during this chapter.

3. Explain the benefits of the adapter pattern.

4. Are there any projects that you are currently working on that implement the adapter pattern?

Key terms

*   **Adapter**: An architectural concept in software development that allows us to build intermediate layers between components that have different protocols.

*   **Integration points**: Components in a system that requires interfaces and intermediate applications and protocols to state a proper communication.

CHAPTER 12

Composite

The representation of hierarchical and recursive structures in any programming language is always a massive challenge in terms of performance, design, and complexity. The composite design pattern allows us to abstract the entanglement behind scenarios where multiple related levels of an object are required. This will result in keeping the original classes involved independent from each other. This pattern is closely associated with the Liskov principle previously explained in this book. Regarding design patterns, you will be able to realize the correlation between concepts and good practices of software development that come from different knowledge areas, such as SOLID principles, object-oriented programming, software architecture, and software quality assurance.

Learning the composite pattern gives you the chance to understand important principles of inheritance. You will also learn the main purpose behind the correct use of interfaces. You will also have the opportunity to apply advanced concepts of software architecture related to extensibility, maintainability, and testability.

With this chapter, you will have the opportunity to apply the composite pattern in a practical example using the C# language and by building a real-world program step-by-step.

Structure

In this chapter, we will discuss the following topics:

- Composite pattern concept
- Examples in C# and .NET Core

Objectives

After studying this unit, you should be able to:

- Understand the composite pattern
- Identify the use of SOLID principles presented in this pattern
- Apply the composite pattern in a real-world program

12.1 Composite pattern definition

The composite pattern states that a group of objects must have the same behavior as all the individual elements in the group. In other words, the composite pattern abstracts the relationship between distinct components or objects and allows to call methods from a child element in the same way it is done for the parent elements. In real-world scenarios, an element might have many children from the same type, as shown in *figure 12.1*:

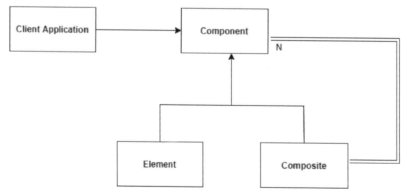

Figure 12.1: Composite pattern diagram

In this specific context, a component could be composed of a single element or a parent element that has many associated sub-elements. The client application does not have any knowledge of an element's composition. All elements are considered the same, abstracting the difference between the parent and child elements. As was previously stated, all the components and classes involved in this process belong to the same type or share the same interface, which allows hiding the aspects of implementation from the client application using the encapsulation concept. This is the principle behind the Liskov principle explained in *Chapters 3: Basic Concepts of Object-Oriented Programming*.

Alternatively, the composite pattern can be represented using a hierarchical diagram, which is visually easier to understand, and it is closer to the situations in which the pattern is most used. As shown in *figure 12.2*, a specific element might have multiple sub-elements; even they belong to the same kind:

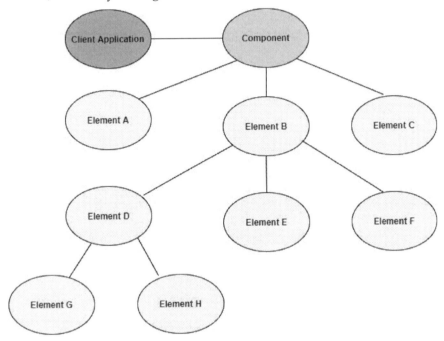

Figure 12.2: Hierarchical representation

This structure is found in many applications, including menu interface components in the Web, mobile, and desktop applications. Considering the composite pattern has an analog architecture as a tree, a single element in the diagram could be called a *leaf*, and all the elements that contain sub-elements could be called *composite*. It is easier to understand the pattern with a practical real-world example, and you will have the opportunity to see and implement a project that involves this pattern in the next section.

In many cases, composite elements may have other composites as child elements, depending on the requirements. The composite pattern allows us to implement a solution that allows us to have unlimited hierarchical relations between classes of the same type or between the elements that share the same interface. Furthermore, this pattern is an elegant and flexible solution that gives us the possibility to reduce the number of necessary classes. This allows us to be able to build a complex structure if a pattern can be defined that could be applied equally to all the elements involved in the solution, and at all the levels.

12.2 Composite pattern implementation

The best way to understand any design pattern is to implement in a program and experience all of its benefits and limitations. The technical decision behind the use of the design pattern must be focused on a problem that needs to be solved. The use of the composite pattern should only be justified if the system is required to implement hierarchical relationships between classes that share the same interface. Imagine the scenario in which an online store contains individual products, and the company decides to sell not only the products themselves but a group of them as a whole product. Although the whole product is considered a group of products, the whole product should be considered as a product as well, as it has specifications such as price, name, barcode, among other characteristics.

The system may change over time. In the future, the hypothetical company may decide to provide different combinations of products as composite single items. This will lead to increasing the complexity, and it would become harder and harder to maintain the system. This is the exact problem that the composite pattern tries to solve, the possibility of having unlimited number of sub elements with in parent elements. The full implementation of this specification creates new challenges in terms of database structure, performance, and the relationship between entities. However, the example scenario in this section is focused on the implementation part of the application, using the C# language.

Considering the given scenario, according to the architecture proposed by the composite pattern, our system would require the following tasks:

- Creation of a common interface for the **Product** entity.

- Development of the **Product** concrete class that implements the **Product** interface.

- Definition of the composite classes and their methods responsible for adding and removing child elements.

- Specification of the custom methods that belong only to the child class.

As shown in the composite pattern definition and based on the requirements, an element may or may not have child elements. In this case, despite all the elements sharing the same interface, a specific custom method needs to be defined in the composite class to distinguish between single elements and composite ones. According to all the requirements specified in this section, our online store implementation would have the structure represented in *figure 12.3*:

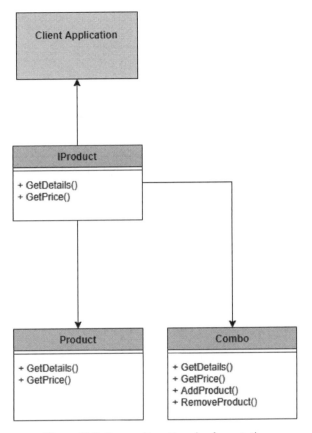

Figure 12.3: Composite pattern implementation

As shown in the previous figure, the combo and product classes share the same interface, but only the combo class has methods responsible for adding and removing products. Considering the combo class is a product that contains other products, this class represents the composite class stated by the composite pattern. It is important to highlight that the correct use of interfaces allows us to create useful abstractions, similar to what has been shown by implementing other design patterns.

It is important is to learn the more advanced concepts of interfaces, inheritance, and abstract classes. If you are not familiar with these concept, it is recommend that you take a look at *Chapter 5: Encapsulation and Polymorphism in C#* where detailed explanation and practical examples are illustrated using the C# language.

The intention in this section is to build an online store that allows us to create products, but with the requirement that some of them may represent a list of several products, but that are sold as a single product. As was previously explained in this section, in terms of implementation, the first thing that needs to be developed to achieve all the objectives is to create a common interface used by all the products. A group of products is called *combo* in this context. Therefore, using Visual Studio, create a Console Application and create an interface with the structure represented in the following screenshot:

```
IProduct.cs  ⊕ ×
[C#] BPBCompositePattern
  1      ⊟namespace BPBCompositePattern
  2       {
           6 references
  3      ⊟    public interface IProduct
  4           {
               2 references
  5               int Id { get; set; }
               8 references
  6               string Name { get; set; }
               11 references
  7               decimal Price { get; set; }
               8 references
  8               string Category { get; set; }
               5 references
  9               void GetProductDetails();
               5 references
 10               decimal GetProductPrice();
 11           }
 12       }
 13
```

Figure 12.4: IProduct interface

The interface must contain all the properties and methods that need to be shared between the individual product and combo classes. Each type of class will implement distinct logic in terms of details and pricing. Not all products contain sub-products. Further more, only the composite classes should have a routine to add and remove sub-elements. These methods are not placed in the interface to avoid mistakes regarding the implementation and erroneous use of the composite pattern. The concrete class will use the **Category** property stated in the interface to distinguish between the single product and combos for demonstration purposes.

Considering the interface is already created, the next step is the creation of the **Product** and **Combo** classes. Create a new class called **Product** in your Console application project and implement the **IProduct** interface, as shown in the following screenshot:

```
Product.cs ● ×
BPBCompositePattern                                                    BPBCompositePattern.Product
     1        using System;
     2
     3       namespace BPBCompositePattern
     4       {
             6 references
     5           public class Product : IProduct
     6           {
                 2 references
     7               public int Id { get; set; }
                 8 references
     8               public string Name { get; set; }
                 11 references
     9               public decimal Price { get; set; }
                 8 references
    10               public string Category { get; set; }
    11
                 5 references
    12               public void GetProductDetails()
    13               {
    14                   Console.WriteLine($"Name:{ Name }. Price: {Price}. Category: { Category }");
    15               }
    16
                 5 references
    17               public decimal GetProductPrice()
    18               {
    19                   return this.Price;
    20               }
    21           }
    22       }
```

Figure 12.5: Product class

As shown in the code sample, the class contains all the properties and methods stated by the interface, and the implementation of the **GetProductDetails** method is showing a resume of the product details, such as name, price, and category. This is only for demonstration purposes. In a real scenario, this method would contain implementation to get information from a database or a more complex logic to build the product details. However, the current implementation is enough to get you familiar with the behavior of the composite pattern and to track the difference between a single **Product** and a composite one that contains child products.

Additionally, the **GetPriceDetails** in the **Product** class implements the functionality to show the original price of the product. It currently does not allow the application of a special discount. In that case, all the objects that will have the individual product as part of their sub product list (**Combo** class) will inherit it is value automatically. This structure allows us to keep a single product and the composite objects independent of each other, even though they share a similar interface. In the end, all of the composite objects are products themselves.

The next step requires the creation of the **Combo** class, which is a product, but it contains other products associated with it. Realize that this concept is different from only a group of objects. The **Combo** class would still have the same characteristics as an individual product, such as name, price, and other properties. In this case, considering the diagram demonstrated in *figure 12.2*, a combo is a product and contains other nodes. Each individual node could contain one sub product. And, recursively, a subproduct could be made from several subproducts. This is a powerful and flexible structure to represent a business process that requires a hierarchical relationship between products and sub products. The implementation of the **Combo** class is presented in the following screenshot:

```csharp
    4   namespace BPBCompositePattern
    5   {
        3 references
    6       public class Combo : IProduct
    7       {
    8
    9           private List<IProduct> _subProducts;
            1 reference
   10           public Combo()
   11           {
   12               _subProducts = new List<IProduct>();
   13           }
   14
            2 references
   15           public int Id { get; set; }
            8 references
   16           public string Name { get; set; }
            11 references
   17           public decimal Price { get; set; }
            8 references
   18           public string Category { get; set; }
   19
            5 references
   20           public void GetProductDetails()...
   31
            5 references
   32           public decimal GetProductPrice()...
            3 references
   44           public void AddProduct(IProduct product)...
            0 references
   48           public void RemoveProduct(IProduct product)...
   52       }
```

Figure 12.6: Combo class

The **Combo** class implements the **IProduct** interface and has a significant difference from the **Product** class. In the **Combo** class, a private property that represents the sub-products associated with the combo has been added. Additionally, two other methods belong to the class, which are responsible for adding new products to the list and remove an existing product from the subproduct list, the **AddProduct** method, and the **RemoveProduct** method. For demonstration purposes, the content of the methods is hidden, but details of their implementation are shown below.

The existence of a list of **IProducts** in the **Combo** class illustrates how to transform a regular individual class in a composite one. Realizing that the **Product** and **Combo** classes are similar, however, the **Combo** class contains an additional logic to handle the subproducts associated with the combo instance. As shown in *figure 12.5*, the **GetProductDetails** and **GetProductPrice** of the **Product** class contain logic to only address the product it self. Conversely, the same methods in the **Combo** class are much more complex, containing code to also manage their sub-products. Notice that the details for each sub-product use the methods from the child element, as shown in the following screenshot:

```
20   public void GetProductDetails()
21   {
22       Console.WriteLine($"Name:{ Name }.  Category: { Category }");
23
24       Console.WriteLine("****All the products in this combo****");
25
26       foreach(var subProduct in _subProducts)
27       {
28           subProduct.GetProductDetails();
29       }
30   }
31
32   public decimal GetProductPrice()
33   {
34       this.Price = 0;
35
36       foreach (var subProduct in _subProducts)
37       {
38           this.Price += subProduct.GetProductPrice();
39       }
40
41       Console.WriteLine($"***Total Price: {this.Price}***");
42       return this.Price;
43   }
```

Figure 12.7: Combo class detail methods

The **GetProductDetails** method contains a custom implementation, and beyond showing the **Combo** details, it executes a loop through the sub product list running the same method from the child element. That way, the implementation of the child class is preserved, and the parent class has the autonomy to decide what to do with its own method. Remember that a composite object could be a child of other composite objects, establishing unlimited set of relations between all the objects that share the same **IProduct** interface. If the developed implementation does not allow this behavior, the implementation of the composite pattern has likely been coded incorrectly.

Continuing with the **Combo** class methods, as shown in the previous screenshot, the **GetPriceDetails** method iterates over each sub-product and increments the **Price** property of the **Combo** class to compute the final price. Therefore, the same method in the child class has a different implementation than the composite one. Our full composite pattern implementation is ready at this point. Now, it is time to use the classes in our client console application.

For example, imagine a scenario in which there are three products (book, laptop, and monitor) and the online store company wants to sell each of them separately with their own individual price. However, on one occasion, there is a promotion that allows the online store to offer a combo called **techCombo**. This offering includes the three products packaged as one. In the composite pattern concept, the book, the laptop, and the monitor should be specified using the **Product** class, and the **techCombo** should be created using the **Combo** class, considering the combo contains sub-products. After creating each individual instance for the three first products, you must add the products to the **combo** object, as shown in the following screenshot:

```
5    class Program
6    {
         0 references
7        static void Main(string[] args)
8        {
9            Product book = new Product() { Name = "Book", Price = 35.00m, Category = "Product" };
10           Product laptop = new Product() { Name = "Laptop", Price = 1200.00m, Category = "Product" };
11           Product monitor = new Product() { Name = "Monitor", Price = 150.00m, Category = "Product" };
12
13           Combo techCombo = new Combo() { Name = "Tech Combo", Category = "Combo" };
14           techCombo.AddProduct(book);
15           techCombo.AddProduct(laptop);
16           techCombo.AddProduct(monitor);
17
18           book.GetProductDetails();
19           book.GetProductPrice();
20
21           techCombo.GetProductDetails();
22           techCombo.GetProductPrice();
23
24           Console.Read();
```

Figure 12.8: The client application

The first three lines of the main method create the three products assigning the **Name**, **Price**, and **Category** properties for each of them. After ward, on line 13, the **techCombo** object is created. In the next lines, the three products are added to the **techCombo** object. Considering the **Combo** class has extra methods to handle the addition and removal of new sub-products, you must take a look in the methods that belong only to the **Combo** class, which are highlighted in the following screenshot:

```
        5 references
33      public decimal GetProductPrice()[...]
        3 references
45      public void AddProduct(IProduct product)
46      {
47          _subProducts.Add(product);
48      }
        0 references
49      public void RemoveProduct(IProduct product)
50      {
51          _subProducts.Remove(product);
52      }
```

Figure 12.9: Addition (AddProduct) and removal (RemoveProduct) methods

More details on the **Combo** class can be seen in the *figure 12.6*, but regarding these two methods, as shown in the previous screenshot, they receive an object that implements the **IProduct** interface. The **AddProduct** method adds a product to the private list specified at the beginning of the **Combo** class, and the **RemoveProduct** method removes a product from the same list. If you run the Console application, you will get the result as shown in the following screenshot:

```
C:\Users\Alexandre Malavasi\source\repos\BPBCompositePattern\
Name:Book. Price: 35.00. Category: Product
Name:Tech Combo.  Category: Combo
****All the products in this combo****
Name:Book. Price: 35.00. Category: Product
Name:Laptop. Price: 1200.00. Category: Product
Name:Monitor. Price: 150.00. Category: Product
***Total Price: 1385.00***
```

Figure 12.10: Client application result

The Console application prints details of the book product, laptop, and monitor first, then prints the details of the **techCombo** object (**Total Price**). You can verify in the total price that the implementation is working as expected. The final price of the combo represents a sum of the prices of all the products associated with the combo.

The **Composite** pattern also allows us to make more complex structures using the same classes, what can be achieved associating a combo object to another **combo** object, as shown in the following screenshot:

```
static void Main(string[] args)
{
    Product book = new Product() { Name = "Book", Price = 35.00m, Category = "Product" };
    Product laptop = new Product() { Name = "Laptop", Price = 1200.00m, Category = "Product" };
    Product monitor = new Product() { Name = "Monitor", Price = 150.00m, Category = "Product" };

    Combo comboOne = new Combo() { Name = "Combo One", Category = "Combo" };
    comboOne.AddProduct(book);
    comboOne.AddProduct(laptop);
    comboOne.AddProduct(monitor);

    Product keyboard = new Product() { Name = "Keyboard", Price = 20.00m, Category = "Product" };
    Product mouse = new Product() { Name = "Mouse", Price = 15.00m, Category = "Product" };
    Product mousePad = new Product() { Name = "Mouse Pad", Price = 25.00m, Category = "Product" };

    Combo comboTwo = new Combo() { Name = "Combo Two", Category = "Combo" };
    comboTwo.AddProduct(keyboard);
    comboTwo.AddProduct(mouse);
    comboTwo.AddProduct(mousePad);

    comboOne.AddProduct(comboTwo);

    comboOne.GetProductDetails();
    comboOne.GetProductPrice();

    Console.Read();
}
```

Figure 12.11: Composite aggregation

In this new example, two combo objects are created. Each **combo** object is created with three different products. The first combo contains a book, a laptop, and a monitor. The second combo contains a mouse, a keyboard, and a mouse pad. At the end of the routine, the second combo is added as a product to the first one. There fore, it does not matter if the child element in the composition is a product or a combo because both of them implement the same **IProduct** interface.

If you run the application after these changes, you get the results as shown in the following screenshot:

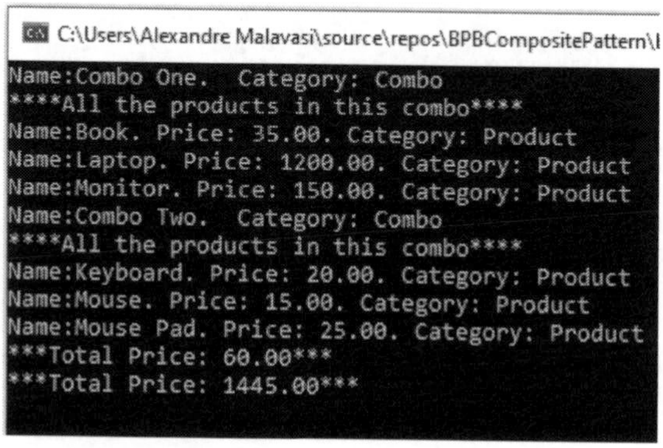

Figure 12.12: Composite aggregation results

The final price still being calculated correctly even though the sub-product associated with the first combo contains products and another combo. The flexibility that the composite pattern gives us is powerful. The implementation of recursive algorithms is always a huge challenge, and the object-oriented programming paradigm adds extra challenges to this equation.

Finally, it is hoped that the content of this chapter helped you to understand and get familiarize yourself with the composite design pattern, which is one of the most widely used patterns in software development for many years. I encourage you to build your own project, creating another hypothetical scenario that would give you the chance to apply what you have learned in this chapter, to other situations.

Conclusion

As learned in this chapter, the composite pattern allows us to create a sophisticated and simple solution for a complex problem, which consists of having hierarchical structures recursively in an application. The composite pattern is one of the most used widely used patterns in software development. However, its implementation is some what difficult and complex. To effectively apply this pattern requires the complete understanding of business of the application. The abstraction of the hierarchical dependence between an element and its sub-elements can sometimes become challenging. The composite pattern gives us an elegant architecture that allows us to scale and extend the functionality, limitlessly. This pattern is commonly found in systems responsible for creating workflows, which consist of steps and sub-steps for execution. Additionally, this pattern can easily be found in libraries that provide graphical hierarchical visual structures, such as diagram tools.

In this chapter, you have learned how to implement the composite pattern using the C# language. You should now be able to understand how to apply simple solutions for complex problems, applying the best practices of object-oriented programming, using the composite pattern.

In the next chapter, you will have the chance to continue your journey into the design patterns using the C# language and the .NET Core platform, learn the proxy pattern, and apply all the general knowledge you have received in the preceding chapters of this book.

Points to remember

- The composite pattern uses the same interfaces between the classes and subclasses.

- Implementation of the composite pattern requires that the composite class contains a list of subclasses in its construction.

- The composite pattern is able to accept the specification of a composite class as a sub class of another composite structure. There is no limit in this abstraction, being recursively flexible.

Multiple-choice questions

1. **In which of the following is the composite pattern suitable?**

   a. Systems that require non-hierarchical architecture.

   b. Systems that contain a huge amount of types.

   c. Any software based on the object-oriented programming paradigm.

   d. Functionalities where elements must be represented hierarchically.

2. **Looking at the example given in this chapter, which alternative contains the composite class?**

   a. IProduct interface

   b. Client application

   c. Combo class

   d. Product class

Answer

1. d
2. c

Questions

1. Explain the primary purpose of the composite pattern.

2. According to what you have learned in this chapter, create a hypothetical scenario in which the composite pattern could be applied, apart from the example given during this chapter.

3. Explain the type of scenarios in which the composite pattern can be used.

4. Are there any projects that you are currently working on that implement the composite pattern?

Key terms

- **Hierarchical structure**: The relationship between the parent and child objects.

- **Recursion**: A technique of making a function calls itself. This technique provides a way to break down the complicated problems into simple problems, which are easier to solve.

CHAPTER 13
Proxy

Security and access control are essential aspects of most software applications. Security and access control are also vital for a company's operation, which generally include the correct implementation of policies that guarantee that only the applicable resources are being accessed by other systems or internally or externally.

The proxy pattern helps us to build an architecture that allows us to control access to a specific resource from an external source by allowing only the operations and data available for that its client needs. Additionally, this pattern represents an elegant way to intercept requests to APIs and to add extra functionality for client applications, without changing the regular behavior of the source application.

Learning the proxy pattern gives you a chance to understand how you can implement access control for simple and complex integrations between systems that share the same interface but whose data and operations needs to be limited for the client application because of business and security requirements.

With in this chapter, you will have the opportunity to apply the proxy pattern in a practical example using the C# language, building anapplication step-by-step.

Structure

In this chapter, we will discuss the following topics:

- Proxy pattern concept

- Examples in C# and .NET Core

Objectives

After studying this unit, you should be able to:

- Understand the proxypattern
- Identify the use of the proxy pattern in .NET applications and existing projects
- Apply the proxy pattern in real-world applications

13.1 Proxy pattern definition

The proxy pattern goal is to mediate the communication between two or more components, with the purpose of controlling the access to the source functionalities.

The proxy pattern, by definition, can easily be confused with the adapter pattern. Both of the patterns have the purpose of mediating the direct access to a specific resource, class, or functionality. However, their purposes seem to be quite similar, but the intention behind each of them is completely different. The adapter patternhas the goal of providing an output understandable to a client application, in case another class has a different interface or output.

This proxy pattern is not involved in changing the output or data format for the client applications, but only to filter and limit the access to certain functionality.

13.1.1 Proxy pattern types

Considering the many reasons to use the proxy pattern, it is possible to split it into the following types:

- **Smart**: This type has the purpose of making extra operations if a client application accesses a specific other resource or class. This kind of proxy is useful to provide an extra functionality to a client application, without the client application knowing it, such as logging in operations.
- **Protection**: This proxy type has the primary intention of adding security control and limits the access to certain functionality. This type is commonly used in APIs where the methods available should be limited by profile or user from the client application.
- **Cache**: In many scenarios, the data returned by a method or API is not frequently changed. In that case, a proxy class can be implemented to handle cache operations in order to avoid extra unnecessary calls to a certain expensive resource such as a database.

- **Virtual**: Sometimes, the proxy pattern can be used to simplify the output provided from a resource to a client application. Simplification in that case means to reduce the methods or functions and not necessarily parse the output to another format.

- **Remote**: This is one of the most common uses of the proxy pattern, which consists of creating a middle ware responsible for intermediate access to a remote resource. The client application does not necessarily know where the resource is hosted, and all the complexity behind the communication with the remote component is abstracted by the proxy component.

One of the good practices presented in software development is the loose-coupling relationship between components. In that context, the proxy pattern allows us to protect an original system from the requirements established by other external systems. There fore, if a client application needs to integrate with an existing third-party or external resource, both of them can co-exist independent from each other at the same time. This is accomplished by using a mediator in order to preserve the source and target systems and implement all the requirements for the integration.

13.1.2 Proxy pattern structure

As part of the structural design patterns, the proxy pattern allows us to control the access to other objects or resources. This makes it possible to run extra routines in the request lifecycle to a certain resource.

Visually, the proxy pattern representation has the structure represented in *figure 13.1*:

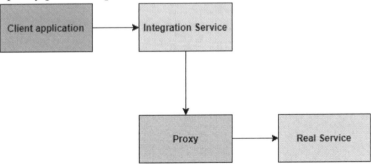

Figure 13.1: *Proxy pattern diagram*

In the *figure 13.1*, a client application needs to access a specific service called *Real Service*. In this scenario, the request to the resource is intercepted by a proxy layer, which allows us to apply extra operations such as access control and filtering. Examples of this include application log on operations and calls to other internal services. According to the solution proposed by the proxy pattern, a client application never accesses the service directly. This restriction may have different reasons for projects with different requirements, but following are the most common reasons:

- The client application should not have access to all services provided by the other application.

- The access to methods and features provided by the service is limited by a legal contract.

- The resource provided by the external service is significantly expensive in terms of costs and performance. This makes it desirable to intercept the requests and provide alternatives to the access of the original resources. This scenario is commonly found when a data cache is used to return information to a client application instead of constantly bringing data from a database.

- In the case where the external resource should be controlled by a distinct profile and the original system does not have support to an access control system in the same format as the client application expects to receive. This is commonly found in integrations between systems developed by different companies that do not share the same requirements.

- In situations where a resource is consumed by many client applications that have different requirements and expectation in terms of features. The proxy pattern can be used to redirect the request from a client application to the correct resource or feature, without changing the implementation of the underlying code in both source and target projects.

- When the security policies are constantly changed by legal or business requirements involving a specific system consumed by many client applications.

In any integration between systems, the full access to the source is usually limited to the scope of the integration considering all the existing legal restrictions between two or more companies. For instance, many large information technology companies provide Artificial Intelligence services based on REST APIs. The access to the resources may be limited to a pricing tier, a security policy, a payment confirmation, or other underlying business rule. Following the best practices of software architecture, features such as access control may not be directly to the Artificial Intelligencere source that the company is offering to their customers. The original service should remain free of external interference, such as financial information and other business requirements beyond the original service. In that scenario, the Artificial Intelligence service can be kept intact, and a proxy layer can be developed to handle authentication, security, user profile, and other information. Therefore, this is one more example of how the proxy design pattern can be applied.

13.1.3 Common use in real projects

The proxy pattern is widely used in the market considering all of its application capabilities. Solutions are made more capable and robust by utilizing the proxy pattern. Many of the APIs used in industry involve certain level of security and commonly implement the proxy pattern, with out many developers being aware that this pattern is actually being used.

It is quite common in solutions used by millions of users to provide alternatives in terms of proper responses based upon the type of devices be accessed. Considering this context, imagine a scenario in which a social media application has several users and the amount of data returned by the application must be customized by the type of device. That means certain kind of devices may receive a greater amount of data, and other ones based upon their capabilities in terms of memory and processor capability. Considering this scenario, a proxy layer can be used to intercept the requests from each device and apply the appropriate custom operations, based upon device capability, before the response, as shown in *figure 13.2*:

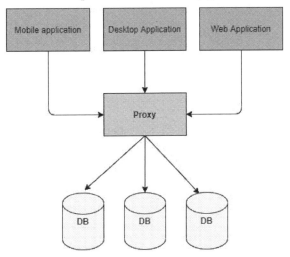

Figure 13.2: *Alternative proxy pattern representation*

Originally, the information requested by the client applications is essentially the same, but the proxy application applies custom policies for each kind of client application, restricting the quantity of data for mobile devices and returning the full content for desktop applications. Additionally, the proxy might be responsible for applying security verification, such as **JSON Web Token (JWT)** for the mobile application, and applying different authentication methods for the Web and desktop applications. All these aspects do not affect the original source application, which in this context are one or more databases.

In the next section, you will have the opportunity to implement the proxy design pattern for a hypothetical application. This application follows similar requirements that commonly exist in real-world applications in order to get experience in the implementation of this pattern using the .NET platform with the C# language.

13.2 Proxy pattern implementation

This section contains a sample application that handles a common requirement found in real-world projects that require the use of the proxy pattern. The use of any design pattern is not mandatory to solve a specific problem. However, the use of design patterns, effectively, usually provide a common, maintainable, and efficient solution for common issues found in various projects across many industries in the market. Therefore, the example in this chapter is one of the ways to handle the given problem.

13.2.1 Scenario requirements

Imagine the hypothetical scenario in which there is an application responsible to store and manage information relating to online news. Each news story or article will have an advertisement associated.

The scenario has the following requirements:

- The news story or article has to be viewable on desktop, mobile, and Web platforms.

- Each individual news story or article must have a category and may be associated with multiple advertisements.

- Accessing the story or article from the Web platform should not have access to any content related to the **Lifestyle** category.

- Advertisement will not be included with the article or story for the mobile platform.

Considering the given scenario, the three distinct platforms (desktop, mobile, and Web) will all consume the information from the same repository. The repository consists of a database that stores the content related to news, categories, and advertisements. However, to increase the complexity of the context, it is established that other applications are consuming the same application responsible for making the communication with the database. That intermediate application is called **ContentRepository**. Therefore, any changes in that application are not allowed, considering all the other applications should not be affected in any case.

13.2.2 Practical example

To create this application, start by creating a Console Application using Visual Studio, and then add the classes related to the example. The first class created is the **News** class, which will contain information relevant to a news story or article, as shown in the following screenshot:

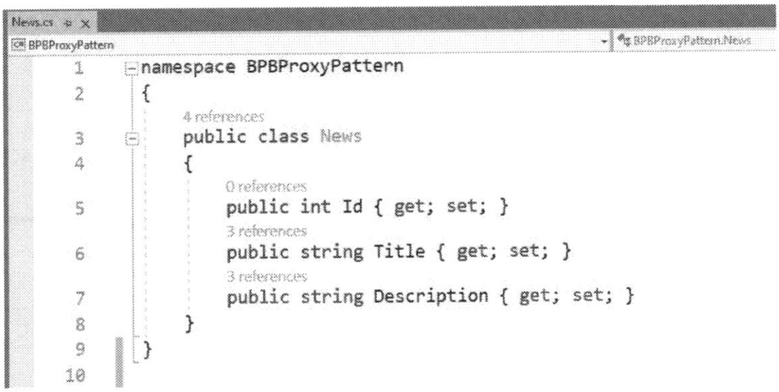

Figure 13.3*: News class structure*

The second class created is the **Advertisement** class, which will be a property from the **Content** class, as discussed below. The **Advertisement** class has the structure represented in the following screenshot:

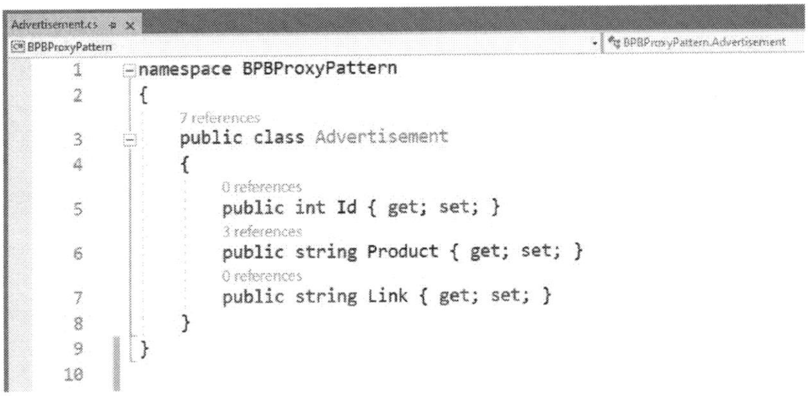

Figure 13.4*: Advertisement class structure*

The **Advertisement** class contains only **Id**, the **Product**name, and the hyperlink to redirect to the advertisement. As was previously stated, the **Advertisement** class will be part of the **Content** class and havea one-to-many relationship, in that the content (news story or article) may have multiple advertisements associated.

The **Content** class contains the news, a list of advertisements, and a category, as shown in the following screenshot:

```
Content.cs ↔ ×
BPBProxyPattern                                                              BPBProxyPattern.Content
 1        using System.Collections.Generic;
 2
 3      namespace BPBProxyPattern
 4      {
            10 references
 5          public class Content
 6          {
                3 references
 7              public Content()
 8              {
 9                  this.Advertisements = new List<Advertisement>();
10              }
                0 references
11              public int Id { get; set; }
                3 references
12              public News News { get; set; }
                8 references
13              public List<Advertisement> Advertisements { get; set; }
                4 references
14              public CategoryEnum Category { get; set; }
15          }
16
            5 references
17          public enum CategoryEnum
18          {
19              Sports = 1,
20              Technology = 2,
21              Health = 3,
22              Lifestyle = 4,
23              Education = 5
24          }
25      }
26
```

Figure 13.5: Content class structure

As shown, the previous code in the preceding screenshot contains the **CategoryEnum** enum definition, which contains 5 category types. At this point, all the necessary models are created, and it is now possible to implement the **Content** repository class, its interface, and finally, the proxy pattern.

An application called **ContentRepository** is responsible for communicating with the database and for returning the necessary information. For demonstration purposes, in this section, the implementation of the content repository application is reduced to a simple **ContentRepository** class that simulates its behavior. There fore, the hypothetical class will return the necessary information regarding content, news, and categories.

In the proxy pattern implementation, it is highly recommended that the **Proxy** class and the real class share the same interface for keeping the method names and properties with the same signature, and thus, remain transparent to the client application. There fore, the client application does not know that the real repository is not being accessed directly, but actually accessed through a proxy in the middle. This proxy will manage permissions, security, filters, and other processes.

The next step in the sample implementation is to create the **IContentRepository** interface that will be shared by the real repository and proxy class, with the implementation as shown in the following screenshot:

```csharp
using System.Collections.Generic;

namespace BPBProxyPattern
{
    public interface IContentRepository
    {
        List<Content> GetContent();
    }
}
```

Figure 13.6: Content repository interface

The **IContentRepository** interface contains only one method for demonstration purposes. The **ContentRepository** class and the proxy class each need to implement their own **GetContent** method, based on theirown requirements.

With the interface already created, the next step is to create the **ContentRepository** class, which has the implementation presented in the following screenshot:

```csharp
public class ContentRepository : IContentRepository
{
    public List<Content> GetContent()
    {
        List<Content> contentList = new List<Content>();
        var advertisements = new List<Advertisement>()
        {
            new Advertisement { Product = "T-Shirt"},
            new Advertisement { Product = "Energy Drink"},
            new Advertisement { Product = "Game ticket"}
        };

        var content1 = new Content();
        content1.News = new News
        {
            Title = "Football",
            Description = "Sport news description"
        };
        content1.Category = CategoryEnum.Sports;
        content1.Advertisements = advertisements;

        var content2 = new Content();
        content2.News = new News
        {
            Title = "Book",
            Description = "Education news description"
        };
        content2.Category = CategoryEnum.Education;
        content2.Advertisements = advertisements;

        var content3 = new Content();
        content3.News = new News
        {
            Title = "Lifestyle",
            Description = "Lifestyle news description"
        };
        content3.Category = CategoryEnum.Lifestyle;
        content3.Advertisements = advertisements;

        contentList.Add(content1);
        contentList.Add(content2);
        contentList.Add(content3);

        return contentList;
    }
}
```

Figure 13.7: ContentRepository class

In this case, the **GetContent** method simulates the database access and creates sample data that consists of a content list with three distinct elements with the information:

- Content with the **Sport** category that has three advertisements
- Content with the **Education** category that has three advertisements
- Content with the **Lifestyle** category that has three advertisements

This content is enough to simulate all the requirements defined in the beginning of this section for the three different platforms. The last very step in the proxy pattern implementation is to create a class or application responsible for intercepting the request from a client application, and based on the requirements, apply all the policies regarding security, authentication, and data filter.

The purpose of the proxy pattern is to provide an intermediate layer to manage a specific resource that needs to have security and filters applied, without affecting the original real source application. In the context of the scenario given in this section, the requests come from applications for desktop, mobile, and Web platforms. A proxy has been created to accept the requests and apply the requirements associated with each platform, avoiding the client application accessing the content repository directly.

Following the best practices of the proxy pattern implementation, the **Proxy** class must implement the same interfaces as the original class. Considering the given scenario, it means that the proxy class should implement the **IContentRepository** interface. The details of the **ContentRepositoryProxy** class needs to implement all the requirements stated for each type of platform and category. Further more, the **ContentRepositoryProxy** class may contain rules regarding authentication, security policies, and any other custom implementation that goes beyond the functionality provided by the original class. This means that the **ContentRepositoryProxy** class only includes logic that is related to the content. The extra responsibilities are applicable only to the **Proxy** class in order to keep the implementation of the proxy class as it currently is.

The design patterns concept is closely related to other practices in software development, such as the SOLID principles. They represent a combination of many good practices that are focused in writing high-standard code and on providing efficient solutions for complex problems. As such, the best practices of the object-oriented programming paradigm are being strictly followed.

The **ContentRepositoryProxy** class implementation is presented in the following screenshot:

```
1    using System.Collections.Generic;
2    using System.Linq;
3
4    namespace BPBProxyPattern
5    {
         5 references
6        public class ContentRepositoryProxy : IContentRepository
7        {
8            private DeviceType _deviceType;
9            ContentRepository contentRepository = new ContentRepository();
             3 references
10           public ContentRepositoryProxy(DeviceType deviceType)
11           {
12               _deviceType = deviceType;
13           }
             6 references
14           public List<Content> GetContent()
15           {
16               List<Content> contentList = contentRepository.GetContent();
17
18               switch (_deviceType)
19               {
20                   case DeviceType.Mobile:
21                       contentList.ForEach(x => { x.Advertisements = new List<Advertisement>(); });
22                       break;
23                   case DeviceType.Web:
24                       contentList = contentList.Where(x => x.Category != CategoryEnum.Lifestyle).ToList();
25                       break;
26               }
27
28
29               return contentList;
30           }
31       }
32
         7 references
33       public enum DeviceType
34       {
35           Desktop = 1,
36           Mobile = 2,
37           Web = 3
38       }
39   }
40
```

Figure 13.8: Proxy class implementation

For clarification purposes, the **DeviceType** enum was created to create a device type with three different values (desktop, mobile, and Web) in order to have more readable code. The class constructor receives a device type as a parameter, and the **GetContent** method has a statement to handle the different rules for each device type.

After bringing the data from the original repository, the returns all of the advertisement information if the client application is from a mobile platform, and in case the requests comes from the Web platform, the method filters the content returned by the original repository, excluding any content of the **Lifestyle** category.

As shown in this example, the client application does not directly access the content repository, but it uses the **ContentRepositoryProxy** proxy class instead, where rules are implemented in code as the business requirements.

To see the results of the proxy class, you can call the proxy class in the Console Application passing distinct parameters, as shown in the following screenshot:

```
Program.cs
BPBProxyPattern                                   BPBProxyPattern.Program
using System;
using System.Linq;

namespace BPBProxyPattern
{
    class Program
    {
        static void Main(string[] args)
        {
            ContentRepositoryProxy contentRepositoryProxy =
                new ContentRepositoryProxy(DeviceType.Web);

            var contentListForWeb = contentRepositoryProxy.GetContent();

            Console.WriteLine("Web: " + contentListForWeb.Count +
                ". Has ads: " + contentListForWeb.Any(x=> x.Advertisements.Count > 0));

            contentRepositoryProxy =
               new ContentRepositoryProxy(DeviceType.Desktop);

            var contentListForDesktop = contentRepositoryProxy.GetContent();

            Console.WriteLine("Desktop: " + contentListForDesktop.Count +
                ". Has ads: " + contentListForWeb.Any(x => x.Advertisements.Count > 0));

            contentRepositoryProxy =
               new ContentRepositoryProxy(DeviceType.Mobile);

            var contentListForMobile = contentRepositoryProxy.GetContent();

            Console.WriteLine("Mobile: " + contentListForMobile.Count +
                ". Has ads: " + contentListForMobile.Any(x => x.Advertisements.Count > 0));

            Console.Read();

        }
    }
}
```

Figure 13.9: Console application

In this small program, the **Proxy** class is instantiated three times, one for each type of device, and the console prints the information about the number of contents returned by the proxy and then checks if there are advertisements associated with them. Considering the requirements, the mobile platform should receive all advertisements, and the Web platform should receive advertisements from all the categories, except from the lifestyle category. If you run the Console application with the given implementation, you will get the results as shown in the following screenshot:

```
C:\Users\Alexandre Malavasi\source\repos\BPBProxyPattern\
Web: 2. Has ads: True
Desktop: 3. Has ads: True
Mobile: 3. Has ads: False
```

Figure 13.10: Proxy pattern results

The **Proxy** class works as expected and illustrates that the content repository class is not affected by any extra needs from the business requirement. Further more, any requirement changes to the ones already specified would only be implemented with in the `ContentRepositoryProxy` proxy class, keeping the original content `Repository` class safe from external interference.

Conclusion

As you have learned in this chapter, the proxy pattern allows us to create a simple solution for scenarios in which it is necessary to mediate the communication between two distinct components, applying policies between them and keeping all the changes in the proxy class transparent to the client applications. The use of this pattern is common in the case of external applications, databases, and APIs, allowing us to keep the integration safe from the modification to the core source application and protecting the original source system from external interference. The proxy pattern represents one of the more simple patterns used in the market. This design pattern is one of the most important solutions largely used in the market, considering almost all the companies across the world need to integrate their projects with third-party systems.

With this chapter, you have learned how to implement in a real scenario the proxy pattern using the C# language and have learned how to apply simple solutions for complex problems, applying the best practices of the object-oriented programming.

In the next chapter, you will have the chance to continue your journey into the design patterns using the C# language and the .NET Core platform, by learning the command pattern and by applying all the general knowledge you have received in the preceding chapters of this book.

Points to remember

- The proxy pattern gives us the chance to intercept the access to functionalities and apply business requirements, with out affecting the original source class.
- The proxy pattern can be combined with SOLID principles in a single solution.
- It is possible to apply the proxy pattern in any situation in which the access to certain functionality needs to be restricted because of security reasons or other similar requirements.

Multiple-choice questions

1. **In which scenario is the proxy pattern suitable?**

   a. Integration between systems

   b. Scenarios in which security is not a concern

   c. Any project that uses the C# as language

   d. None of them

2. **Looking at the example given in this chapter, which class contains the necessary implementation for the proxy pattern?**

   a. Content repository class

   b. Client application

   c. ContentRepositoryProxy class

   d. News class

Answers

1. a

2. c

Questions

1. Explain the primary purpose of the proxypattern.

2. According to what you have learned in this chapter, create a hypothetical scenario in which the proxy pattern could be applied a part from the example given in this chapter.

3. Explain the types of scenarios in whichtheproxy pattern can be used.

4. Are there any projects that you are currently working on that implement the proxy pattern?

Key terms

- **Client application**: The layer of a system that usually contains a user interface and has the higher level in terms of abstraction.

- **System integration**: Communication between two or more components using defined protocols.

- **API**: Application programming interface usually made for allowing integration between different systems.

- **Cache**: In software development, it consists in storing data in a place that has better performance than the original source.

CHAPTER 14
Command

The command design pattern allows us to aggregate in a single object all the necessary information regarding a complex operation. This includes database transactions, API requests, and many types of integration, simplifying the whole process for a client application and encapsulating all the internal operations made by the command class. Considering this pattern is largely used by database providers that integrate various programming languages, it surely is one of the most used design patterns used in software development and used in a huge amount of projects across the globe.

Learning the command pattern gives you the chance to identify its use in legacy projects, optimizing the time spent in understanding the existing code and saving resources and implementing a new software using the C# language and .NET platform.

With this chapter, you will have the opportunity to apply the command pattern in a practical example using the C# language, building a realscenario step-by-step.

Structure

In this chapter, we will discuss the following topics:

- Command pattern concept
- Examples in C# and .NET Core

Objectives

After studying this unit, you should be able to:

- Understand the command pattern

- Identify the use of the command pattern in .NET applications and existing projects

- Apply the command pattern in real-world scenarios

14.1 Command pattern definition

Design patterns, in general, have aprimary purpose of simplifying the solution for complex problems following the best practices of the object-oriented programming paradigm, software architecture, and SOLID principles. Although each of them varies in terms of implementation and concrete intention, it is much easier to understand them to be able to focus on their principles instead of their actual implementation.

In this chapter, you will walk through the details behind the command design pattern and will also have a chance to understand how to apply its concept in a real-world scenario, implementing integration with an external financial service for an online store. But, first of all, it is essential to get yourself familiar with the command pattern structure and its primary purpose.

The command pattern hides from a client application (requester) the complexity of an operation executed by the other layer of the application (receiver). As the receiver is fully responsible for executing actions, it does not matter how many sub-actions the request actually requires. The central idea behind that pattern is to allow the execution of many complex tasks and combine the result in a single high-level operation called by the client application, being possible to not only execute actions but revert those as well, implementing the concept as transactions, largely used in database operations and the execution of a large business process.

In a high-level abstraction of the command pattern, the structure looks like *figure 14.1*, which shows the interaction between a client application and the command pattern, even the responsibilities that are proper to each of the layers, as shown in *figure 14.1*:

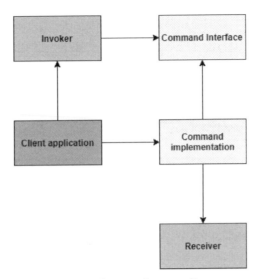

***Figure 14.1**: Command pattern diagram*

As shown in the previous figure, the command pattern implementation requires the following parts: client application, invoker, command interface, command implementation, and receiver. At the first moment, this representation generally represents the implementation of this design pattern in almost all cases.

However, the implementation can be a little different in more complex scenarios in which multiple commands need to be executed.

The use of a common interface for all the commands in the same context allows us to increase the testability of the application considering a command can be injected in a class and simulate the behavior of a real concrete command class. As the command pattern definition may be abstract, it is always recommended to experience the underlying design pattern implementing something similar you would find in a real-world scenario. Because of that, you must follow the practical tutorial presented along with this chapter.

14.2 Command pattern implementation

Considering the command pattern has the purpose of abstracting the execution of complex operations from a client application, a real experience with this pattern requires the implementation of an application that has the purpose of solving the same problem as the command pattern tries to solve. As was said in the first section of this chapter, as shown in subsequent pages, you will have the opportunity to implement a project that contains an abstraction for a financial transaction related to a process that is usually made by an online store, which contains the following requirements:

- The online store should allow the user to pay with a credit card.

- Once a purchase is made by a user, the system should decrease the quantity available for the same product.

- The third-party suppliers must be notified if a product provided by them was sold.

- In case there is any failure in any of the operations above, the system should roll back all the operations.

Considering the given scenario, the system would require the development of a common command interface to be implemented by all the operations, and although they are completely different from each other, the implementation of the operations must be hidden from the client application. Inevitably, the full implementation of this example would involve calls to external APIs, database integration, and integrations with third-party systems. This would include communications with the suppliers, but the underlying implementation will be simulated to be focused only on the command pattern implementation.

Regarding the business model classes, the example requires the creation of models for the purchase data and related data, such as customer, product, and supplier, as represented in *figure 14.2*:

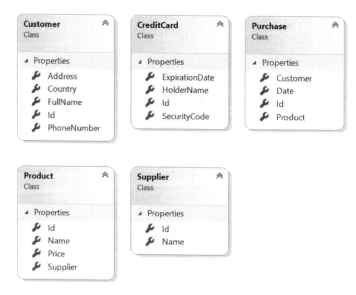

Figure 14.2: Command Pattern class diagram

The purchase class is the main class, considering that the class will be used in the command pattern implementation as a parameter, and it stores all the necessary information for the operations stated in the requirements. The implementation of this class is illustrated in the following screenshot:

```
 7   □namespace BPBCommandPattern
 8    {
           0 references
 9    □     public class Purchase
10          {
                 0 references
11               public int Id { get; set; }
                 0 references
12               public DateTime Date { get; set; }
                 0 references
13               public Product Product { get; set; }
                 0 references
14               public Customer Customer { get; set; }
                 0 references
15               public CreditCard CreditCard { get; set; }
16          }
17    }
18
```

Figure 14.3: *Purchase class*

Considering the relationship between the **Purchase** class and the **Product** and **Customer** entities, for the full implementation of the hypothetical scenario, requires the implementation of the **Customer** class as the next step, as shown in the following screenshot:

```
Customer.cs  ⯎ ✕
[C#] BPBCommandPattern                              ▾ ⚙ BPBCommandPattern.Customer
 1   □namespace BPBCommandPattern
 2    {
           1 reference
 3    □     public class Customer
 4          {
                 0 references
 5               public int Id { get; set; }
                 0 references
 6               public string FullName { get; set; }
                 0 references
 7               public string PhoneNumber { get; set; }
                 0 references
 8               public string Address { get; set; }
                 0 references
 9               public string Country { get; set; }
10          }
11    }
12
```

Figure 14.4: *Customer class*

The product class contains a one-to-one relationship with the supplier class, and for demonstration purposes, the supplier class has only the properties referenced to the model. There fore, this example hides the methods responsible for making the integration process with the suppliers.

14.2.1 Extra classes

Following the requirements stated by the given scenario, the **Product** and **Supplier** class in the example of this chapter has implementation shown in the following screenshot:

```csharp
namespace BPBCommandPattern
{
    public class Product
    {
        public int Id { get; set; }
        public string Name { get; set; }
        public decimal Price { get; set; }
        public Supplier Supplier { get; set; }
    }

    public class Supplier
    {
        public int Id { get; set; }
        public string Name { get; set; }
    }
}
```

Figure 14.5: Product and supplier classes

The following is the **CreditCard** class, which is related to the **Purchase** class, whose implementation can be seen in the following screenshot:

```csharp
using System;

namespace BPBCommandPattern
{
    public class CreditCard
    {
        public int Id { get; set; }
        public string Number { get; set; }
        public string HolderName { get; set; }
        public DateTime ExpirationDate { get; set; }
        public int SecurityCode { get; set; }
    }
}
```

Figure 14.6: Credit card class

At this point, we have created all of the necessary classes regarding the models to implement the example of this chapter. In that context, the command pattern will be responsible for making distinct operations implementing a common interface. The constructor will include a purchase object. Therefore, the next step is the creation of the interface with the same implementation, as shown in the following screenshot:

```csharp
namespace BPBCommandPattern
{
    public interface IPurchaseCommand
    {
        void ExecuteOperation();
        void RevertOperation();
    }
}
```

Figure 14.7: Common interface

The given interface requires the implementation of two methods, one responsible for making a custom operation and the other responsible for reverting the operation in case any exception occurs. Considering the scenario proposed in this section, three distinct command classes must be created, one for each operation: credit card payment, storage product information, and supplier notification. Of course, it is not necessary to implement the real actions for any of the command classes for this example. For demonstration purposes, you can specify only a **Console. Writeline** method to show the behavior of the implementation. The first command class demonstrates the credit card operation, which has the implementation shown in the following screenshot:

```csharp
using System;

namespace BPBCommandPattern
{
    public class CreditCardPaymentCommand : IPurchaseCommand
    {
        private readonly Purchase _purchase;

        public CreditCardPaymentCommand(Purchase purchase)
        {
            this._purchase = purchase;
        }

        public void ExecuteOperation()
        {
            Console.WriteLine("Integration with the credit card provider");
        }

        public void RevertOperation()
        {
            Console.WriteLine("Something failed in the payment");
        }
    }
}
```

Figure 14.8: Payment command class

As shown in the previous screenshot, the class implements the **IPurchaseCommand** interface and receives in the constructor a **purchase** object. This is the pattern used in all the command classes in the example. Considering the full purchase process involves three different operations, the implementation of two of them is missing, including supplier notification and storage product management. Therefore, the next command pattern implementation that needs to be created is the one responsible for decreasing the product quantity information in the storage as a part of the process. The underlying command class for this operation has the implementation, as shown in the following screenshot:

```csharp
1    using System;
2
3    namespace BPBCommandPattern
4    {
        2 references
5        public class StorageManagerCommand : IPurchaseCommand
6        {
7            private readonly Purchase _purchase;
8
            1 reference
9            public StorageManagerCommand(Purchase purchase)
10           {
11               this._purchase = purchase;
12           }
13
            4 references
14           public void ExecuteOperation()
15           {
16               Console.WriteLine("Operation to decrease the product quantity availability");
17           }
18
            4 references
19           public void RevertOperation()
20           {
21               Console.WriteLine("Something failed in the storage operation");
22           }
23       }
24   }
```

Figure 14.9: Storage command implementation

As shown in the previous screenshot, the storage command class follows the same pattern as the payment command, only the implementation of the two methods will change to execute the custom operations regarding each of them. The use of the same interface is important from an architecture point of view to ensure that all the command classes across the system will implement a revert process stated by the requirements given at the beginning of this section. From that point, only one command class is missing to be implemented regarding the supplier notification. Each supplier must have a specific way for integration, which means that the command design pattern could be used combined with other patterns, such as strategy pattern explained in *Chapter 15: Strategy*. After simplifying the supplier command class, it has the implementation shown in the following screenshot:

```
1     using System;
2
3    namespace BPBCommandPattern
4    {
        2 references
5        public class SupplierCommand : IPurchaseCommand
6        {
7            private readonly Purchase _purchase;
8
          1 reference
9            public SupplierCommand(Purchase purchase)
10           {
11               this._purchase = purchase;
12           }
13
          4 references
14           public void ExecuteOperation()
15           {
16               Console.WriteLine("Operation to notify the supplier");
17           }
18
          4 references
19           public void RevertOperation()
20           {
21               Console.WriteLine("Something failed in the supplier notification");
22           }
23       }
24   }
```

Figure 14.10: *Supplier command implementation*

With the three necessary command classes already created, the next step is the creation of the class responsible for encapsulating the operations made by the command classes. According to the requirements, if the execution of an operation throws an exception or has an unexpected result, the system should execute the revert process regarding the same operation. Therefore, the class that directly manages the command classes must guarantee the expected behavior, as shown in the following screenshot:

```
1     using System;
2
3    namespace BPBCommandPattern
4    {
        4 references
5        public class PurchaseLogic
6        {
7            private readonly IPurchaseCommand _purchaseCommand;
          3 references
8            public PurchaseLogic(IPurchaseCommand purchaseCommand)
9            {
10               this._purchaseCommand = purchaseCommand;
11           }
          3 references
12           public void ConfirmPurchase()
13           {
14               try
15               {
16                   this._purchaseCommand.ExecuteOperation();
17               }
18               catch(Exception)
19               {
20                   this._purchaseCommand.RevertOperation();
21               }
22           }
23       }
24   }
25
```

Figure 14.11: *Purchase logic class*

The **PurchaseLogic** class receives a **purchaseCommand** class that implements the **purchaseCommand** interface and has a method responsible for managing the execution of the existing operation provided by the concrete command class. As you can see in the code presented in the preceding screenshot, the confirm purchase method has a **try-catch** block to handle failures in the purchase execution. Considering the client application must use the purchase logic class to execute the operations instead of calling the underlying methods directly from the command class, this approach guarantees that the revert operation will always be executed in case some unexpected event occurs.

All the necessary classes are already created to consume the command design pattern infrastructure. You can use the sample classes in a Console application or in another type of project that is suitable for you to execute the operations implemented in each class.

In this chapter, a Console application is used to create multiple instances of the command classes and to instantiate the model classes, which means the information regarding the customer, supplier, product, and purchase.

To implement this, first of all, create the instances for the **Customer** and **CreditCard** objects with hypothetical data, as shown in the following screenshot:

```
 9      Customer customer = new Customer()
10      {
11          Id = 1,
12          FullName = "Customer example"
13      };
14
15      CreditCard creditCard = new CreditCard()
16      {
17          Id = 1,
18          ExpirationDate = new DateTime(2030, 12, 31),
19          HolderName = "Customer example",
20          Number = "1111222233334444",
21          SecurityCode = 123
22      };
```

Figure 14.12: Customer and credit card objects

At this point, all the main classes are already created, and you are able to implement the next classes related to the client application.

14.2.2 Client application

With the initial objects created, the next step is to generate a new instance of the purchase object, associating the **Customer** and **CreditCard** just created, as shown in the following screenshot:

```
24    Purchase purchase = new Purchase()
25    {
26        CreditCard = creditCard,
27        Date = DateTime.UtcNow,
28        Customer = customer,
29        Product = new Product
30        {
31            Name = "Book",
32            Supplier = new Supplier
33            {
34                Name = "Book store"
35            }
36        }
37    };
```

Figure 14.13: *Purchase object*

The **purchase** object has only one product with a supplier associated. In a real scenario, this information might be retrieved from a database or external API, but for demonstration purposes, the instance of these objects is being created manually in this example. Each command class expects to receive a purchase object in the constructor; therefore, the same instance of the **purchase** object will be passed for each type of command class instance, including payment, storage manager, and supplier notification. Remember that a full purchase process in this context must involve the operations made by all the three command classes.

In the client application, it is necessary to create an instance for each type of command and pass each of them as a parameter for the **PurchaseLogic** class instances, as shown in the following screenshot:

```
IPurchaseCommand paymentCommand = new CreditCardPaymentCommand(purchase);
IPurchaseCommand storageCommand = new StorageManagerCommand(purchase);
IPurchaseCommand supplierCommand = new SupplierCommand(purchase);

new PurchaseLogic(paymentCommand).ConfirmPurchase();
new PurchaseLogic(storageCommand).ConfirmPurchase();
new PurchaseLogic(supplierCommand).ConfirmPurchase();
```

Figure 14.14: *Client application implementation*

Realize that the **Purchase** class object is responsible for calling the **ConfirmPurchase** method, which contains the **try-catch** block to manage the underlying execution for the purchase operation. In this example, even the three necessary operations are being executed, the implementation is wrong because it does not have a routine that guarantees that all the operations will be reverted in case of one of three operations fails. The given implementation would not be complete if it did not include a complete process reversion, if any one of the three operations in a single transaction fails. Therefore, the implementation needs to change a little bit to ensure this requirement is being met, what can be achieved implementing the transaction class shown in the following screenshot:

```
1    using System;
2    using System.Collections.Generic;
3    using System.Linq;
4
5    namespace BPBCommandPattern
6    {
7        public class TransactionPurchaseCommand : IPurchaseCommand
8        {
9            private readonly List<IPurchaseCommand> _purchaseCommands;
10           private List<IPurchaseCommand> executedPurchaseCommands;
11           private List<IPurchaseCommand> failedPurchaseCommands;
12
13           public TransactionPurchaseCommand(List<IPurchaseCommand> purchaseCommands)
14           {
15               this._purchaseCommands = purchaseCommands;
16               executedPurchaseCommands = new List<IPurchaseCommand>();
17               failedPurchaseCommands = new List<IPurchaseCommand>();
18
19           }
20           public void ExecuteOperation()
21           {
22               foreach (var purchaseCommand in _purchaseCommands)
23               {
24                   try
25                   {
26                       purchaseCommand.ExecuteOperation();
27                       executedPurchaseCommands.Add(purchaseCommand);
28                   }
29                   catch (Exception)
30                   {
31                       failedPurchaseCommands.Add(purchaseCommand);
32                   }
33               }
34
35               if (failedPurchaseCommands.Any())
36               {
37                   RevertOperation();
38               }
39           }
40
41           public void RevertOperation()
42           {
43               foreach (var purchaseCommand in executedPurchaseCommands)
44               {
45                   purchaseCommand.RevertOperation();
46               }
47           }
48       }
49   }
```

Figure 14.15: Transaction purchase command class

The **TransactionPurchaseCommand** class receives a list of **purchaseCommands** and implements the same **purchaseCommand** interface to follow the same pattern. This implementation meets the requirement that becomes mandatory to revert all the operations if only one fails. This approach is a little more complex than the previous implementation, but on the other hand, itbetter represents the requirements. In the client application, it is necessary to create an instance of the transaction command class and replace the creation of the three instances of the **PurchaseLogic** class, as shown in the following screenshot:

```
40       IPurchaseCommand paymentCommand = new CreditCardPaymentCommand(purchase);
41       IPurchaseCommand storageCommand = new StorageManagerCommand(purchase);
42       IPurchaseCommand supplierCommand = new SupplierCommand(purchase);
43
44       List<IPurchaseCommand> purchaseCommands = new List<IPurchaseCommand>
45       {
46           paymentCommand,
47           storageCommand,
48           supplierCommand
49       };
50
51       new TransactionPurchaseCommand(purchaseCommands).ExecuteOperation();
```

Figure 14.16: Client application with a transaction

The use of the command design pattern allows us to implement a readable code that clearly shows the intention of the requirements. In the given scenario in this chapter, the intention of the requirements were to guarantee that all the necessary operations regarding a purchase in the online store would run, and in case of one or more of them failing, the full purchase operation should be reverted as they were a single process. It is particularly a handful in this context, and it is hoped that this example helped you to properly understand the command pattern and also give you the necessary ability to identify its use in legacy projects.

Conclusion

As learnedin this chapter, the command pattern is extremely useful in the scenarios in which multiple operations need to be made as a group of operations, and their complexity must be abstract from the client application. This pattern is largely used in .NET applications once almost all the database providers commonly implement the command pattern to abstract the execution of database operations for an application developed using the C# language. The knowledge gained during this chapter allows you to create your own command structure from scratch and apply it in real projects, being possible to combine this pattern with others that have the purpose of encapsulating the execution of operations from the client application.

With this chapter, you have learned how to implement in a real scenario the command pattern usingthe C# language and became able to understand how to apply simple solutions for complex problems, applying the best practices of OOP.

In the next chapter, you will have the chance to continue your journey into the design patterns using the C# language and .NET Core platform, learn the strategy pattern, and apply all the general knowledge you have got in the first chapters of this book.

Points to remember

- The command pattern allows the hiding from the client application all the complexity behind the execution of operations, always sharing the same interface and following the same pattern.

- The command pattern can be used combined with other patterns, such as the strategy design pattern.

- The command pattern is highly recommended in scenarios in which multiple operations require to be handle as a single transaction.

Multiple-choice questions

1. **In which scenario is the command pattern recommended?**
   a. For simple operations
   b. When the integration between systems is complex
   c. When operations need to be executed and handled as a transaction
   d. None of them

2. **Looking at the example given in this chapter, which class contains the necessary implementation for the proxy pattern?**
   a. Purchase logic
   b. Customer
   c. Purchase
   d. Purchase command

Answers

1. c
2. d

Questions

1. Explain the primary purpose of the command pattern.

2. According to what you have learned in this chapter, create a hypothetical scenario where the command pattern could be applied apart from the example given in this chapter.

3. Give examples of scenarios in which the command pattern can be used.

4. Are there any projects that you are currently working on that implement the command pattern?

Key terms

- **Transaction**: In software development, a transaction represents a group of tasks that need to be executed successfully. If one task fails, a roll back process is executed for all the tasks in case of at least one of them fails.

- **Receiver**: In the context of the command design pattern implementation, a receiver is the source class responsible for executing a certain operation.

- **Invoker**: In the context of the command design pattern implementation, an invoker is an intermediate class or layer responsible for calling a command class.

CHAPTER 15
Strategy

In software development, there are many ways to solve a specific problem, and distinct approaches can be taken to achieve the same result. However, the design patterns represent a toolbox solution for frequent issues found across many companies and a huge number of project types.

In that context, the strategy pattern represents an efficient and straightforward pattern that simplifies the complex algorithms implemented in multiple classes that have a similar purpose.

Learning the strategy pattern gives you the opportunity to identify its use in legacy projects based on the C# language and .NET platform, and also helps you to apply a high-level abstraction for managing distinct operations that can be made on new and existing projects of any kind.

With this chapter, you will have the opportunity to applythe strategy pattern in a practical example using the C# language, building a real-world scenario step-by-step.

Structure

In this chapter, we will discuss the following topics:

- Strategy pattern concept

- Examples in C# and .NET Core

Objectives

After studying this unit, you should be able to:

- Understand the strategy pattern
- Identify the use of the strategy pattern in .NET applications and existing projects
- Apply the strategy pattern in real-world scenarios

15.1 Strategypattern definition

Before the concrete definition of the strategy pattern, it is essential to properly understand the difference between runtime and compiletime in the C# language. Compile time means any operation that can be identified and recognized while the application is built, and before the project runs. For instance, if there is a Web application developed using the ASP.Net Core technology, this project needs to be built, compiled, and published to a web server. If there are issues in terms of C# implementation, such as a syntax error, the Visual Studio IDE will generate a build error and not allow the program to be fully compiled and built. This means that all the types and classes identified by the compiler must be valid and present, in that context, specifically for the C# language. Therefore, the types and classes must be known at compile time, including their implementation.

On the other hand, the application runtime means that a specific behavior of the application will only be identified when the application is actually running. Generally, small issues in interfaces and logical implementation issues are identified at this time, because they depend on specific conditions to be verified, such as page request, database connection, among others. It is possible to say that, in a high-level definition of the difference between compiletime and runtime, the first one knows the types and classes, including their behavior in terms of syntax. The second one is more related to unknown behavior that does not necessarily happen all the time, depending on certain factors that need to be checked and validated.

Given this brief explanation, the strategy pattern allows us to change the type of a method or implementation in run time, which means that based on certain conditions, the code would assume the creation of different classes in distinct scenarios. This flexible behavior helps us to develop solutions that encapsulate the complexity of a sort of operations from a client application. This is similar towhat happens with other patterns, such as the factory method explained in the factory method in C# and .NET Core chapter.

The strategy pattern consists of the specification of a common interface that needs to be implemented by all the classes that belong to the same family or have similar purposes. The strategy pattern class, in that case, is responsible for deciding which concrete class needs to be instantiated based on parameters, conditions, or custom verification implemented based on the business and technical requirements.

15.2 Strategy pattern structure

In this chapter, you will walk through the details of the strategy design pattern and will also have a chance to understand how to apply its concept in a real scenario, implementing the business requirements for a global delivery application. But, first of all, it is essential to get yourself familiar with the strategy pattern structure and its primary purpose.

The strategy pattern contains a context class that manages the decision of which concrete class needs to be created, defining in runtime the strategy class that will be used by the primary routine, as represented in *figure 15.1*:

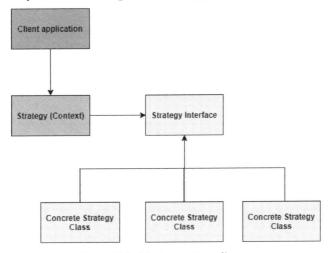

Figure 15.1: *Strategy pattern diagram*

As shown in *figure 15.1*, all the concrete classes implement the same interface, and the logic behind the creation of the correct object is hidden from the client application once a specific routine has multiple options to choose from. The client application does not necessarily know which class needs to be created, with the full strategy being handled by the context class.

A real-world scenario example may involve hundreds of classes if the project contains many complex micro-operations that need to be executed, but abstracting their complexity from the client application. The creation of the context class in that represents the biggest challenge in the strategy pattern implementation. In with this chapter, you will have the opportunity to implement from scratch this design pattern, following the requirements of a hypothetical scenario that is close to a real-world scenario.

15.3 Strategypattern implementation

The use of any design pattern in software development must be restricted to the problems that they have the intention to solve. Therefore, different problems require distinct solutions as well, and distinct requirements demand custom implementation for covering all the necessary aspects of them, with out violating the good practices of the object-oriented programming. For that reason, this section contains a hypothetical scenario that consists of a global delivery company that wants to control the process per city where the services are being executed. Each city has its own rules regarding taxes, revenue, employment, and price, as the following requirements:

- New York City has a 10% tax for any transaction made in the application and 25% profits for the delivery.

- Los Angeles city has a 20% tax for any transaction and 10% profit for the delivery.

- Sao Paulo city has 10% tax, 15% profit, and the requirement to have permanent employees.

- In case the user is from a city that does have any implementation regarding any rules, all the requirements from New York should be applied by default.

Given this scenario, there are many ways to properly implement all the requirements. But, one thing that is really important to keep in mind is this kind of application usually has the potential to scale globally across many cities, each of which may have different business rules. A single application that would support all the legal requirements for all the contexts would be a challenging one to implement, as the complexity behind legal requirements may vary between cities. Some of them may have extra laws, and others may have simpler regulations.

In order to keep the consistency in the application in terms of technical architecture, it is possible to use the strategy pattern in that context. This considers that the instantiation of the object by the client application could involve complex implementation being interesting for the higher level of the application to have the API calls as simple as possible. Therefore, a strategy infrastructure would be responsible for creating the correct instance regarding each city, loading all the local regulations for taxes, employment, and profitability correctly.

The creation of the models to support the example will consist of the classes regarding the user and delivery entities. Considering this chapter is focused on the strategy pattern implementation, these models have been simplified and do not have all the properties and methods that would exist in a real-world scenario.

The first class that needs to be created is the **User** class, as shown in the following screenshot:

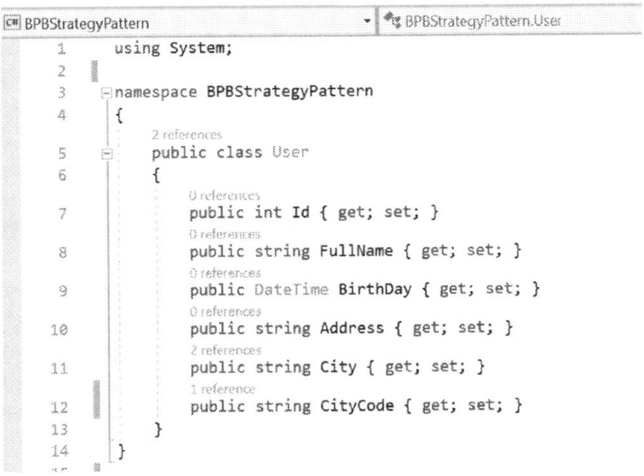

Figure 15.2: User class

The **User** class contains only the information that will be used further in the strategy pattern class, including the city code property. In the example in this section, a different instance of the strategy object needs to be created, as the implementation for each city is different. Also, the **Delivery** class needs to be created with the basic information regarding the entity, as shown in the following screenshot:

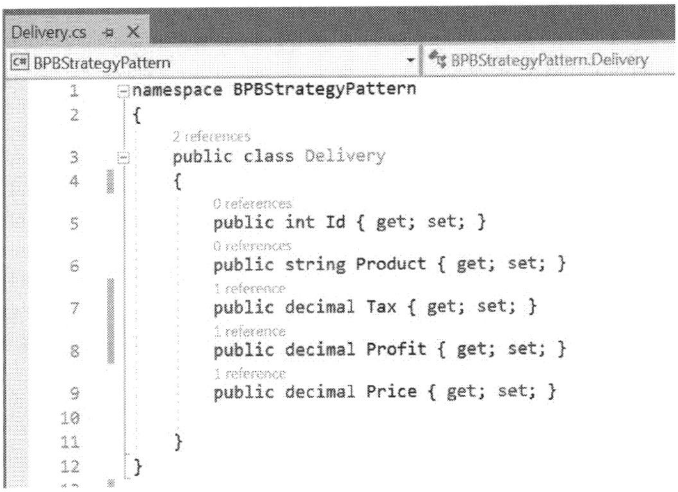

Figure 15.3: Delivery class

According to the requirements, each city has its own rules regarding tax and profit, which means that the underlying properties of the delivery class must be changed using the strategy class. There fore, after the creation of the class presented in the preceding screenshot, the implementation of this class will change to receive the injection of the necessary logic to change the tax and profit values based on the custom city rules.

15.4 Creating the city strategy class

In order to increase the testability and extensibility of the strategy pattern implementation, it is recommended to use interfaces rather than abstract classes for the base classes. Given this important aspect, the next structure that needs to be created is the city strategy class, which will contain in the contract the methods responsible for applying the requirements regarding tax, profit, and employment rules, as shown in the following screenshot:

```
ICityStrategy.cs
BPBStrategyPattern    BPBStrategyPattern.ICityStrategy

namespace BPBStrategyPattern
{
    6 references
    public interface ICityStrategy
    {
        3 references
        decimal ApplyTax(decimal price);
        4 references
        void ApplyEmploymentRules();
        3 references
        decimal ApplyProfit(decimal price);
    }
}
```

***Figure 15.4**: City strategy interface*

Notice that the city strategy interface does not have any specification for properties, but only methods because the class is only responsible for handling the custom implementation for the specific requirements for each city. Therefore, it does not need to have properties to keep the correct state of the delivery or user objects. Considering different objects need to be created for each city, instead of having complicated business logic under a unique complex class, it is better to have a concrete class for each city, implementing the city strategy interface. Another good practice is to name the classes involved in a design pattern implementation with the pattern name as a suffix. It helps other developers in the project identify the pattern, and it saves time in the analysis process in case of legacy projects.

With the city strategy interface already created, it is time to change the `Delivery` class previously specified, injecting the interface in the constructor method of the `Delivery` class. Additionally, the `get` method of the tax and profit properties are being determined by the underlying methods presented in the interface, as shown in the following screenshot:

```
1   namespace BPBStrategyPattern
2   {
        3 references
3       public class Delivery
4       {
5           ICityStrategy _cityStrategy;
            1 reference
6           public Delivery(ICityStrategy cityStrategy)
7           {
8               _cityStrategy = cityStrategy;
9           }
            0 references
10          public int Id { get; set; }
            0 references
11          public string Product { get; set; }
            1 reference
12          public decimal Tax => _cityStrategy.ApplyTax(this.Price);
            1 reference
13          public decimal Profit => _cityStrategy.ApplyProfit(this.Price);
            3 references
14          public decimal Price { get; set; }
15
16      }
17  }
```

Figure 15.5: Delivery class with the strategy interface

The constructor of the delivery does not receive a concrete city strategy class considering it must be dynamic following the purpose of the strategy design pattern. The concrete class to be instantiated needs to be defined in runtime, which means that the class type is unknown until the routine that contains the strategy implementation runs. As there is already the entire infrastructure for the concrete strategy classes, it is necessary now to create one class for each city, implementing the city strategy interface.

In case the client application is to be suddenly started to be used in a huge number of different cities, this situation would require the implementation of many extra classes, keeping the pattern of one for each individual city, which would not be easy to maintain. This would require the application to be re-deployed many times when new cities must be supported by the application. There fore, in specific scenarios, another approach should be taken, such as the implementation of a single class whose states might be controlled by a complex database structure correctly supporting the rules for each city.

The current example states the requirements for three cities (New York, Los Angeles, and Sao Paulo), and in that case, the three classes need to be created. The first could be the New York City class, as shown in the following screenshot:

```
BPBStrategyPattern                              BPBStrategyPattern.NewYorkStrategy
1        using System;
2
3      namespace BPBStrategyPattern
4      {
         2 references
5          public class NewYorkStrategy : ICityStrategy
6          {
             4 references
7              public void ApplyEmploymentRules()
8              {
9                  Console.WriteLine("No permanent employees");
10             }
11
             4 references
12             public decimal ApplyProfit(decimal price)
13             {
14                 return  price * 0.25m;
15             }
16
             4 references
17             public decimal ApplyTax(decimal price)
18             {
19                 return price * 0.10m;
20             }
21         }
22     }
```

Figure 15.6: New York strategy class

The mechanism responsible for determining the employment rules for the city are included as an input, in this case, the **NewYorkStrategy** class, which has the **ICityStrategy** interface, to the constructor of the **Delivery** class. The methods responsible for applying the tax and profit under the delivery price are implemented in the underlying class, which implements the **ICityStrategy** interface and follows the requirements stated at the beginning of this section.

Following the same approach taken for the New York City class, there are two additional classes that are needed to be created, one for Sao Paulo and another for Los Angeles. Both of these classes need to implement the same **ICityStrategy** interface, which will be injected via the constructor into the **Delivery** class based on the user city. The development of a class, in that case, one for each city, looks like a huge effort, judging by the amount of cities that need to be implemented.

However, the main objective of the strategy pattern is to keep client application simple. This requires the building of a more complex infrastructure in the lowest layers of the application.

With the first concrete class already created, the next step is to specify the classes for the Sao Paulo and Los Angeles cities, implementing the same interface. The following represents the implementation of the **LosAngelesStrategy** class:

```
1      using System;
2
3    ┌ namespace BPBStrategyPattern
4    │  {
            1 reference
5    ┌     public class LosAngelesStrategy : ICityStrategy
6    │     {
              4 references
7    ┌        public void ApplyEmploymentRules()
8    │        {
9    │            Console.WriteLine("No permanent employees");
10   │        }
11
              4 references
12   ┌        public decimal ApplyProfit(decimal price)
13   │        {
14   │            return  price * 0.10m;
15   │        }
16
              4 references
17   ┌        public decimal ApplyTax(decimal price)
18   │        {
19   │            return price * 0.20m;
20   │        }
21   │     }
22   │  }
23   ▌
```

Figure 15.7: Los Angeles strategy class

As shown in the preceding screenshot, the class name has the suffix strategyto facilitate the identification of the strategy pattern for maintenance purposes. The implementation of the class seems to be redundant, but in real-world scenarios, the specification of the profit and tax values may involve more complex operations, such as database calls or integration with external services. Thus, it is recommended to keep the implementation free of external changes, such as extra parameters to define the values provided by the tax and profit methods. This approach follows the good software development practices stated by the SOLID principles as well. Implementation of the strategy pattern requires only the changing of a single class if a change is only applicable to one city.

According to the **Single Responsibility Principle (SRP)**, a class must have only one reason to change. For instance, in the context of the delivery client application, a change in city rules for New York only requires the underlying class to be affected, and nothing else.

With the specification of the concrete classes regarding cities almost done, the final step is to create the **SaoPauloStrategy** class, which can be achieved as shown in the following screenshot:

```csharp
1    using System;
2
3    namespace BPBStrategyPattern
4    {
         1 reference
5        public class SaoPauloStrategy : ICityStrategy
6        {
             4 references
7            public void ApplyEmploymentRules()
8            {
9                Console.WriteLine("Must have permanent employees");
10           }
11
             4 references
12           public decimal ApplyProfit(decimal price)
13           {
14               return price * 0.15m;
15           }
16
             4 references
17           public decimal ApplyTax(decimal price)
18           {
19               return price * 0.10m;
20           }
21       }
22   }
```

Figure 15.8: Sao Paulo strategy class

At this point, all of the concrete classes regarding the cities have been created, and all the requirements defined by the client application have been implemented inside each strategy city class. Considering the architecture proposed by the strategy design pattern, the next step is to build the context class responsible for creating the correct instance of the city strategy class. In that way, the client application will not have any responsibility related to the decision behind each class that needs to be created in each case.

Given that, it is necessary to create a strategy method class that returns the correct concrete class based on some criteria. In the context of this chapter, the criterion used will be the city code information presented on the **User** class. There fore, depending on the city code, the system must create the correct instance of the city strategy class. The creation of this extra structure is optional, but it keeps the code more readable for developers and increases the possibility of implementing a meaningful unit and integration tests for the strategy design pattern classes.

Usually, to handle multiple options, a **switch-case** statement is used for handling the creation of the concrete object in the strategy method class, in case of multiple options. In other scenarios, a more complex condition must be defined to handle the strategy behind the creation of the correct instance. But, according to the requirements of this example, a simple **switch-case** statement can be used, as shown in the following screenshot:

```
1    namespace BPBStrategyPattern
2    {
         2 references
3        public class CityStrategyMethod
4        {
             1 reference
5            public ICityStrategy SetCityStrategy(string cityPrefix)
6            {
7                ICityStrategy cityStrategy;
8
9                switch (cityPrefix)
10               {
11                   case "NYC":
12                       cityStrategy = new NewYorkStrategy();
13                       break;
14                   case "LAC":
15                       cityStrategy = new LosAngelesStrategy();
16                       break;
17                   case "SPC":
18                       cityStrategy = new SaoPauloStrategy();
19                       break;
20                   default:
21                       cityStrategy = new NewYorkStrategy();
22                       break;
23               }
24
25               return cityStrategy;
26           }
27       }
28   }
```

***Figure 15.9**: Strategy method class*

As shown in the preceding screenshot, the class has a single method that receives the city code as a parameter, and based on its value, the switch-case statement selects a different city strategy class to create the concrete object. In the case where there is no matching city code and thus no city strategy, per the requirements, the New York City class is being created by default.

The last step for the practical experience is to call the classes in the client application, which could be a simple Console application that creates an instance of the user and delivery objects. For the study purposes, it is important to create instances that will cover the implementation for all the cities created in this example. Unit tests can be created as well in order to verify that the appropriate profit, tax, and employment rules' information is being correctly applied by each concrete class.

You can start the consumption of the classes by creating a **user** object, specifying the city of New York with the code NYC for the strategy method class, as shown in the following screenshot:

```
1       using System;
2
3       namespace BPBStrategyPattern
4       {
            0 references
5           class Program
6           {
                0 references
7               static void Main(string[] args)
8               {
9                   User user = new User();
10                  user.CityCode = "NYC";
11                  user.City = "New York";
12
13                  CityStrategyMethod cityStrategyMethod = new CityStrategyMethod();
14                  ICityStrategy cityStrategy = cityStrategyMethod.SetCityStrategy(user
15
16                  Delivery delivery = new Delivery(cityStrategy);
17                  delivery.Price = 10.00m;
18
19                  cityStrategy.ApplyEmploymentRules();
20                  Console.WriteLine($"Tax: {delivery.Tax}");
21                  Console.WriteLine($"Profit: {delivery.Profit}");
22
23
```

Figure 15.10: The client application

As shown in the implementation existing in the preceding screenshot, on lines 13 and 14, the city strategy method object is created, and after that, a concrete city strategy class is created in runtime, passing the city code to the method **SetCityStrategy**. After that, a **delivery** object is generated, passing the city strategy object as a parameter, on Line 16.

If you print on the screen the values for tax, profit, and employment values, as it is done between lines 19 and 21 in the preceding screenshot, you will get the correct values for the New York City, based on the requirements for the city for employment rules, tax, and profit, as shown in the following screenshot:

```
C:\Users\Alexandre Malavasi\source\repos\BPBStrategyPattern\
No permanent employees
Tax: 1.0000
Profit: 2.5000
```

Figure 15.11: Client application result

As demonstrated in this chapter, the consumption of the strategy pattern infrastructure by the client application is quite simple, illustrating the good practices of OOP, encapsulating the implementation from the target class, a tenet of OOP.

Once the strategy pattern is fully understood, it is recommended to create other instances of the **user** and **delivery** objects for all the possible cities in this example and create unit tests to evaluate the results.

Conclusion

As learned in this chapter, the strategy pattern is recommended in scenarios in which the same business logic needs to be followed across the application, but distinct rules are required to be applied based on the business requirements.

The correct use of this pattern is extremely useful in complex projects, to keep things simple and thus more maintainable, and it helps developers to safely extend functionalities with out affecting the legacy code.

With this chapter, you have learned how to implement a real scenario using the strategy pattern and the C# language. Also, you have understood how to apply simple solutions to complex problems, applying the best practices of the objected-oriented programming.

In the next chapter, you will have the chance to continue your journey into the design patterns using the C# language and .NET Core platform, learn the observer pattern, and apply all the general knowledge you have gained in the first chapters of this book.

Points to remember

- The strategy pattern gives us the possibility of encapsulating from the client application all the logic behind the creation of concrete classes, being a flexible alternative to extend existing functionalities with out impacting the legacy code.

- In the cases where the application requires the implementation of a highly divergent set of rules between scenarios, the use of the strategy pattern is not recommended.

- The use of interfaces in the strategy pattern implementation helps us to implement unit and integrations tests and to cover 100% of the cases by testing a single strategy method class. There fore, the specification of tests is not expensive and has huge benefits.

Multiple-choice questions

1. **In which scenario is the strategy pattern recommended?**

   a. When objects need to be created in compiletime

   b. When dynamic objects need to be created in runtime

   c. When the classes share the same requirements

   d. None of them

2. **Looking at the example given in this chapter, which class does not contain the necessary implementation for the proxy pattern?**

   a. New York Strategy class

   b. Los Angeles Strategy class

   c. City Strategy Method class

   d. User class

Answers

1. b
2. d

Questions

1. Explain the primary purpose of the strategy pattern.

2. According to what you have learned in this chapter, create a hypothetical scenario in which the strategy pattern can be applied, a part from the example given during this chapter.

3. Explain the type of scenarios where the strategy pattern can be used.

4. Are there any projects that you are currently working on that implement the strategy pattern?

Key terms

• **Compile time**: Any operations that can be identified and recognized before the project runs.

• **Run time**: A specific behavior of the application will only be identified when the application is actually running.

CHAPTER 16
Observer

M odern applications involve the use of notifications based on the events defined by business requirements, which requires the implementation of a reliable software architecture that guarantees all the subscribers to a certain event will receive the notification on time and with the correct information. The observer design pattern explained in this chapter helps us to implement routines that allow us not only to identify changes of a certain object but also give us a way to notify correctly all the users or a client application that is expecting to receive information in case of any changes occurring in an object.

Learning the observer pattern gives you the opportunity to identify its use in the legacy projects based on the C# language and .NET platform and also helps you to apply this pattern in many kinds of applications for any platform, such as mobile, desktop, and Web applications.

With this chapter, you will have the opportunity to apply theobserver pattern in a practical example using the C# language, building a realscenario step-by-step.

Structure

In this chapter, we will discuss the following topics:

- Observer pattern concept
- Examples in C# and .NET Core

Objectives

After studying this unit, you should be able to:

- Understand the observer pattern

- Identify the use of the observer pattern in .NET applications and existing projects

- Apply the observer pattern in realscenarios

16.1 Observerpattern definition

Now a days, it is quite common to find applications that are available on multiple devices and platforms at the same time in order to give users a rich experience and to notify the users synchronously in case an event happens. The use of notifications, manly in mobile applications, has become something available in any application, with many ways to implement that feature. Considering it represents a common problem that needs to be solved by many companies globally, it is not necessary to reinvent the solution applied by them, but just to adapt it to our own custom scenario.

Since the beginning of the modern programming languages, the use of an event-driven architecture is widely used in the market. The use typically consists of the application that uses events to start processes between distinct components or even between different services. There fore, the reaction of an application based on a particular event is not something new in software development, but it has been intrinsically used for many years.

The social media applications used globally by millions of users increased the challenge behind the use of notifications, considering the vast amount of users who need to be notified in certain conditions. At a certain point, it is possible to say that a simple social media application may have hundreds of events that may require the sending of notifications to users, always based on complicated rules, permissions, and conditions. The use of a common and simple pattern is essential in that case, considering the core of this kind application is not about the notification itself, and a good software architecture needs to be built in order to support this important requirement without affecting the implementation of the other functionalities.

The observer design pattern represents an elegant and efficient way to implement applications that need to support notification features, being largely used in the C# language and .NET applications. All the logic behind this pattern is related to having subscribers associated with a specific object. Therefore, if an object needs to receive notifications based on changes in another object, the object responsible for sending the notifications must support the subscription process.

In order to clearly understand how the observer pattern works, look at *figure 16.1,* which contains the basic structure of this pattern and shows the relationship between the class that has to receive notification (observer) and the class the needs to be responsible for the notification (subject):

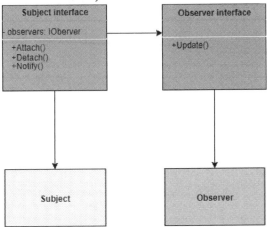

Figure 16.1: Observer pattern diagram

The **Subject** class contains timely information that other classes may have an interest in receiving notifications based on the changes in its state or contents. Because of this, the concrete **Subject** class has a private property responsible for storing the list of subscribers, which are the objects that are interested in receiving the notification. There are methods in the class responsible for attaching and detaching an observer in the private list, which, in a real-world example, could have methods named as **subscribe** and **unsubscribe**.

As shown in *figure 16.1,* the **Observer** interface contains a method called **Update** that needs to be implemented by all the concrete observer classes. This update method needs to be called by the **Subject** class in the **Notify** method for each individual object presented in the observer list. Considering interfaces can be used for the entire observer design pattern implementation, different concrete classes can subscribe to receive notifications, giving to the pattern flexibility and extensibility.

Further in this chapter, you will have the opportunity to implement from scratch a practical real-world application using the observer pattern. The sample implementation consists of a blog application that allows the users to subscribe to receiving notifications, in this case, a new post that is created in a blog.

16.2 Observer pattern implementation

Similar to what was done in the previous chapters regarding other design patterns, the current chapter will give you the chance to implement the design pattern the oretically explained at the beginning of the chapter. With this short experience, you will be able to identify the use of the observer pattern in legacy projects, and you will also be capable of implementing this pattern in any scenario that requires the implementation of notifications or any routine that is based on events.

The practical example of this section consists of blog application that allows the users to subscribe to a blog in order to receive notifications in case any new post is created. The blog application can contain many micro-blogs managed by the users, and the application should allow multiple users to subscribe to multiple blogs.

First of all, it is necessary to create all the interfaces that are common to any application that uses the observer design pattern. Despite the fact that the context of the applications may change for different systems, the concept of subject and observer remains the same considering for all of them. There fore, the first interface is going to be the **ISubject** interface, as shown in the following screenshot:

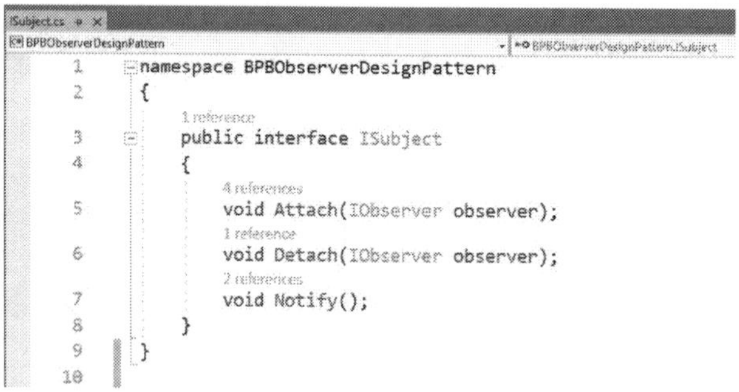

```
namespace BPBObserverDesignPattern
{
    public interface ISubject
    {
        void Attach(IObserver observer);
        void Detach(IObserver observer);
        void Notify();
    }
}
```

***Figure 16.2**: Subject interface*

The **ISubject** interface contains two methods that have the purpose of handling the addition and removal of observers in the subject concrete classes. There is a **Notify** method included as well in order to force the concrete class to implement the necessary logic behind the notification process, which can vary between different classes. The **IObserver** interface must be specified as well in order to contain the contract for all the **observer** classes, as shown in the following screenshot:

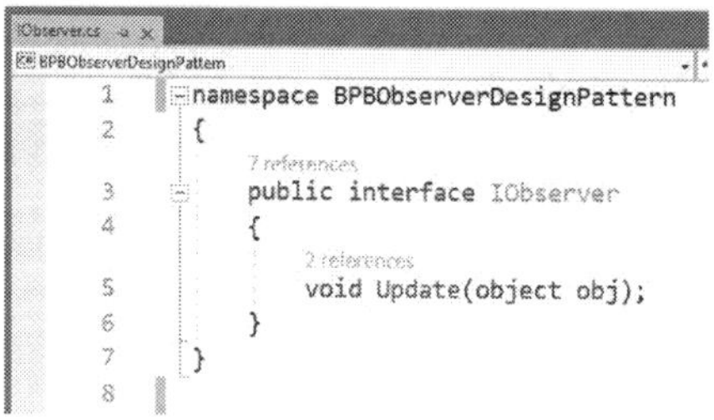

```
namespace BPBObserverDesignPattern
{
    public interface IObserver
    {
        void Update(object obj);
    }
}
```

***Figure 16.3**: Observer interface*

The **Update** method specified in the **Observer** interface must be implemented by all the concrete classes in order to define the action taken in case the **observer** class receives a notification from the subject class. Considering the same interface may be used for different types of situations, the update method receives a generic object as a parameter, and each concrete class has to cast the object to the correct type.

In the given scenario of this section, the user represents the observer, and the blog represents the subject, which means that the observer expects to receive a notification from the blog.

Making a comparison between the observer pattern structure and concrete example regarding blogs and users, the result is like *figure 16.4*:

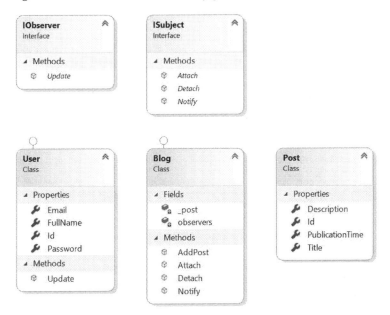

Figure 16.4: *Class diagram*

In this case, the blog class implements the **ISubject** interface, and the **User** class implements the observer interface.

16.3 Creating the User class

The concrete **User** class has the implementation presented as shown in the following screenshot:

```
1    using System;
2
3    namespace BPBObserverDesignPattern
4    {
         6 references
5        public class User:IObserver
6        {
             0 references
7            public int Id { get; set; }
             4 references
8            public string FullName { get; set; }
             0 references
9            public string Email { get; set; }
             0 references
10           public string Password { get; set; }
11
             2 references
12           public void Update(object obj)
13           {
14               var post = (Post)obj;
15
16               Console.WriteLine($"User: {this.FullName} - New Post: {post.Title} ");
17           }
18       }
```

Figure 16.5: User class

In the **User** class implementation, the **Update** method receives an object as a parameter and casts it to a **post** object. The method will be called by the **subject** class upon the occurrence of a notification event. There is a huge benefit of using a generic object in this case for the notification because different classes may expect to receive a different type of notification.

As shown before, the **Update** method prints on the screen the user name and the blog post title for demonstration purposes. In this way, you can follow what is happening in the observer pattern implementation. In a real-world implementation, the same method could be used for showing an inbox notification to users in a mobile application or even update the screen with the new blog post.

On the other hand, the **Blog** class represents the **Subject** class in this context and needs to implement the underlying interface that requires the custom specification for the methods responsible for attaching and detaching observers. Further more, the **Blog** class must implement the method responsible for notifying all the subscribed observers. Keeping the **Blog** class implementation simple for demonstration purposes, it would have the structure represented in the following screenshot:

```
1    using System.Collections.Generic;
2
3    namespace BPBObserverDesignPattern
4    {
         2 references
5        public class Blog : ISubject
6        {
7            private Post _post = new Post();
8            private List<IObserver> observers = new List<IObserver>();
             4 references
9            public void Attach(IObserver observer)
10           {
11               observers.Add(observer);
12           }
13
             1 reference
14           public void Detach(IObserver observer)
15           {
16               observers.Remove(observer);
17           }
18
             2 references
19           public void Notify()
20           {
21               foreach (var observer in observers)
22               {
23                   observer.Update(_post);
24               }
25           }
26
             1 reference
27           public void AddPost(Post post)
28           {
29               _post = post;
30               Notify();
31           }
32       }
33   }
```

Figure 16.6: Blog class

As shown in the preceding screenshot, the **Attach** and **Detach** methods have the single responsibility of updating the private observer list in the class. These methods must be called for handling the subscription events that may occur in the client application. The **Notify** method iterates through the observer list and executes the update method present on the **observer** object, following the requirements stated by the observer design pattern.

Finally, the **Notify** method is being called by the **AddPost** method, which is used every time a new post is created in the blog. Considering the concept of event-driven development, the strong relationship between the two methods (**AddPost** and **Notify**) gives the application a reliable behavior in terms of the purpose of sending notifications when a new post is created.

16.4 Creating the Blog Post class

The blog post, when implemented, is shown in the following screenshot:

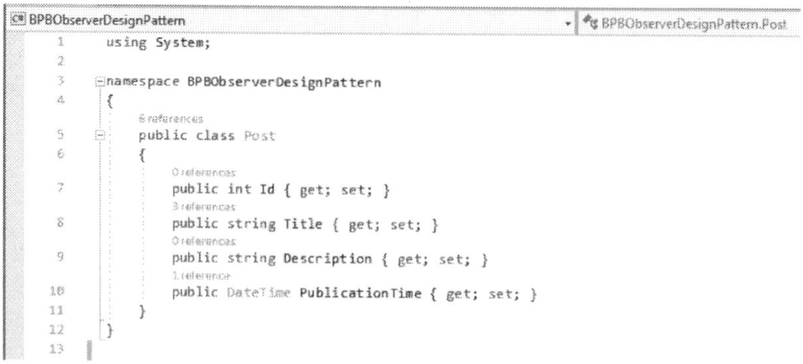

Figure 16.7: Post class

In cloud applications, it is quite common to use the concept of a queue to manage the notifications involving a huge number of devices that need to receive notifications when the demand by a certain process is critical. For real-time notifications, the .NET platform contains the Sign a lR technology, which allows us to create real-time communication between the client and server, following the same concept of subscribers stated by the observer pattern. In that context, the client application, which could be a web page, opens in a browser or a desktop application, assumes the subject role in the observer design pattern implementation. In case of any changes in the client application, the server needs to be notified, and all the necessary changes need to be synced between all the multiple devices that are subscribed to a certain event. It represents such a powerful technology and simplifies the development of a real-time application, such as a chat application or real-time screens.

At this point, you already have all the necessary infrastructure to implement the observer pattern and test the full implementation using hypothetical data. Given the custom implementation in the **Update** method presented in the user class, you can use the output of this method to verify the exact behavior of the solution.

16.5 Client application

To simulate a real-world scenario properly, you can manually create multiple new instances of the **User** class, create a new instance of the **Blog** class and, finally, attach the **user** objects to the **Blog** class, as shown in the following screenshot:

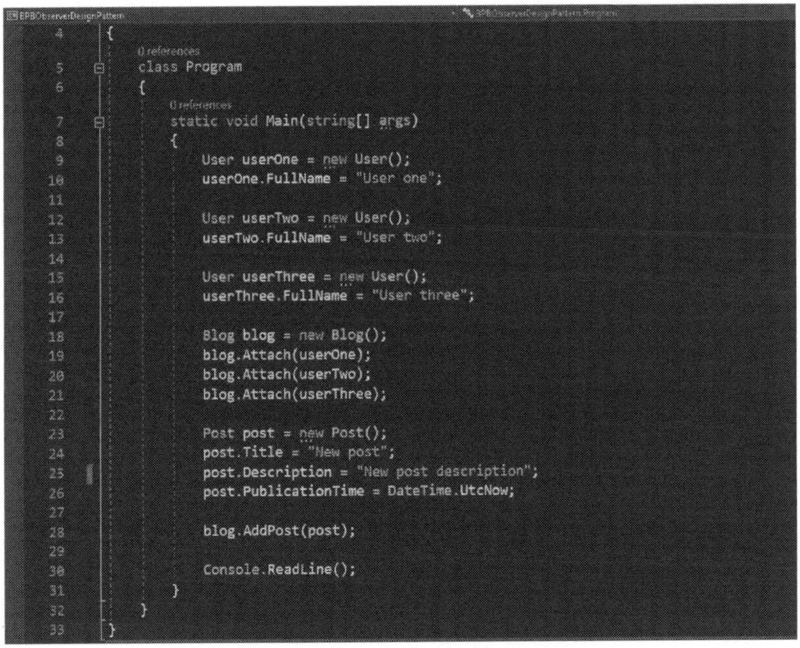

Figure 16.8: The client application

As shown in the preceding screenshot, which demonstrates a Console application, three user objects are being created at the beginning of the program, which include **userOne**, **userTwo**, and **userThree**. Each of these objects is then attached to the **blog** object. Then, a new post is created and then added to the blog.

The results produced are presented in the following screenshot if you run the application:

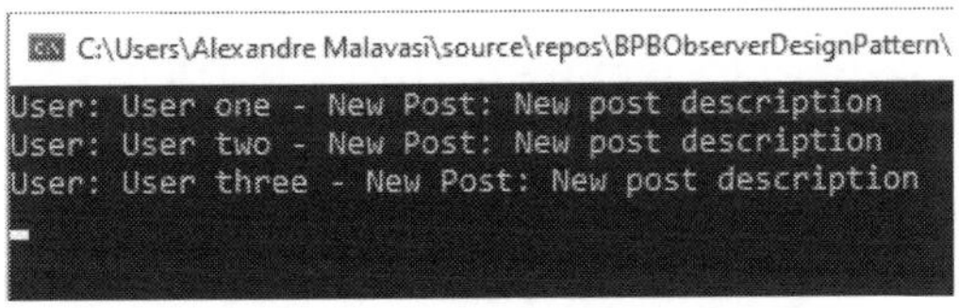

Figure 16.9: Client application result

In order to understand the result of the implementation correctly, it is essential to remember that the application executes the following process:

1. Create new instances of the **User** class.

2. Create a new instance of the **Blog** class.

3. Attach the user objects to the **Blog** class, subscribing those to receive the notification when a new post is created.

4. Add a new post object using the method presented in the **Blog** class.

5. The **AddPost** triggers the **Notify** method, which calls the **Update** method presented in the user class, for which the implementation is highlighted in the following screenshot:

```
     6 references
5    public class User:IObserver
6    {
         0 references
7        public int Id { get; set; }
         4 references
8        public string FullName { get; set; }
         0 references
9        public string Email { get; set; }
         0 references
10       public string Password { get; set; }
11
         2 references
12       public void Update(object obj)
13       {
14           var post = (Post)obj;
15
16           Console.WriteLine($"User: {this.FullName} - New Post: {post.Title} ");
17       }
18   }
```

Figure 16.10: Update method

As shown in the examples of this chapter, the observer design pattern implementation requires modification in the class responsible for sending the notification. Additionally, changes are necessary for the class that receives the notification as well. To easily identify the use of this pattern, it is highly recommended that you use friendly names in all the interfaces involved in the implementation. It will help other developers in the project in the maintenance process and ensure that the principle behind this design pattern will be strictly followed, in case the application needs to be extended.

I hope this chapter helped you to understand the observer pattern. Considering the knowledge you gained along with this practical example, it is recommended that you try creating other scenarios demonstrating the observer pattern, in addition to the one given in this section in order to give yourself extra practice.

Conclusion

As learned in this chapter, the observer pattern is useful in scenarios in which the notifications need to be sent to multiple objects across the application.

This design pattern is one of the most commonly used design patterns in software development and is largely applied in real-world scenarios, such as social media applications and any other application that requires the sending and receiving of notifications across multiple devices and a large user base.

In this chapter, you have learned how to implement the observer pattern in a real-world scenario, using the C# language, following all the good practices regarding SOLID principles and the object-oriented programming paradigm.

In the next chapter, you will have the opportunity to walk through a brief overview of the other common design patterns used in the .NET applications that are not covered in the other chapter of this book. Additionally, you will learn important good practices and recommendations regarding the use of design patterns in real-world applications.

Points to remember

- The observer pattern allows implementing the necessary logic to send a notification to multiple objects based on events.

- It is highly recommended to use interfaces in the observer design pattern implementation in order to have a more flexible and extensible software architecture.

Multiple-choice questions

1. **According to what you have learned and the practical example given in this chapter, in which class should the Notify method be implemented?**

   a. In the subject class

   b. In a static class

   c. In an external service

   d. In the observer class

2. **Which class represents the observer class in the practical example given in this chapter?**

   a. The blog class

   b. The post class

   c. The user class

   d. None of them

Answers

1. a
2. c

Questions

1. Explain the primary purpose of the observer pattern.

2. According to what you have learned in this chapter, create a hypothetical scenario in which the observer pattern could be applied apart from the example given during this chapter.

3. Explain in which type of scenarios the observer pattern can be used.

4. Are there any projects that you are currently working on that implement the observer pattern?

Key terms

- **Observer class**: The class that expects to receive notifications.

- **Subject class**: The class responsible for sending the notification to all subscribed objects.

CHAPTER 17

Good Practices and Additional Design Patterns

There are many additional design patterns existing for the OOP paradigm that can be used in real-world scenarios using the C# language, beyond the ones that we studied in the previous chapters of this book.

While studying the previouschapters of this book, you had a chance to implement practical examples of the most widely used design patterns for .NET applications, and now, in this concluding chapter, you will have a chance to learn good practices and recommendations, and also have a brief overview of other patterns that are not presented in other chapters.

Learning the good practices regarding the design patterns implementation gives you the opportunity to make better decisions in terms of which pattern can be used and in which scenarios the use of any pattern is not recommended.

Structure

In this chapter, we will discuss the following topics:

- Good practices and recommendations
- Builder, bridge, and decorator patterns
- Chain of responsibility, facade, and interpreter patterns
- Iterator, mediator, and memento patterns

Objectives

After studying this unit, you should be able to:

- Understand the good practices related to design patterns

- Comprehend the general idea behind the builder, bridge, and decorator patterns

- Get familiar with the concepts of chain of responsibility, façade, and interpreter patters

- Identify the use of the iterator, mediator, and memento patterns

17.1 Good practices and recommendations

The correct use of any design pattern in a real-world project requires a strong background in terms of the OOP paradigm knowledge and also requires a deep comprehension of the all the technical and business requirements behind the project that is being built. The design patterns used in the market were defined to solve specific problems in software development. The successful use of a design pattern involves assessing the business problems that the applications must solve and to identify if a design pattern or patterns can be used to solve the problem.

As illustrated in previous chapters, some of the design patterns use many different concepts related to the OOP paradigm, such as interface, inheritance, polymorphism, abstraction, protection modifiers, and other important concepts that affect directly the development of components and a complete application. For that reason, it is extremely important to become familiar with all the object-oriented programming paradigm explained in the first six chapters of this book.

Software development is a complex process that involves the employment of many distinct techniques. It is important to become acquainted with the basic concepts of the C# language and then take on the advance features until their use becomes naturalon a daily basis. The majority of good practices in software development are common sense among developers, including for projects built using the .NET platform and the C# language. Therefore, in many cases, some good practices, such as the SOLID principles, will be used in real-world projects, but they will not be explicitly mentioned, and their identification will not be so clear.

Simplicity must be a concern of any project regarding the technical aspects, and the code should be readable and easy to maintain. Therefore, this should be considered in the technical decisions when the software architecture is being defined in a planning process. Design patterns andany other technique represent solutions for specific problems, and they should be carefully used so as to not include extra complexity in projects that do not require the use of them.

If the development team is not familiar with design patterns, it is highly recommended that the team be educated on the basic concepts of the object-oriented programming paradigm, SOLID principles, and design patterns. After appropriately educated, the team will be better able to determine which patterns need to be applied in the project. If the members of the team are not familiar with design patterns, it is highly recommended to start a training process in order to have all the developers on the same page, and be able to work on creating and maintaining the application while following all the recommended approaches when a design pattern is used.

The complexity of software development has increased exponentially over the last several years. This is due to all the requirements behind global projects, such as social medias, streaming platforms, online banks, and entertainment and mobile applications. All these kinds of applications have something in common: they face huge challenges in terms of scalability, being a cloud-based solution, which means that the complexity of these projects is not only related to the programming language aspect, but also in terms of software architecture and infrastructure. There fore, the approach to take is to keep any application as simple as possible.

A single project may have any extra concerns during the development process, and simplicity, readability, and the correct observance of the SOLID principles might represent the key of technical success of the projects.

17.2 Builder, bridge, and decorator patterns

In this section, you will have the opportunity to learn in a brief overview the concept of three important design patterns presented in .NET projects, which will help you to solve common problems that majorly exist in real-world scenarios. Despite of the huge amount of existing design patterns, the learning of each of pattern should be taken gradually in order to apply those concepts in suitable situations. Design patterns serve as a toolbox from where you can pick the necessary tools for whatever situation of condition you need to. In the next sections, you will learn the general theory of builder, bridge, and decorator patterns.

17.2.1 Builder pattern

The builder pattern is one of the most useful patterns for helping in the creation of complex objects, splitting the complexity of the building process in multiple small steps, reducing the risks of the operations, increasing the possibilities in terms of extensibility, and having the code more readable for developers. The approach followed by the builder pattern is consistent with the SOLID principles and demonstrates individual steps for the creation of complex objects that have a unique and single responsibility.

Imagine the scenario in which the creation of an object involves many lines of code, including calls to external services in the middle of the entire operation. This whole process could involve building hundreds lines of code, which could hamper maintainability, and a good understanding by developers would be compromised. Beyond that, any changes in the code would represent a huge risks in terms of new issues being introduced, considering keeping the creation process in a single method or constructor would delegate to a single method several multiple responsibilities.

The build pattern states that a concrete class must implement a builder interfaces that has multiple methods responsible for creating a different part of the complex object. The concrete class is also responsible for returning the full object as shown in *figure 17.1*:

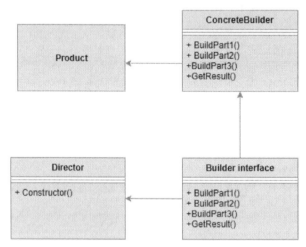

Figure 17.1: *Build pattern*

The implementation of any solution is quite flexible; the achievement of the main goal is the most important point of any software architecture. There fore, regarding the build pattern, more than the relations between the client application, interfaces, and concrete class, the central point is to provide an implementation that splits the creation of a complex object into multiple small parts, and each part should be testable, extensible, and easy to use and maintain.

17.2.2 Bridge pattern

The bridge pattern allows to specify multiple different behaviors for child classes that share the same inheritance from an abstract class, keeping the implementation of the child and parent classes totally independent from each other, allowing to extend a functionality with out affecting any legacy implementation. As shown in *figure 17.2*, the child classes refer to an interface, the same one used by an abstract class:

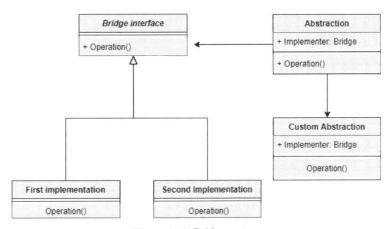

Figure 17.2: *Bridge pattern*

This pattern is extremely useful when there are new requirements to extend functionalities of a legacy project and the old classes need to be kept intact. This approach is in total compatibility with the good practices stated by the SOLID principles in the object-oriented programming paradigm, specifically the Liskov principle. As shown in the previous chapters of this book, the SOLID principles and design patterns are some what related, and the correct use of any pattern must require proper knowledge of the generic principles that would be applicable to any software project. Generally, it is possible to say that the bridge pattern is suitable for the scenarios in which the old and new functionalities of the same system should coexist in production environments in order to enable and disabled functions according to the version that the client application should use.

17.2.3 Decorator pattern

The decorator pattern is closely related to the concept of dependency injection, which exists to extend the behavior of certain class without changing the actual class, but injecting a new object using interfaces. The .NET Core platform introduced an easier way to handle dependency injection in general, being possible to specify an interface in the application start class, globally, and every class in the project that has the interface specified in the constructor will automatically receive an instance of the concrete object. This is largely used for injecting repositories in controllers for Asp.Net Core **MVC (Model View Controller)** projects. As shown in the following screenshot, in the **Startup.cs** class of the Asp.Net project, it is possible to register services that will be globally used across the project:

```
10    using Microsoft.Extensions.Hosting;
11
12    namespace DecoratorDesignPattern
13    {
          2 references
14        public class Startup
15        {
              0 references
16            public Startup(IConfiguration configuration)
17            {
18                Configuration = configuration;
19            }
20
              1 reference
21            public IConfiguration Configuration { get; }
22
              0 references
23            public void ConfigureServices(IServiceCollection services)
24            {
25                services.AddControllersWithViews();
26
27
28                services.AddScoped<ICustomService, CustomService>();
29
30
31            }
32
              0 references
33            public void Configure(IApplicationBuilder app, IWebHostEnvironment env)...
59        }
60    }
61
```

Figure 17.3: Dependency injection

Once an interface and the underlying concrete class are registered in the services, all the controllers in the Asp.Net Core project will receive a concrete instance of the object in case of there is a constructor referencing the interface, as shown in the following screenshot:

```
DecoratorDesignPattern                                    DecoratorDesignPattern.Controllers.HomeController
1     using Microsoft.AspNetCore.Mvc;
2
3     namespace DecoratorDesignPattern.Controllers
4     {
          1 reference
5         public class HomeController : Controller
6         {
7             private readonly ICustomService _customService;
8
              0 references
9             public HomeController(ICustomService customService)
10            {
11                _customService = customService;
12            }
13
              0 references
14            public IActionResult Index()
15            {
16                return View();
17            }
18        }
19    }
20
```

Figure 17.4: Injection in the Controller

The transparent handler for dependency injection is one of the main innovations presented in Asp.Net Core in comparison to the previous versions because it does not require the use of external libraries, being natively part of the Asp.Net Core project. The correct use of the dependency injection allows us to have an extensible and testable class, being possible to create mock classes that implement the same interface that is injected in the controllers.

17.3 Chain of responsibility and patterns

In this section, you will have the opportunity to learn in a brief overview the concept of two more essential design patterns used in .NET projects by many companies, including thechain of responsibility andfaçade patterns.

17.3.1 Chain of responsibility pattern

The chain of responsibility pattern is used in scenarios in which multiple requests need to be made in a certain service and the process must be split into multiple requests in order to give to each individual request less data to process. If we compare this pattern with the bridge one, it is possible to see similarities in terms of purpose: split the responsibility into multiple smaller methods or objects. Imagine a scenario that consists of requesting thousands of distinct objects, individually and sequentially to a specific service and, according to the infrastructure limitation of the service, there is a maximum of objects that can be requested in a single session or authentication process. In that case, multiple handlers can be created, each of them responsible for requesting a specific range of objects. The representation of the chain of responsibility pattern can be seen in *figure 17.5*:

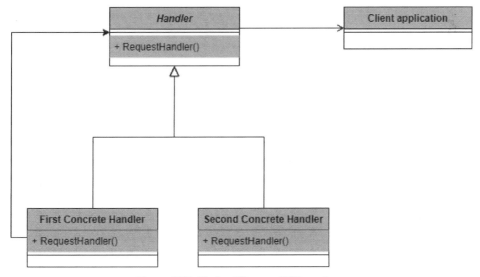

Figure 17.5: Chain of Responsibility pattern

Each handler used by the client application can have a custom implementation responsible for handling different parts of a larger request. This represents such a good practice in terms of splitting the responsibility of objects created at run time, but in the cases where a single transaction needs to be made, the use of this pattern may represent a huge challenge, considering the process that is being processed by each instance may be quite independent from each other.

17.3.2 Façade pattern

The façade pattern represents one of the most common patterns used in .NET applications. This pattern allows the abstraction of the business requirements from implementation details, hiding the complexity between distinct systems. For instance, in cases where an integration requires to connect to and bring data back from a database, there is always a ready connector or a library that facilitates that process, such as connector for SQL Server, Oracle, or other databases. The Entity Framework is a good example of this. This allows us to make operations on the databases without necessarily needing to write a single line of code to handle all the complex operations regarding protocols, security, and other aspects of database access. Therefore, it is possible to say that any layer in an application that facilitates the access to another system could be considered as a façade implementation.

There are many scenarios in which a single client application needs to access multiple other systems that have different ways of authentication and distinct patterns in terms of objects. The best approach in the case is to create an intermediate layer to handle the communication between the two or more systems, and keep the client application and the source applications safe from interference that comes from the integration.

Conclusion

As learnedin this chapter and in previous chapters, the correct understanding of design patterns allows us to more efficiently and reliably builds software for real projects, solving complex problems in simple ways, following the best practices of the OOP paradigm, including SOLID principles and practices related to QA. I hope that all the chapters of this book have contributed to help you in understanding how the design patterns can be applied in .NET projects.

Additionally, you had the opportunity to learn and understand the difference between .NET Frame work and .NET Core, including the most important new features presented in the newest version of the C# language. In this chapter, you have learned good practices in the use of design patterns, including general concepts of the most used design patterns in the C# language, such as façade, chain of responsibility, decorator, build, and bridge patterns.

Points to remember

- The builder pattern allows to split the creation of complex objects.

- The bridge pattern helps to create flexible child classes that can have custom implementation independent from the parent classes.

- The decorator pattern follows the concept of dependency injection.

- The chain of responsibility allows us to split a big request into small parts.

- The façade pattern is one of the simplest patterns used in .NET applications, representing an extra layer to simplify the integration between two components.

Multiple-choice questions

1. **What is the design pattern that uses the concept of a dependency injection?**

   a. The façade pattern

   b. The SOLID principles

   c. The decorator pattern

   d. The builder pattern

2. **Which pattern is largely used for integration between systems and components?**

   a. The façade pattern

   b. The chain of responsibility pattern

   c. The single responsibility principle

   d. Dependency injection

3. **Which patterns represents a challenge in terms of transaction?**

   a. The chain of responsibility pattern

   b. Decorator pattern

   c. Façade pattern

   d. Builder pattern

Answers

1. c
2. a
3. a

Questions

1. Explain the primary purpose of the decoratorpattern.

2. According to what you have learned in this chapter, create a hypothetical scenario in which the chain of responsibility pattern could be applied, apart from the example given in this chapter.

3. Explain in which type of scenarios the builder pattern can be used.

4. Are there any projects that you are currently working on that implement the façade pattern?

Key terms

*   **Dependency injection**: Consists in having another object being injected in another object in order to extend its behavior.

*   **Handler**: A concept that consists in creating a method or a class responsible for handling requests to an external resource or service, hiding the complexity from the client application.

Index

Manufactured by Amazon.ca
Bolton, ON